BLACK SAND
and
BETEL NUT

Childhood Memories of Papua New Guinea

Suellen Holland

BALBOA.
PRESS

A DIVISION OF HAY HOUSE

Balboa Press books may be ordered through booksellers or by contacting:

Balboa Press
A Division of Hay House
1663 Liberty Drive
Bloomington, IN 47403
www.balboapress.com.au
1 (877) 407-4847

Cover Art by Andrew Hamilton

Print information available on the last page.

ISBN: 978-1-5043-0703-1 (sc)
ISBN: 978-1-5043-0704-8 (e)

Balboa Press rev. date: 03/16/2017

This book is dedicated to my parents and to Leanne, Brandon, Ethan and Camryn.

Sometimes, for a fortunate few, the mind immortalizes an image of a face, a place, and an event. The mind holds the picture for evermore—to surface, to linger, to fade, to surface again, and to remind those fortunate few of something that once was.

When I was six years old, my family and I went to live in Rabaul, a quaint little town on the island of New Britain in Papua New Guinea.

This is how it was in the place of my childhood—a place I still hold dear, a place I will *always* call home.

Acknowledgments to Max Hayes, Kathyann Dixon and Andrew Hamilton.

CHAPTER 1

Here We Are

I remember the sky as a majestic sapphire that day: deep deep blue and endless. The arching vault cradled the sun as the golden ball spread her elongated fingers and radiated her splendour over the shimmering land.

It was January, and the monsoon was upon us. The air hung thick with humidity; perspiration poured from every pore. The wetness soaked our dresses, our T-shirts, and our shorts, leaving a salty residue that chaffed and stung the unfortunate who suffered from prickly heat rash. As the day wore on and the temperature soared, the heat drove the population indoors. Metal ceiling fans groaned in protest, cranked to full speed by those seeking solace from the furnace outside.

Earlier that week, Mum had enrolled me in my new school: Court Street Primary "A" School. After a few small hiccups, I had settled in quite well. At 2:30 p.m., the bell rang. School had finished for the day and Mrs. Ross, my second class teacher, dismissed the class. I ran out the door and did not break my stride until I mounted our front veranda steps a few minutes later.

After I had changed out of my new school uniform, Mum and I walked across Queen Elizabeth Oval to Dad's office, borrowed the

1

office car, and drove to Collier Watson's store. Mum bought me a new pair of red swimmers, a red-and-white-striped beach towel, and a red plastic beach bag.

I loved my new swimmers the best of all. This was my very first pair of grown-up swimmers. Not the saggy, baggy, too-big-in-the-bottom type of swimmers that mothers buy for their children to "grow into," but smooth, shiny swimmers that fit me all over.

Later that afternoon, I heard the office car pull into our driveway. Dad was home. I ran outside just as Dad alighted from the car. I was so excited he was home. At breakfast that morning, Dad had promised that, when he had finished at the office for the day, he would drive the family to Pila Pila for a swim.

The "swim" was my first in the ocean. Mum had taught me to swim at the local pool and said that only when I could swim properly, could I swim in the ocean. Now, that day had arrived. I couldn't wait—especially now that I had new swimmers to wear.

"Hello pet," Dad said when he saw me. "How was school?"

Dad strode up the veranda steps followed closely by a rotund bald-headed man. The man, like Dad, was dressed in tropical whites: long socks, knee-length shorts, and an open-necked shirt.

"This is Mr. Weiss," Dad said. "Mr. Weiss is the assistant manager from the office, and he has just come home with me this afternoon on office business. This is our big daughter Susie," Dad added.

"Hello Susie," Mr. Weiss said. "Do you like your new home? Settled in, have you?"

My heart sank. "Yes, thank you," I replied politely. "I think so." I hoped Mr. Weiss wouldn't stay too long on "office business."

Mum walked onto the veranda, kissed Dad *and* Mr. Weiss on the cheek, and said, "Hello Father, hello Frank. I'll make you both a cup of tea."

Dad and Mr. Weiss settled themselves into the cane chairs on the front veranda. Mum emerged from the kitchen a few minutes later with the tea tray, set the tray down on a nearby table, and sat next to

Dad. When Dad and Mr. Weiss had finished their tea, Dad rose from his chair and said, "If you are ready, Frank, I'll show you the trees."

After a few minutes, I followed Dad and Mr. Weiss outside. I knew better than to interrupt them, so I squatted on our back veranda steps, where Dad could see me. Earlier on, I had changed into my new swimmers. I was so very desperate to try my new swimmers in the water; as I ran my hands over the silky material, my skin tingled with excitement and anticipation. I sighed, stretched my legs, drew them back underneath me, and rested my hands on my chin.

It was late in the afternoon, and the sun had mellowed. The high-stilted house water tank cast long dark shadows that ran along the short fat grass and up the wall of the *boi haus*. Dappled light flicked across Dad and the office man as they talked business.

Storm clouds gathered on the horizon, and the temperature had dropped somewhat. I knew a deluge was on its way. The rain settled the fine pumice dust and filled the storm drains until they raged with power, but that was ages away, and I cared little whether it rained or not.

I had grown impatient, and in my opinion, Dad and Mr. Weiss had talked business for long enough. I struggled to understand why the topic of conversation was so important. However, I still remember their discussion—in fact my memory so clear, I remember it as if it was yesterday.

"Frank, these are teak trees," Dad said as he reached above his head and plucked a large shiny leaf. "I've seen hundreds of teak trees in India, and I know this is a leaf from a teak tree." Dad rubbed the leaf between his thumb and forefinger. "Most definitely teak," he nodded.

"No, Cyril, I beg to differ," Mr. Weiss stated. "These trees are not teak, they are avocado. I know that for sure. They are most definitely avocado." Mr. Weiss slapped the leaf against his palm to emphasize his point. "I have lived in Rabaul for years," he continued, "and I know: these are avocado trees. You see them all over the place, Cyril, everywhere. They are like a damn weed."

Dad scoffed and raised his eyebrows. "Well," he said "*I* lived in India for years, and you are wrong, Frank. These trees are teak. Teak. Not, as you say, avocado. I know they are teak. I've walked through hundreds of teak forests—*hundreds*—and these are teak trees. I know that for sure."

As Dad and Mr. Weiss debated the question of the trees, Mr. Weiss became increasingly frustrated. His face turned red, and as he became more and more agitated, the tip of his nose took on a purple hue. The humidity was crushing, and the office man was uncomfortable.

At a pause in the conversation, the office man grappled in his shorts pocket and took out a light blue handkerchief. He took off his glasses, glanced over at me, and mopped his red face with his still folded hanky. He gave a long quiet sigh, shook his hanky vigorously, and blew on the lens of his glasses. In quiet resignation, the office man wiped his lens furiously.

I didn't care that the office man was uncomfortable. I was glad. Maybe he would leave soon.

Alas, my dad, however, relished a good debate, and I could tell he was eager to continue their discussion.

Dad wasn't hot or uncomfortable, but I was. The back steps were hard, and my new swimmers, now moist with perspiration, stuck to my bottom. I was tired of sitting and waiting, tired of hearing about Dad's silly Indian trees, and even more tired of the office man's even sillier arvacar-something (whatever they were) trees. I just wanted to go swimming, that's all. I just wanted to go swimming, and I wished and wished the office man would believe my dad about our backyard trees and go home.

I stared hard at my father and willed him with all my might to look up and see me sitting there waiting so patiently. *Please, Daddy,* I thought to myself, *please, please hurry up and stop talking about those trees.*

Dad glanced in my direction. His deep cornflower-blue eyes lit up as he smiled at me.

"What's the matter, pet?" he called out. "Are you getting impatient?"

I shook my head. I did not want to appear rude.

"Come," he said and beckoned me over.

I jumped off the steps, skipped over the shadow lines, and landed at Dads feet.

"What kind of trees are they, Daddy?" I asked as I stretched out my hand. "Are these trees the same trees we used to get in India?"

I didn't really care what sort of trees they were. I just thought if Dad noticed I was wearing my new red swimmers, he might see it was already late and remember his promise to take the family for a swim.

"Yes, pet," Dad nodded and dropped the leaf into my palm, "these trees are the same trees we used to get in India. They are called teak trees, and they are growing right here in our new backyard. Aren't we lucky? Teak trees, just like we used to get in India."

The office man glared at Dad and looked down at me. He shook his head in resignation and blew his nose loudly. I smiled weakly at the office man and edged closer to Dad. Dad put his arm around me and patted me on the shoulder.

"When are we going swimming, Daddy?" I asked. "You promised, and soon it will be too late."

Before Dad could answer, Mum appeared at the back door. She had changed into her swimmers and had a black-and-white beach towel tied around her waist.

"Gentlemen," Mum called loudly, "would you care for a drink before we take Suellen for a swim?"

Mum's voice carried a tone of annoyance. She too had heard the conversation. Her tone meant the subject of trees was now closed, and we had been summoned.

I dropped the leaf, and we walked quickly towards the house.

Incidentally, in the years that followed, Frank Weiss, his wife Louisa, and their daughter Orana became family friends. In fact, on my birthday that year, Uncle Frank gave me a multicoloured plastic woven Chinese dragon. The dragon, Uncle Frank told me, was an Imperial Dragon, with five toes on each foot. The Imperial Dragon is owned by royalty and is considered very lucky. For many years, the Imperial Dragon hung on my bedroom wall, and when I came to live in Australia, the Imperial Dragon came with me. In fact, the Imperial Dragon still holds pride of place on my bedroom wall today.

The vision of my dad as he stood under his teak trees was my very first memory of Rabaul, a quaint little town in a strange new land—a land that was to leave its mark on me forever. My family and I had lived in Rabaul but a few short weeks, and little did I know how this town, this land, and its people would change our lives dramatically, mould and shape my character, and bring my family once-in-a-lifetime adventures and experiences beyond belief. My beloved childhood home would leave me with a cavernous hole of homesickness and deprivation when I left.

A quirk of fate had brought my family to Rabaul. It was the second time in five years my parents and I had moved from one country to another. In 1956, we left India to start a new life in Australia, and in 1960, we packed up again and came to live in Papua New Guinea.

CHAPTER 2

The Big Grey Painted House with the Outside Staircase

The big grey house with the outside staircase was our first home in Rabaul. The house sat on large corner block, which was surrounded by gardens and fronted on a dusty half-tarred street lined with dense casuarina trees.

Our home was situated within walking distance of Dad's office, Queen Elizabeth Oval, and the primary school I attended. Like all of the dwellings in Rabaul at that time, our house was constructed from wood and had a tin roof. However, unlike many of the other houses around, our home was double-story and was therefore considered by many of the town folk to be "nice."

Interestingly enough, an Australian architect had designed our home. It had many redeeming features: two bedrooms, a bathroom, sundeck on the top level, a very large lounge-dining area, a kitchen, and a two-car garage on the ground level. However, the fact that we had a "nice" house did not impress my mother. Mum had lived in "nice" houses all her life and thus expected nothing less. She disliked this house immensely; actually, quite simply, Mum detested the house.

A week or so after we had arrived in Rabaul, Mum decided

the house was unsuitable for her family and informed Dad that she wished to move to a better house. Mum vividly remembers her horror and subsequent anger when she discovered that her new home lacked many of the household items and appliances she deemed necessary for everyday living.

"There was no stove in the kitchen," Mum stated upon reflection, "only this gaping hole that I assumed was for a stove. On a whim," Mum added, "I stuffed a large electric frypan into my suitcase before we left Sydney, and just as well," she laughed, "because that frypan saved us all from starvation. When my new stove arrived, I was so sick to death of cooking in that damn frypan, I gave the bloody thing to Phyllis Skinner."

Mum continued, "Apart from the stove business, there was no washing machine. Instead, there was this dirty-looking copper in a humpy in the back garden. I assumed the humpy was the laundry, but it had a dirt floor. There was a concrete tub in there, however, so the *haus boi* could at least hand wash the clothes. The copper was filthy; it was filled with rubbish, old tennis shoes, and suchlike. When I instructed the *haus boi* to clear the rubbish, I found, if you please, that the copper had a bloody great hole in the bottom of it, so it was useless."

Mum also discovered, to her annoyance, that many of the rooms in the house had only one power point in them, and that the only telephone was situated stupidly, in of all places, the garage.

I suppose my Dad was somewhat oblivious to the lack of household appliances and the needs and wants of a family, and he thought the house "marvellous." Dad also thought Mum had a "most unreasonable attitude" in her desire to move. Consequently, each time Mum broached the subject of moving, Dad evaded the issue.

"What have you been cooking on?" Mum asked Dad the day we arrived in Rabaul. "There is no stove in this kitchen."

"Oh … I've been eating at the New Guinea Club," Dad replied. "It's good food there, too."

"I see," replied Mum, "and do you expect to eat at the New Guinea Club for the rest of your life?" she asked with sarcasm.

"Oh no, darling," smiled Dad, "not now that you are finally here. I have missed your cooking—and you and Susie too," he added.

"Ah ha, and might I ask," stated Mum, "do you expect me to cook in the bloody backyard over an open fire, like a villager or something?"

"Absolutely not, darling," Dad exclaimed. "I wouldn't expect anything of the sort. I'll see about a stove as soon as I have time ..."

"Well," Mum replied angrily, "if you expect to be fed, one requires a stove to cook on. I have a family to feed every day, and I want a stove now—today. And while we are on the subject, I want power points in every room. I am sick of tripping over those extension cords. And I want a washing machine, a very large washing machine, so the *haus boi* can wash our clothes. Today, understand? *Today.* Otherwise, Suellen and I will be returning to Australia tomorrow on the morning aircraft. I left a fully equipped house in Sydney to come here, and I am not compromising."

Mum glared at Dad and reached for a cigarette. She lit her cigarette, drew back deeply, and stormed off.

Dad was in big trouble and he knew it. Bachelorhood loomed just around the corner.

Dad wrung his hands and ran after her. "Please, darling," he begged, "please try to be reasonable. You and Susie have only just arrived. You know there are no stoves here in Rabaul. You know that anything like that has to be ordered from Australia and it takes six weeks on the ship, even after it's ordered, before anything gets here."

Mum was unmoved by Dad's pleading. She stood her ground, and with arms crossed, declared that she would deal with the situation herself.

"How could you bring us here," Mum stated angrily, "when this house is so ill-equipped for my family?"

My mother certainly dealt with the situation herself. That day, she placed an international telephone call to the head office of Nelson and Robertson.

Mum politely informed the general manager that the new Rabaul manager's wife required these items. She read from the list in her hand: a stove, a washing machine, and a vacuum cleaner. She also required more power points in all the rooms and the telephone moved into the house.

In a clipped voice, Mum informed the general manager that if confirmation of these goods was not received via telex by five p.m. that afternoon, the new manager's wife and daughter would be leaving Rabaul. She added that the company—having contributed to the breakdown of her marriage—would pay for her divorce.

Later that day, Dad received a telex from the company head office. The telex advised him that all the household goods requested by Mrs. Holland that morning had been purchased. The goods were to be conveyed to Rabaul on the next available ship.

Mum said she also found the big grey house rather uncomfortable. She maintained that the bedrooms were hot, cramped, and pokey. The bedroom windows were fitted with louvers that Mum said seemed to trap rather than expel the hot air.

Mum also loathed the fact that the house only had one bathroom. The bathroom was small and was fitted with a toilet, hand basin, and a shower over the bathtub.

"That shower is dangerous," Mum told Dad. "The sides of the bathtub are too high. You have to have a pole vault stick to jump over the side. The floor is always wet because nobody pulls the shower curtain across properly when they shower. Somebody will slip and break their bloody neck—and while we are on the subject of the bath, the bloody house is supplied by tank water, and because we only have one bloody tank, we never have enough water to run a bath anyway. What a stupid idea."

Mum also scoffed at and refused to set foot on a deck that sat on top of the garage. The deck lay adjacent to my bedroom and was only accessible via my bedroom.

"That bloody deck frightens the life out of me," Mum often said to Dad. "It's a death trap. I won't allow Suellen to go up there. It doesn't have a guardrail around it, and she will fall off and that will be that. Apart from that, it's too hot to sit there during the day, because there's no roof over it. Without a roof, that black tar stuff that's painted on the floor burns the very soles off my shoes. Therefore the deck is of no use to man or beast. It's a stupid design, just like everything else in this bloody house."

Unlike the upstairs, the downstairs of the house was open plan. The large living-dining area had high ceilings, was panelled in darkish wood, and had highly polished wooden floors. At the front of the living area, three sets of French doors swung onto a covered veranda that overlooked an enclosed garden. The garden was ringed with hibiscus and sweet smelling frangipani trees; dappled sunlight filtered through the gnarled branches of the frangipani and settled over the clumps of large-leafed green and pink striped caladiums that thrived below. Luckily for us, the trees provided the house with total privacy from the road in front.

One afternoon after school, I sat on our front veranda flipping through Mum's latest *National Geographic* magazine. I was enthralled by the photos of the Tahitian girls depicted in the film *Mutiny on the Bounty*. The young girls all wore leis made from frangipani flowers around their necks. The leis and the girls looked beautiful, and I decided to make a lei for myself.

I threw the magazine aside, ran into the kitchen, and found scissors and a roll of string in a bottom drawer. I then raided Mum's sewing box for a large darning needle. I knew exactly what to do.

The frangipani trees were filled with bunches of white yellow-centred blooms. I broke off a bunch, settled myself on a carpet of fallen flowers, and set about my task. By the time Dad arrived home from the office, I had draped myself in layer upon layer of frangipani leis. I felt compelled to share my leis with Mum and Dad, and my dad gracefully wore his lei for the rest of the afternoon.

The kitchen, although not overly large, had a whole wall of storage cupboards along the back and a double door that opened into the garage. At the back of the house stood a water tank on very high stilts, a hand water pump with a long handle attached at the base, and the one feature Mum hated above all: an outside staircase. The open-air staircase was the only way upstairs to the bedrooms and bathroom from the main living areas of the house, and it was totally exposed to the sun and rain. That, along with the single bathroom, irritated Mum immensely.

"Oh this stupid, stupid house," Mum complained with monotonous regularity. "It makes my life a misery. Who in God's name," she often added, "would design a tropical house with an outside staircase and only one godforsaken miserable bloody bathroom?"

Sometimes, to Dads' acute embarrassment, Mum even complained about the house when she and Dad socialized.

"Who in Gods' name," Mum stated to whomever she managed to corner, "would design a house with the bloody main staircase outside, and only one bloody bathroom inside? Who? Well I'll tell you who. An idiot-madman, that's who, a stupid bloody idiot-madman who has no idea whatsoever what is required in the design of a house suitable for the tropics, or a house a child is required to live in harmoniously with her parents. And how can she, I ask you? How can any of us live harmoniously when we are all required to share one bathroom? We cannot. We simply cannot. We all fight—fight like madmen because of one stupid bloody idiot architect who designed a stupid house!"

Mum's hatred for the house and staircase intensified during the northwest monsoon season. Almost every afternoon, the sky darkened, the heavens opened, and it rained. More often than not, it rained *hard*. Sometimes it rained so hard that walls of water rolled down the back staircase, rushed under the back door, and flooded the dining room.

At the first sign of the pooling water, Mum stuffed towels and old sheets under the door. With mounting anger, she instructed us that the door was to remain closed at all costs, and so we stayed, often until quite late at night, trapped downstairs, waiting for a break in the weather.

Mum was strict about "early to bed" nights for me, and she was no doubt sick of me by seven o'clock. She complained endlessly to Dad about "that bloody staircase" and the fact that the staircase was "keeping Suellen up late again on a school night."

Dad was typical in his colonial attitude to petty domestic trivia and didn't think there was a problem with the open-air staircase. However, he always tried to keep the peace with Mum, and so to appease her, he agreed wholeheartedly, saying, "Yes, yes, darling, the stair business, it's terrible … terrible. Susie will get all wet, and she might get sick, and we can't have that, now, can we? We will have to do something about those back steps soon."

One evening during the monsoon season of our second year in Rabaul, Mum was party to an unfortunate incident. The consequences of that incident intensified Mum's unrelenting demands for a new abode.

The violent tropical storms that were so very typical of Rabaul in the monsoon season rocked the land to its very core. As the great claps of thunder rolled around the volcanoes, electrified fingers of lightning probed and blinded in an instant. The noise frightened the young, terrified the dogs, and unnerved the cats. The rain hammered down unrelentingly until the heavens ran dry, and when all was finished, the land was clean and replenished and the sun shone again. The monsoonal storms of Rabaul were wonderful, and I miss them terribly.

It was early evening and already pitch black outside. The Southern Cross and Milky Way were hidden by dark moisture-laden clouds.

Mum and Dad were going to a cocktail party—a "do," as it was commonly known.

As usual, Dad showered and dressed first, and when he had finished, he came downstairs for a quiet brandy and a smoke of his pipe. Mum could then shower and dress uninterrupted; Mum disliked sharing a bathroom with anybody (let alone Dad) and called the bathroom sharing "uncivilized" and "undignified."

From past experience, Dad and I had learned that whenever it was required, we would leave Mum in peace and quiet to shower and dress.

Dad walked onto the veranda and looked towards the sky.

"Run upstairs, Susie, there's a pet," he called to me, "and ask your mother to hurry and finish dressing, please. It's going to rain again soon, and your mother will have a fit if her party frock gets wet. You know how she carries on about those stairs when it rains."

'Yes, Daddy," I nodded and ran up the steps two at a time.

I rapped loudly on Mum's closed bedroom door.

"Mummy," I called loudly, "Daddy said it's going to rain again soon. He said you'd better hurry up and come on down."

The bedroom door sprung from its latch, and I stepped inside Mum's bedroom. Mum sat at her at her dressing table, brushing her hair.

"Mummy," I repeated, "Daddy said ...."

"Yes, Suellen," Mum cut me off, "I heard you." Without turning around, she added impatiently, "just tell your father to stop agitating, please, I'm almost ready."

Mum reached for her bottle of Worth perfume, pulled the glass stopper off, and tipped the bottle. She dabbed some perfume behind her ear, replaced the stopper, and stood up. Satisfied with her smart full-skirted black cocktail dress, strand of pearls, and hair, Mum picked up her black evening bag and turned to walk to the door.

I have often wondered at the perfect timing of fate, for at that precise moment, the heavens opened and a blast of wet wind caught the bedroom curtain. The curtain billowed like an open parachute, and the hem blew straight into the path of the ceiling fan. The curtain twirled and twisted and knotted tightly around the spinning fan blades. The fan slowed momentarily and gave a deep violent shudder. As the fan gathered momentum again, spinning faster and faster, the force ripped the wooden curtain rod clean off the wall. The rod dipped and swayed like a Korean fighting stick, broke free from the curtain, and sailed across the room. The rod slammed into the far wall, fell to the floor, and rolled under the bed. The white muslin curtain danced around the room like a ribboned-baton. Before Mum could duck, the curtain slapped her hard across her face.

Mum yelped and dropped to her knees.

"Turn off the bloody fan," she screamed, "before the bloody curtain strangles me!"

The bedroom door slammed shut behind me. The noise of rain on the tin roof drowned Mum's angry words as she shook her fist at the heavens.

I reached for the door handle behind me, flung open the door, and flew down the stairs. I did not want to be in the same room as my mother as she vented her anger on the fan, the rain, and the stupid, stupid house with the outside staircase.

Dad, brandy in hand, looked up as I burst into the lounge room. From the look on his face, I could tell he was extremely agitated.

"Oh! For Pete's sake, damn it," Dad cursed. He looked at his Omega watch. "I hate being late. The damn rain's hammering down now, and your mother won't come down now until it stops."

I related the episode of the fan and the curtain to Dad. He sighed and muttered, "Oh, for mercy's sake," and poured himself another brandy, a double shot this time—Dutch courage for when Mum came down.

The rain gradually eased after twenty minutes or so and finally stopped altogether. Suddenly, the night was still and quiet expect for the echo of water droplets that splashed into the puddles outside.

Dad and I waited in silence. Finally Mum stepped through the back door and stood in the dining room, stony-faced.

Dad put down his brandy balloon on the coffee table and smiled sweetly at Mum.

"Oh, that's a nice frock, darling. Er, is it new? Susie tells me you had a problem with the fan or curtain or something. Well … er … we had better get on. Please say goodnight to your mother, pet. I'll get the car. It's already twenty-five past seven."

Mum's face grew dark with anger.

"I don't bloody well care if we are late," she exploded. "They can all damn well wait for their bloody cocktails."

Mum fumbled in her bag and took out her black cigarette case. Dad quickly stepped forward and offered Mum a light. Mum angrily waved Dad away, flicked her own lighter, held it to her cigarette, and inhaled deeply.

"You get on to Sydney head office tomorrow morning," Mum demanded, "and," Mum exhaled sharply, "you … you tell those bastards down there … you make it quite clear to them that …' Mum's voice rose in octaves, "I want another house to live in. Do you understand me? Another *house!*" Mum spat the word in Dads face.

"I am not putting up with that—" Mum jabbed at the back door with her cigarette "that bloody staircase, or this bloody stupid house any longer. Do you hear me? Do you? Oh, I'd like to get my hands on the idiot …"

"Yes, yes, darling, I will, I will," Dad mumbled. "I will—terrible business, the staircase, terrible. I'll get the car." Dad disappeared through the kitchen and into the garage.

It wasn't long afterwards, though, that "the stupid, stupid house" revealed a very surprising secret. The secret pleased my Mum greatly and pacified her for a day or so at least.

As I ran up the driveway after school one afternoon, I noticed Mum on the front veranda. As soon as she saw me, she gestured wildly for me to come inside.

As I mounted the front steps, Mum rushed forward and took hold of my arm. My feet barely touched the ground as she propelled me in to the dining room.

"Oh, Suellen," she exclaimed, "look what I found this morning!"

Mum raised her fist and thumped the dining room wall. As if by magic, a panel dislodged and sprang open. Behind the panel, hidden all this time, was a dream come true for Mum.

"Wow, Mummy," I exclaimed and dropped my school bag, "a bathroom! It's another bathroom, you found another bathroom!"

"Yes indeed," Mum nodded, "I did, and fancy that, if you please. I found the damn thing quite by accident this morning. I thumped the wall here," Mum explained, "and this door opened, and there was this bathroom, hiding all this time. Oh, thank the good Lord," she sighed, "that that idiot architect had some forethought after all."

I grinned at Mum and stepped inside the bathroom. The walls were tiled a pale jade colour, an oval gilt-edged mirror hung above a green marble hand basin, and a short squat toilet stood in the corner. The bathroom taps and towel rails shone like silver, and I noticed that Mum had placed soap in the soap dish and towels near the basin.

"Mummy," I grinned, "now you can have your own bathroom upstairs and everybody else can have this one downstairs."

"Yes, that's right," Mum nodded, "and now maybe all of us can start living like civilized human beings again."

I played thump-the-wall all afternoon until Mum's patience wore thin. She banished me outside to play until Dad came home from the office to take Mum and me for our daily swim.

I enjoyed exceptionally good health in my childhood years. However, in our second year in Rabaul, a fistful of small yellow tablets, forced down my throat, held the power to render me senseless.

We had been on annual holidays in Australia, and as Mum recalled, I had not been well. After some tests, the local doctor informed Mum that I was infected with hookworm (from the family *Ancylostomatidae*), and I required treatment to kill the worms.

Hookworm, an internal parasite, invaded all human life in Rabaul, and every year the family had to be "wormed" to ensure a parasite-free existence. Mind you, I never saw Mum or Dad being "wormed."

How I hated the de-worming process! Year in year out, after I had swallowed the tablets, I suffered gut-wrenching pain, projectile vomiting, and diarrhoea that debilitated me for hours. The aftermath left me helpless with exhaustion and bedridden well into the next day.

On the morning of my de-worming, I was forbidden breakfast. The tablets had to work on an empty stomach. The required dosage was one tablet per year of your age, so ten tablets if you were ten years old, eight tablets if you were eight, etc. The dosage was clearly marked on the back of the packet, and I often wondered who set the dosage. l guess whoever just assumed that all children who had to be de-wormed were the same weight and height at eight or ten years old.

I hated the tables. They smelt foul and tasted vile, and I drank glass after glass of water to swallow them. However, the tablets rarely stayed down, and within seconds, yellow water and tablets shot up my throat and out my nose and mouth.

Mum had no mercy for my plight. Each time I vomited, Mum handed me a wad of toilet paper. I was told to pick up the tables, wipe them clean, and swallow them again.

As the morning progressed, the tablets festered and gurgled inside my tummy. I remember the feeling oh so well. By lunchtime, however, I was hungry, and I was allowed a "light lunch"—a few chunks of tomato, some lettuce leaves, and a slice or two of cucumber.

Inevitably, after I had eaten lunch, my stomach revolted. Time and time again, I sprayed the walls of my bedroom (for I rarely made it to the bathroom) with a steady yellow stream of vomit until I was spent with exhaustion. Only then, when there was nothing left to eject, could I finally sleep. My dreams were tortured by big-eyed hook-mouthed worms.

The microscopic eggs of the parasite hookworm live in dirt and invade the human body through the soft flesh around one's ankles.

As Rabaul was rife with hookworm, I was never allowed to walk around in bare feet. If, by chance, Mum caught me without my shoes on, she threatened me with "a double dose of worm medicine" next time. Mum's warning always sent me at high speed to find my shoes.

Hookworm and worm tablets still terrify me to the very core, and the memory of my de-worming is still very much etched in my mind—so much so that to this day, I still gag whenever I swallow a tablet. Consequently, I admit, I have two psychotic afflictions: I break out in a cold sweat at the sight of a yellow tablet, and I will never ever, for the life of me, allow my feet to touch the ground without shoes on.

Many years later, Mum and I visited Espritu Santo Island in Vanuatu. We stayed in a scuba diving lodge I had visited many times before. We spent the week swimming and taking in the local sites, and in the evening, after Mum had showered, padded about our room in bare feet.

I reminded Mum of the threat of hookworm and suggested that she put on her sandals. Mum gave me one of her looks and informed me that she had lived in the tropics all her life and knew what she was doing. Far be it for me to question my mother.

Upon our return to Australia, I swallowed my anti-worm tablet (thank goodness the treatment had changed and now one only required a single tablet to kill the parasites). Mum, however, declined my offer of a tablet, and a few days later returned to her home in Queensland.

One morning not long after, I received an early morning phone call from Mum.

"Suellen," Mum said, "er ... I have hookworm. I did not feel well and ... er ... well ...anyway ... I saw my doctor, and I had to have a tablet. I felt so dreadful, but now I feel better. And you are *not* to laugh"

"Oh dear Mum," I said as I supressed a giggle, "I'm glad the worms are gone. At least you didn't have to have seventy-five tablets!

Poor Mum ... now *that* is poetic justice.

On a lighter note, a few months after we arrived in Rabaul, Dad's teak trees bore fruit: shiny green tear-drop-shaped avocados. Dad eyed the fruit sheepishly as Mum pointed to them one evening and said he wasn't particularly fond of avocados anyway, and therefore didn't much care one way or another.

"Well, I do care," Mum stated as she and Dad walked back to the house. "And what's the good in having teak trees anyway, Father? At least Suellen and I can eat the avocados, even if you don't like them. You can't eat a teak tree, can you? Thank the good Lord," Mum continued, "that somebody, obviously not the architect of this stupid house, displayed some forethought and planted avocado trees in the backyard and not teak."

Even if Dad did like avocados, he wouldn't admit that he did, for I know he secretly wanted the trees to be teak, so our new backyard would be "just like India."

Now that I have lived in Australia for many years, I am full of empathy for Dad and his teak trees. As I sit on my veranda now and gaze into my back garden, a large flowering plum tree comes in to view. I love my flowering plum tree—the bare branches in the winter, the burst of pink blossom in the spring, and the deep purple leaves in the summer. However, if I close my eyes and wish with all might, I hope that, if I am lucky, when I open my eyes again, my plum tree will have transformed itself and drip not with purple leaves but with glossy green tear-drop-shaped avocados instead, just like Rabaul.

Not so long ago my girlfriend Jane and I spent some time as volunteers at an elephant rescue centre in Thailand. The sanctuary was dotted with tall straight-trunked trees. I recognised the trees as teak, and I giggled to myself (for the trees were nothing like avocado trees) as I remembered Dad and Uncle Frank arguing about the 'teak' trees that grew in our new back yard.

When I lived in the big grey-painted wooden house, I learned to speak Pidgin English (the universal language of Papua New Guinea)—complete, I might add, with all the appropriate swear words. I also had my first taste of a rambutan.

When I lived in the big grey-painted wooden house, I learned of the World War II Japanese tunnels along the Kokopo Road. Many a time, I stood in awe inside the tunnels and wondered if there were Japanese bodies inside.

When I lived in the big grey-painted wooden house, I felt my first real earthquake and sat enthralled as the house rocked and rolled and settled again.

When I lived in the big grey-painted wooden house, I experienced the wonder of a virgin coral reef and learned to whistle a hermit crab from its shell.

When I lived in the big grey-painted wooden house, I did not realise that I was blessed—immeasurably blessed. I was too young to know that the halcyon days of my childhood would pass in the blink of an eye.

CHAPTER 3

My Mum

My mother was twenty-six years old when it became apparent to her that it was time to leave India, the land of her birth.

In that era, as a married woman, Mum was expected to stand by her husband, support him in whatever he did or chose to do, and be guided by his wishes. For the best part, Mum *did* support Dad, in every aspect of their daily lives. However, Mum displayed maturity and courage well beyond her years when she realised that their future in India lay very much in hands of the new Indian government and not the (very familiar) British government.

In Australia four years later, tormented by constant struggle and fraught with sheer desperation, Mum instigated a move for the second time. Our family left Australia and went to live in Papua New Guinea. My mum's forethought bought our family experiences beyond belief and blessed me with a childhood filled with adventures, wonder and opportunity.

In 1947, India became independent of British rule and increasingly, as she gathered confidence, sought to rid herself of all things British. Under the new Indian government, "British businesses"—including

Dad's family business—were bound by law to employ Indians in managerial positions and have a high proportion of Indian staff.

British judges, doctors, and suchlike were replaced with Indian professionals of equal standard, and British schools were handed over and became Indian schools. Indeed, my mother's old school, the Lawrence Memorial Royal Military School, now became known simply as the Lawrence School.

In a short period of time, British Europeans were feeling increasingly uncomfortable. Even though, Mum and Dad did not experience any animosity towards them, the era known as the British Raj had ended, and our future was now uncertain.

My mother's family had been very much part of that era. The family had been in India for more than two hundred years. My maternal great-grandfather was posted, with his British Army regiment, to North India, to guard the border between what was then a part of India (now Pakistan) and Afghanistan. Great-grandfather gladly fought for India and loved her so much, he never returned to England.

India became the home for three generations: the Rishworths, the Middletons, and now that Mum had married, the Hollands. As hurtful as it was, however, India wanted the British and everything that was British out. By 1956, most of the British Europeans had gone "home" to England, and only the most ardent colonials were left. There was much discussion among Mum, Dad, and Dad's family as to where we would all go. Mum said many a cross word was exchanged when she announced to all that she would not leave India to live in England.

Mum already had a reputation with Dad's family. In 1953, she exercised her right as a mother over my impending birth and informed the family that her baby was to be born in India and not in England. Mum refused to change her mind, and to everyone's disgust, engaged the services of an Indian lady doctor. Suffice to say that on June 27, 1953, Dr. Mary Proudfoot delivered me (with minimal fuss, Mum said) at the Kalyani Methodist Mission Hospital in Mylapor Madras, South India.

When I was three years old, Mum told Dad's family that she was not going to subject me to "a life of misery in England." In Mum's opinion, England was "too small" (Mum said wanted open spaces for me to run in) and "too bloody cold" because the "sun never shone" there.

Mum told Dad that if he wished to go to England to live, he was quite welcome to do so. However, he would go by himself!

Dad suggested we go to Canada. Mum's elder sister, Alexia; her husband, Leslie; and their children had resided quite happily there for many years. Mum said Canada sounded fine, except that it snowed in Canada for six months of the year. Mum did give Canada some thought. It was the gateway to America, and maybe in time we could find our way to Florida, where it was warm.

However, as Mum advised Dad in a later conversation, if we did go to America, I would grow up as an American and speak with an American accent. As an ardent colonial Englishman, the thought that a "Holland child" would grow up as an American did not sit well with my Dad. Thus, all thoughts of Canada vanished from Dad's mind.

South Africa also came up for discussion; however, Mum said she knew that sometime in the future, South Africa would also become independent, and we would be faced with the same problem again.

By 1951, my maternal grandmother, Marjorie Middleton, could see that India had changed. She wished an alternative future for her only son, Kenneth. Uncle Ken was sixteen years old when Granny sent him to live in Australia, and therefore it seemed that Australia was the logical place for us to go as well. It wasn't until Mum and Dad attended a cocktail party at Government House in Madras and met the Australian High Commissioner, though, that Mum really gave Australia some thought.

Over the next few days, Mum spoke at length with the High

Commissioner about Australia. The High Commissioner told Mum that in Australia, the sun shone every day of the year. There were vast open spaces and endless opportunities for new families.

In later discussions, the High Commissioner furnished Mum and Dad with pictures of healthy sun-bronzed children at play on Bondi Beach. He also casually mentioned that free milk was given to all schoolchildren. The High Commissioner also said that Sydney was the best place to go, for Sydney was on the coast. If we chose Sydney, we shouldn't bother with warm clothes, because "Sydney never gets cold."

In Australia, he advised Mum and Dad, furniture and household goods were "very cheap." If we decided to go to Australia, we should not to "burden" ourselves with unnecessary household items.

In 1956, the "White Australia" policy was in force, which meant Australia was closed to many who sought a new home there. The Australian High Commissioner knew Mum, Dad, and I as Europeans, and therefore he signed our necessary papers without the usual fuss. Soon after, our request for residency in Australia was granted.

However, the High Commissioner informed Mum and Dad, our permanent residency status came with conditions. Dad had to find employment within three months of arrival, and if any of us became ill and needed to attend a hospital, we would be admitted as private patients (at our own cost) and not public patients.

As to the question of our accommodation in Australia, the Commissioner offered us a room in a Migrant Hostel in Western Sydney. If that was not suitable, he required confirmation of our living arrangements before we left India. Mum declined the offer of a room in a Migrant Hostel and wrote to Uncle Kenny, who found a small apartment for us to rent in Cremorne, a suburb on the North Shore of Sydney.

Five weeks later, Mum, Dad, and I bade an emotional farewell to family and friends and embarked aboard a small Norwegian passenger liner bound for Ceylon, now Sri Lanka. After a restless night, our vessel steamed into Colombo harbour. Early the next morning, Mum and Dad settled our luggage aboard the *Orantes*, a passenger ship bound for Australia. A few hours later, the *Orantes* weighed anchor and, with propellers at full trust, headed into the Indian Ocean.

My mother seldom spoke of her early days of adjustment in Australia. All of her life, Mum was used to a variety of household staff who tended to not only her every need but Dad's and mine as well. Mum told me that her life now became one of drudgery and hardship. She recalled later that she sobbed every night for six months as she battled homesickness and isolation from family and friends.

"I hung on by my fingernails for four long years," Mum reflected, "and kicked myself every bloody day for leaving India. I knew too that Father would never adjust to Australia; he was so miserable. I thought he would curl up his toes and die and leave me to bring up you on my own. I had to find him another job, some other place for us to go to, a small town or something. Your father left the house at dawn and didn't return until after you were in bed at night, and he hated catching the bus and train to the office every day. There were other things, too. It was terrible …" Mums voice trailed off. "So every Saturday morning without fail, I bought the *Sydney Morning Herald* newspaper. One day I saw the advertisement for Rabaul, and that was that."

The advertised position was with Nelson and Robertson Pty Ltd. Nelson and Robertson had business interests in Australia and the (then) Territory of Papua New Guinea and wanted a manager for their New Britain (Rabaul) office.

The advertisement provided a brief job description, boasted an attractive salary, included a house and car, and offered four weeks annual leave with fully paid airfare for all family members back to Australia.

"I had never heard of 'New Britain,'" Mum recalled to me, "let alone Rabaul, so I went straight to the book case and pulled out the

Reader's Digest Atlas. I looked in the index and found New Britain. When I saw where it was, I knew we had all been saved."

Mum discovered that New Britain Island lay in the heart of the Bismark Archipelago, just off the east coast of Papua New Guinea. Rabaul, the capital of New Britain Island, was situated on the northern tip of the grub-shaped island and (to Mum's delight) was only a few degrees below the equator.

After dinner that evening—with thoughts of warm weather, household help, and perhaps some rest and recreation—Mum drew the advertisement to Dad's attention. As she and Dad discussed the issue, Mum said, by chance, that Papua New Guinea might be something like India. Mum then asked if Dad would like to arrange an interview with Nelson and Robertson to see if the position was suitable.

The advertised position proved more than suitable, and six weeks later Dad left Sydney for Rabaul. He now held the position as the new manager of the Rabaul Trading Company Pty. Ltd. Mum dispersed our winter woollies among friends and placed our home in the hands of an estate agent to be rented. She packed our goods and chattels in large wooden crates and deposited our dog, Scamp, aboard the ship *Soochow* bound for Rabaul.

Close to midnight on January 4, 1961, Mum and I boarded the DC6B aircraft that waited at the international terminal at Kingsford Smith Airport in Sydney. As the "no smoking" signs lit the cabin, the aircraft taxied to the end of the runway and, with engines at full speed, lifted into the night sky. Seventeen hours and four stops later, the aircraft banked low over Simpson Harbour. Below us, the township of Rabaul basked in the late afternoon sunshine. Below us lay a new and intoxicating land, a lush and exquisite paradise. A paradise that, for my family, became home for many years to come.

Mother was thirty-one years old when she placed her weary feet on Lakanoi Airfield in Rabaul and breathed a sigh of relief - salvation was at hand. In a space of six weeks, she had packed and rented our house in Australia, sold the car, nursed me after my inoculations, and endured a seventeen-hour flight. Now, at last, it was over.

When Mum first arrived in Rabaul, she said she slept for four years straight, relieved at last of what she termed as "coolie work." Certainly the basic housework was taken care of, but Mum's hopes of life as she had known it in India were shattered within the first week.

Mum took longer than Dad to settle in Rabaul. She loved the warm weather, abundance of tropical fruit and vegetables, and the Pacific Ocean—but deep inside I think, Mum wondered if she had made the right choice. Not for her family, for she knew Dad had found his niche again, and I was young and I would adapt quickly, but for her own intellectual well-being.

My mother loved the arts, the theatre, and the opera, none of which existed in Rabaul. She also read extensively, but there was no library to speak of, and therefore no reference books, which were her favourites. She devoured crosswords by the hundreds (if we were lucky, the newspapers and magazines arrived by air once a week) and ruthlessly annihilated her opponents in Scrabble—so much so only a few would consent to a game. Mum only drank alcohol socially, detested women's tea parties, and refused to gossip.

Before my Mother found her feet, she thought Rabaul's womenfolk intellectually barren. My mother was not only academically gifted but blessed with a photographic memory as well, and sometimes the Rabaul folk thought her too smart for her own good.

In the years that followed, Mum's educated voice on certain matters more than once slighted her reputation with the so-called experts. Mum, nonetheless, was happy to be in Rabaul, and she set about adjusting her life and mine to the tropics again.

The commandment "Thou shall not kill" was a policy in our house under my mother's rule, as indeed it had been the policy in *her* mother's house. We did not use pesticides to kill the mossies or any other creepy-crawlies that invaded our house and garden, and we tolerated with benign resignation the little sugar ants that invaded our sugar bowl. My mother believed that every caterpillar, moth, dog, cat, and human had been put on this earth for a purpose. As a family, we lived by Mum's belief without a second thought.

Mum was a greenie long before it became fashionable. She refused to wrap presents in pretty paper. "Save the trees!" she said in her defence if questioned about the reused brown-paper-covered gifts. Mum also detested anything wrapped in plastic (even then, she recycled madly) and complained bitterly about throwaway packages and chemical sprays. She admonished anybody who fished illegally, plundered the coral reefs of too many seashells, or littered the landscape. Very few people argued with her.

In our early days in Rabaul, after a bout of rain, the glow-worms came to life in abundance. I often caught the little insects in my hands and watched fascinated, through half-opened fingers, as the little creatures flashed on-off, on-off. To me, the glow-worms were fairies with lights on their wings—magical, tiny living beings that spoke to me in flashes of Morse code.

Early one hot and sticky evening, just after the start of the monsoon season, I had been banished to our front veranda while Mum cooked dinner. Mum and I had been for our daily swim, and I had already showered and changed into my pyjamas and dressing gown. Dusk had just fallen and I sat quietly in the fading light waiting for the glow-worms to appear.

The air was moist and still, the silence broken now and again by the sound of a distant truck engine. As the minutes ticked by, the engine noise grew louder and closer, louder and closer.

I watched, puzzled, as a strange slow-moving vehicle crawled up our street. The truck was rather old-fashioned and dark in colour, with a square bonnet, square cabin, and large round tank fitted to the back. The truck trailed a thick grey cloud of misty fumes.

Mum was drawn outside by the loud noise. She stepped onto the veranda, and when she saw the truck, her face creased into a frown. She sniffed the air, and her expression quickly turned to horror.

"Oh my God!" Mum whispered. "I know that smell. It's DDT. That thing, that bloody thing," she said a little louder, "is pumping out DDT! Quick," Mum screamed to me, "go inside. Now. Now. Call in the dogs and find the cats, too. Close the windows and shut the doors. What the hell is that machine doing here in my street?"

Mum fumed in anger all evening. She puffed madly on cigarette after cigarette and refused to eat any dinner.

"Who the hell organized that thing?" she asked Dad, grinding another butt into a nearby ashtray. "And why wasn't there some warning about it? That thing is pumping out DDT! It will kill everything. Everything—the insects, the beetles, you, me, Suellen, everything!'

"I don't know, darling," Dad answered. "I don't know who organized the truck. I'll make some inquiries in the morning. See what I can find out."

That night, after the truck had long gone, Mum and I went looking for the glow-worms. There were none to be found, and for the first time ever, we missed the click-click calls of our friendly geckos.

Matters of concern to the family were always discussed at our dinner table. So it was inevitable that the events we had witnessed the evening before were tabled for discussion the *next* evening. Apart from that, Mum was still very angry. That morning, she had found that some of the green frogs that lived near our water tank had died.

Dad advised Mum and me that the truck we had seen carried commercial grade DDT. "I found out that the tank," Dad added, "has been fitted with special sprayer. The sprayer sprays a large area in one go, so the DDT can kill as many mossies as possible."

"Yes," Mum said, "and the bloody DDT kills every other bloody thing as well. It's disgusting. They're idiots if they think they can get away with it."

As expected, the poisonous spray meant certain death for not only the insects but many other little creatures as well. The toxic fumes killed mosquitoes, glow-worms, and winged flying ants. They also suffocated caterpillars, butterflies, rhinoceros beetles, and the sticky-footed geckos. In fact, the DDT annihilated just about everything for miles around.

Mum was murderously angry. She complained loudly to anybody who would listen, and—with a sharp tongue—rejected those who defended the actions of the mosquito-killing truck. Most of the townsfolk thought Mum crazy and laughed at her behind her back.

"What a stupid woman," some said. "She wants to save the mosquitoes. Mosquitoes carry malaria, and malaria is deadly. We have to get rid of the mossies, or the mossies will get rid of *us*. Doesn't the woman know that DDT spray is the only way to kill them? The method is tried and true. It's the only way to control malaria."

Week after week, the toxic-fumed truck chugged up and down our street and spewed a cloud of thick grey mist. Mum's face darkened each time she saw the truck.

"Murderers," she'd mutter to Dad, 'bloody murdering bastards. There will be nothing left soon, nothing at all. I can't stand it. I have to do something."

I don't know if we had a Rabaul council as such, but we did have a collection of administrative personnel who, I suppose, tended to such things as the mosquito-killing machine. Mum decided that, if the little creatures of Rabaul were to be saved, she would have to convince the council people to stop using the toxic spray.

"There are lots of ways to control malaria," Mum said. "We didn't use DDT in India to kill the mossies, and India was full of mossies, especially in Madras."

On many occasions, Mum visited the council office and attempted to tell the council personnel that the poisonous spray killed not only the mosquitoes but lots of other things as well. The bees had suffered—no bees, no pollination of flowers for fruit (New Britain Island was built on the exportation cocoa and copra). The caterpillars had suffered—no caterpillars, no butterflies (the butterflies also assisted in pollination). Perhaps most importantly, the green frog and gecko populations had suffered—and the diet of the green frogs and geckos consisted mainly of insects, such as mosquitoes.

Mum also suggested a public meeting be arranged so everybody could be educated as to the life cycle of the mosquito and therefore act accordingly.

"The mosquito," Mum explained to the Rabaul council, "lay their eggs in any water that's lying around. The eggs then hatch and become larvae. Upon maturity, the mosquitos fly off, mate, find more water, and the cycle begins again. If you educate everybody," Mum added, "to dispose of all old tins and containers lying around, anything that holds water after the rain, empty pot plant trays regularly, and change dog water bowls daily, the mosquitoes would have fewer places to breed, and everybody would be happy. Why don't you approach the ABC?" Mum suggested. "Everybody listens to the radio. And put an article in the newspaper. Education is the key to the mosquito problem, not to kill everything."

At some stage or other, most people in Rabaul (except for my mother—the mosquitoes mysteriously left her alone) succumbed to malaria, and those who didn't were considered lucky. Mum's "get rid of the empty container" theory seemed somewhat far-fetched for the council personnel, and so Mum's public education suggestion fell on deaf ears. The council adhered to its "tried and true" method of malaria control, and as it was the monsoon season, increased the mosquito-killing truck run from weekly to daily.

Dad was secretly pleased that the mosquito population was getting their just deserts; the mossies stung him (and me) viciously at every available opportunity. During Mum's crusade with the Rabaul council, he adopted—just as Mahatma Gandhi did in his Quit India policy with the British—*satyagraha*, a creed of nonviolent resistance, and that made Mum even angrier.

Just after sunrise one morning, as Mum walked in the garden, she discovered that the very last green frog that lived beside our house water tank was dead—poisoned, no doubt, by the DDT spray. The sight of the dead frog was enough for Mum. She was angered to point of insanity, and she wanted somebody's blood.

My mother was not one to do anything by half measures, especially when she was on a mission, nor was she prone to politeness when angered. Promptly at eight a.m., with her dead frog in a shoebox, Mum stormed into the council office. She strode past the counter, flung open the half gate that divided the public from the council personnel, and held her shoebox aloft.

In an explosive volley of insults, Mum attacked the council personnel. When my Mum was angered, she often resorted to character assassination.

"You are all murderers!" she thundered. "Bloody murdering bastards, and you are all ignorant. Ignorant and uneducated, and because of your ignorance, your children won't know what a frog or a glow-worm or a caterpillar is. Your children will grow up ignorant, as ignorant and as uneducated as you all are, because you have killed the green frogs in my garden along with everything else!"

Not surprisingly, Mum was politely asked to leave and promptly escorted to her car. Unperturbed, day after day, week after week, at eight o'clock sharp, Mum presented herself at the council office. Day after day, week after week, Mum thumped the counter and voiced how ignorant the council members were. Day after day, week after week, Mum was politely asked to leave and escorted to her car.

Dad was acutely embarrassed. Mum had developed a reputation of being unreasonable and difficult to deal with, and that just wouldn't do. As the manager of the Rabaul Trading Co., Dad had a reputation to maintain.

Apart from that, at every cocktail party, every dinner, and every "do" he and Mum attended, Mum's only topic of conversation was the council's continued commitment to the "annihilation of the creatures of Rabaul." Many a time, Dad asked Mum to rethink her behaviour and just give up the fight.

"No, I will not *give up*," Mum always responded to Dad. "I will not just give up my fight with these stupid people. I am British, even though I was born in India. I am *British*, and we simply do not *give up*. Look at Churchill in the war. He didn't just *give up* to Hitler's nonsense, did he? I too will fight them on the beaches and in my garden, and I will never ever surrender to their stupidness."

Rabaul and the surrounding areas were now almost devoid of insects and other little creatures; certainly our garden was barren except for the mossies. The mossies proved tough and still bred prolifically.

There were also unconfirmed reports of early signs of dieback in some of the native-owned cocoa trees that grew on the outskirts of town. *Dieback* is a disease transmitted to the cocoa tree by mealy bugs, and the larvae of the mealy bug is a pod borer. The rhinoceros beetle (*Oryctes rhonoceros*) lives in the rotting wood and rotting leaves found at the base of many trees, and the main diet of the rhino beetle is comprised of rotting fruit, fungi, and mealy-bug larvae.

The continued use of the DDT spray in and around the outskirts of town had killed a large number of rhino beetles, and now, it seemed the livelihood of many—or, indeed perhaps our very economy—was threatened. Personal reputations were now very much at stake. Questions now circulated behind closed doors: "Was there an element of truth in what Mrs. Holland said?"

The council held a special meeting, and a motion was passed to "retire" the mosquito-killing truck.

When Mum heard that the mossie-killing truck had been retired, she celebrated with a double shot of Johnny Walker (Black Label, naturally) whiskey, and that night cooked a slap-up curry with all the trimmings for the family.

After dinner, Dad poured himself a brandy. "Darling," he said as he raised his brandy balloon, "'*Never in the field of human conflict was so much owed by so many to so few.*"[1] Dad loved the wartime speeches of Winston Churchill and quoted them often.

"Few?" Mum said. "It was *I* who defeated those idiots, not 'few,' if you please."

We never saw or heard of the truck again, and within a few weeks the glow-worms came back, as did the caterpillars, moths, and butterflies. Mum's little green frogs also returned to the garden, and the geckos click-clicked again at night.

In 2009 I visited Rabaul for a scuba diving holiday; it was the first time I'd been home for many years. My visit not only flooded my mind with memories of my precious childhood, it also saddened me beyond belief.

Andrew and I, along with our diving friends, stayed at a scuba-diving lodge at Kabaira Bay. On the day before we returned to Australia, we planned a visit to the Bita Paka War Memorial. The family often visited Bita Paka when I was growing up. The Japanese forces that occupied Rabaul during World War II used (among other prisoners of war) Indian slave labour to build many of the underground tunnels that dotted the landscape, and Dad still loved anything that was connected to India.

As we drove though the cocoa plantations near Kerevat, I was surprised to see that many of the cocoa trees were affected by dieback. Nearing Vunapope on the outskirts of Kokopo, we passed by a roadside depot. The depot housed a number of council trucks, road graders, and tractors ... and an antiquated truck with a large tank fitted on the back.

I recognised the truck immediately. Was it the same mossie-killing truck that had angered Mum all those years ago? Indeed it was.

The sight of the truck filled me with sadness and anger. No wonder the cocoa trees were disease ridden—there were very few,

---

[1] Quote from the speech Sir Winston Churchill delivered to the House of Commons August 20, 1940.

if any, rhino beetles to feed on the mealy-bug larvae. The mossie-killing truck had seen to that. We really do reap what we sow.

In my opinion, the mossie-killing truck did little to control the mossies anyway. I left Rabaul with eleven infected mossie bites, one of which turned into a topical ulcer. The ulcer plagued me for days and left a nasty scar on my ankle.

Unfortunately, malaria is a fact of life in many of the South Pacific islands, and New Britain was no exception. Malaria is carried by the anopheles mosquito, and when I was a child, many of our friends took quinine as a precaution and or treatment. Unfortunately, some still succumbed to the dreaded fever.

On the odd occasion our native staff contacted malaria, Mum always administered a large dose of quinine to them and sent them off to bed until their rigor abated.

As mentioned, before Mum had an enquiring mind and read extensively, and at times, she recalled information when a related subject was raised.

"You know," Mum said to me one day after she had administered a dose of quinine to our *haus boi* Joseph (at breakfast that morning, Joseph told Mum he had *guria*, a pidgin word for the shakes, a sure sign of malaria), "there is a sunken ship, American I think, somewhere in the New Hebrides (Vanuatu) that is loaded to the gunnels with quinine. I read it somewhere. Apparently, the ship hit a mine and sank with everything on board."

On October 26, 1941, the SS *President Coolidge,* an American troop carrier, hit two friendly mines and sank off the island of Espiritu Santo in Vanuatu. The ship was heavily laden with military equipment and medical supplies to support the American troops stationed throughout the South Pacific. In order to save his stricken vessel Captain Nelson ran the ship aground.

With the *President Coolidge* now "safe" on a coral reef close to shore, the captain gave orders to abandon ship. Five and a half thousand troops scrambled overboard, and as it was low tide, walked over the coral reef to the safety of dry land.

The cargo of the *President Coolidge* was precious and considered vital to the American war effort in the South Pacific. With the ship now high and dry, plans were made to unload her. However, a few hours later, the tide rose, and the two blast holes quickly filled with sea water. As she listed to her port side, sea water poured over her deck and filled her opened cargo holds The *President Coolidge* rolled onto her side and, with most of her cargo still secured below, sank beneath the waves.

It is well documented that just as many American troops died from malaria as were killed or wounded in World War II. As America had now been at war for eleven months, the loss of the *President Coolidge* and her supplies, not to mention the medical supplies which comprised of thousands of boxes of quinine, was to say the least catastrophic.

The bow of the SS *President Coolidge* now lies in eighteen metres of water and her stern in seventy meters. She is considered *the* most accessible shore wreck dive in the world today. I have dived the *Coolidge* (as she is known to divers worldwide) many times, and each time I penetrate one of the flooded cargo holds, I remember the story Mum told me all those years ago.

As usual, Mum was right. The *Coolidge* was full of (among other things) quinine when she went down.

In some cases, the long-term use of quinine during childhood resulted in adult hearing loss. Mum was well aware of the side effects of quinine; she was warned against the drug by her grandmother in India, and therefore she refused to administer the tablets to me. Sadly, some of my school friends who took quinine throughout their childhood now have a varying degrees of hearing loss; some even require a hearing aid.

Mum maintained that if you looked after your body, ate plenty of fresh fruit and vegetables, and swam or exercised every day—in other words, lived a "healthy life," your body would reciprocate and look after you. And Mum was right. In all the years my family lived in Rabaul, I never fell victim to (the sometimes fatal) bite of the malaria-carrying anopheles mosquito.

Ironically, I *did* suffer a bout of malaria after a scuba-diving holiday to the Solomon Islands. The fever ravaged my body for more than a week, and as I shivered and sweated in my bed at home, I cursed the mosquito that had bitten me. In my lucid moments, I vowed to live healthy, drink less coffee, and attempt, at least, to eat breakfast three times a week.

I still today live as I did as a child, upholding my mother's policy of "Thou shall not kill" in my own home. However, that policy does not extend to the mosquito! Now, if I ever hear, see, or even smell a mossie, I reach for the can of spray and, with steady hand and keen eye, blast the offending little blighter off the face of this earth.

However, whenever I visited my Mum in Queensland, I was denied that pleasure. Mum's large garden was a playground for little green frogs, and the garden had a plethora of mossies. Often in the early mornings, I walked with Mum as she watered her plants. Her garden overflowed with bromeliads, and as she filled their throats with water, the mossies buzzed around and stung my ankles.

If I complained loudly enough about being bitten, I was permitted to carry a weapon. As an act of revenge, I leapt about Mum's garden like a demented butterfly catcher, laughing hysterically each time I murdered—with a very large fly swat and amid howls of protest from my mother—one of the little bastards that buzzed my ankles.

As mentioned before, when Mum first arrived in Rabaul, there appeared to be very little to keep her occupied. Not one to be idle, Mum craved an interest that involved not only her, but the whole family.

A seashell found on a beach and a chance conversation with a visiting plantation owner paved the way for a new and interesting hobby. This hobby captured Mums heart completely and held her passion for life. As an added bargain, for many years to come, Mum's hobby also kept me out of mischief. The family became collectors of seashells.

Our interest in shell collecting became a favourite pastime. Mum fostered our enthusiasm. She purchased shell reference books (by mail-order catalogue) and subscribed to shell magazines. Interestingly enough, an enquiry made through a shell magazine afforded the family an opportunity to meet a like-minded person from half a world away.

Mum read that an American university professor wanted a *Promanthellum parafragile,* commonly known as the fragile file shell, for his collection. The fragile file is only found in the South Pacific and northern parts of Australia. Mum responded to the enquiry and stated that although the fragile file shell was uncommon, we had, by chance, found some at Nordup, one of our reefs in Rabaul. The coral reef at Nordup was decayed, even dead in some parts—a perfect habitat for fragile file shells.

Not long after, Mum was surprised to receive a phone call from the professor. He had arrived in Rabaul the evening before and wished meet her.

The professor joined our family for dinner that evening. He told us he had a vast collection of seashells from all over the world. However, he did not have a fragile file shell in his collection, and he had coveted one for a long time.

Our family had, by now, lived in Rabaul for a number of years, and we too had a vast collection of sea shells. However we only collected shells from the South Pacific. Our collection only had two of each kind of shell. Mum insisted that when we found a live shell that we already had two of, we were to leave the shell where we found it.

Mum was very protective of all things nature provided, especially our coral reef and reef inhabitants. She made it quite clear to the professor that *if* we found a fragile file shell at Nordup (and she was quite sure we would), he was to only take two shells for his collection and no more. If he disagreed, Mum added, then he would have to find his fragile file shell "someplace else."

The professor was somewhat taken back by Mum's demand. However, he agreed that *if* we found any fragile file shells, he would only take two.

We did not snorkel at Nordup very often, as the reef was mostly decayed and in parts quite desolate. However, the professor was in Rabaul to find a fragile file shell, so Nordup it was. A decision was made to visit Nordup the next afternoon.

As the professor was in town for a few days, he elected to hire a car and arranged to meet us at Dad's office at 4:30 in the afternoon.

It was low tide when arrived at Nordup. The water had receded well into the distance, and the reef—once a haven for fish and sea creatures—now lay high and dry in the afternoon sun. As it was much too shallow to swim, Mum and I donned our sandshoes and decided to walk the reef instead.

The exposed coral heads camouflaged the muted dark colours of the fragile file shell clam perfectly. However, we knew exactly what to look for, and we were confident the professor would not be disappointed.

The professor and I teamed up. We gingerly trod our way through the coral and, with heads bent low, ever so gently moved the seaweed about in the shallow pools of trapped water.

As expected, with in a short period of time, I found a cluster of file shells—five in fact—nestled against a decayed brain coral. The Professor shouted with joy when I pointed to the shells; he recognised them at once. He now had the shell he had travelled thousands of kilometres for.

The professor picked up two fragile file shells and placed them ever-so-carefully into the plastic (recycled, naturally) bag Mum had given him earlier.

The professor took a shine to me, especially now that I had found his shell, and he asked question after question about the reef, the fish, and the shells we had seen and collected over the years. I regarded myself as reef expert, and I prattled on as I pointed out the different coral, fish, and shells.

A few minutes later, my "expert" knowledge or (should I say) lack thereof created a mind-numbing disaster. The day was only saved, at least for me, by the actions of my quick-thinking Mum. The events that followed are etched deep within my mind and have made me forever cautious whenever I dive or snorkel a dead or decayed reef.

A slash of red in a shallow pool caught my eye. A large plate coral had crumbled and fallen over, and a red jelly-like substance oozed, like an open wound, from the broken stem. I had not seen the coral 'bleed' like this before, and I was puzzled as to what it was.

I plunged my hand into the water. The red jelly felt soft and warm to the touch and disintegrated instantly as I squished it between my fingers. Fascinated, I passed some "red jelly" to the professor.

Within seconds, hot needles of pain jabbed at my fingers and palms, and within minutes my hands were on fire. The pain was excruciating, and I cried out in agony and screamed for Mum to come over to me.

Mum raced over. "What on earth has happened?" she yelled at me. "What's wrong?"

I showed Mum the red jelly I had touched and then showed her my hands.

"Oh my God," Mum said, "I think you have touched some fire coral."

Fire coral, from the genus *Millepora*, is a soft and highly aggressive stinging coral that thrives in dead and decaying reefs. The nematocysts (microscopic stingers) of the coral penetrate the skin and, if left unchecked, fester quickly and infect the surrounding tissue for months to come.

Mum sprinted up the beach and ran into a small clearing. "Help,

help, somebody! Somebody please help me!" she yelled at the top of her voice. "My daughter has touched some fire coral!"

The clearing was surrounded by a native village, and within seconds, a sea of worried native faces surrounded Mum. She pointed to the professor and me and ran towards us. The villages raced into the water. We showed them the red jelly we had touched and held out our palms.

The natives grimaced and urged us to come to their village. They had lived at Nordup for generations and knew exactly what to do.

The professor's was face was frozen in pain. His fingers were bright red and had already swelled to the size of small bananas. He shook his head and shouted, "No bush medicine for me. I'm going straight to the hospital!" and bolted to his car. We had no choice but to let him go.

The Nordup villagers cut some thick stems from a large-leaved plant that grew nearby. A young native squashed the stems between two flat stones, plunged the stems into nearby hot ashes, and loudly summoned an elderly woman.

The old woman gently took my hands and squeezed warm sap from the stems over my stinging palms. The warm sap bought immediate relief, and within seconds, the burning pain abated. Again and again, the old woman applied her "bush medicine," and very soon, my pain and discomfort had vanished completely.

The Nordup villagers assured Mum and Dad that the hot sap had killed the fire coral, and I had not suffered any side effects. Dad offered to pay the villagers for their help, but the kindly natives refused. With a smile and a wave, we thanked them all and went home.

Incidentally, Mum was well known at the little native school situated near Nordup village; she was often invited to present the awards to the schoolchildren at their end-of-year speech night. So when Mum ran into the village and screamed for help that day, the primary-school children recognised her immediately.

When Mum attended the next end-of-year celebrations, the children enquired as to how I was and laughed openly at memory of the "man who ran off."

At dinner that night, the family discussed the events of the afternoon. After a phone call, we learned the professor had been admitted to Nonga Hospital. His hands were red and swollen, and his sting-wounds had already festered.

Not surprisingly, the native bush medicine had worked for me. I was pain-free and my hands appeared normal—as good as new.

Dad was most impressed. "That was a smart idea," he commented to Mum, "asking the villagers to help with the fire coral rather than taking Susie to hospital. Look at the mess that poor old professor is in."

"Well," said Mum, "the silly fool wouldn't listen. So what do you expect? These native people here don't have antibiotic creams and suchlike, so they know what to do in a situation like that. Besides, what did we do, or use, before the intervention of modern medicine? We didn't have a choice and therefore utilized what the good Lord provided. We should learn and take notice of these natural remedies."

"Quite," stated Dad, "we should."

Some weeks later, Mum wrote the professor and asked how he was getting on. She said I had not suffered at all from the fire coral and that the native "bush medicine" had done its job well.

A few months later, Mum received a letter back from the professor. His letter informed us that when he returned to America, he had consulted a specialist about his hands. However, even though he'd received treatment, his hands still itched constantly, were sore, and in some parts were still infected. He added that he wished he'd trusted the Nordup natives and availed himself of their "bush medicine" when it was offered.

Mum's conservation policy included the land *and* the sea. She insisted—nay, demanded—we be respectful of what nature had provided us in our tropical island home.

As a child, I was never allowed to damage any coral or leave any rubbish behind when we picnicked. I was never ever allowed to harass any creatures, be they land or sea, or destroy their homes. And I was only ever allowed to take from the reef the seashells we did not have in our collection.

My mother encouraged me to indulge myself whenever I could in the splendour of Rabaul and be appreciative of the life I led, because she knew that one day, my life would change, and the opportunities offered would be lost forever.

Mum was right ... as usual.

Most mothers are protective of their offspring; it's a natural basic instinct. However, most will agree that a fine line exists between protection and overprotection—to mollycoddle or not to mollycoddle, or is it best just to display indifference at a disadvantage?

I was born with right eye *strabismus*, or a turn in my right eye. Mum said when I was about three weeks old, she noticed something was not quite right with my right eye. She had heard that a Belgian ophthalmologist was on a lecture tour at the hospital where I was born. She contacted the doctor and asked him to Ascot (our home) for dinner.

After dinner, Mum mentioned she thought I had a problem with my right eye asked him if he would "please take a look". The ophthalmologist diagnosed a *strabismus* in my right eye and said to Mum, "Bring Suellen to Belgium when she is about nine or ten, and I will do surgery and fix the problem for her. Do not worry about it until then."

My mother always believed self-confidence was an admiral trait in a person, be that person child or adult, and she firmly believed the seeds of life-long confidence were set at a very young age. Mum wanted my seed to grow and flourish, and she let it be known to all—friends, family, and primary school teachers—that no one was to draw attention to my (very evident) wandering eye, and threatened retribution to anyone disobeyed her. So for the best part of my younger years, I was unaware I had an eye problem.

Mum chose to walk a fine line of indifference towards my *strabismus* rather than mollycoddle me. For most part, my mother hid her indifference well. I was never allowed to tease or make fun of anyone less fortunate than me, and if Mum ever heard me speak of anyone in a derogatory manner, she delivered me a severe tongue-lashing.

"There but for the grace of God go you," she admonished me. "You will keep your comments to yourself. You may think what you like, but you will keep your tongue still."

By the time I was ten years old, the family had resided in Papua New Guinea for a number of years. However, once a year, we returned to Australia for our annual leave—and during our leave, an appointment was made for me to visit a Sydney ophthalmologist to have the *strabismus* in my right eye assessed.

Mum and I caught the bus to Manly and the ferry to Circular Quay and walked to Macquarie Street. My appointment always produced the same result. The ophthalmologist conducted some tests on my eyes, spoke to Mum about things I didn't understand, and then bade us a cheery farewell until the next visit.

One day in Rabaul, when I was about eight or nine years old, I tasted the sting of cruelty for the first time. A few words passed in innocence set me apart from my peers, and even though I was just a young child, the comment momentarily swayed my confidence.

"My Mum said you have funny eyes," my friend Pam told me as we played after school one day. "She said she doesn't know which eye you are looking at her from. Mum said it's funny, and your mother should get your eye fixed. Mum said it makes you look ugly."

I remember I was hurt and puzzled at my friends' comments, and soon after I jumped on my bike and rode home.

Later that evening, I sat next to Mum on the lounge, the "funny eyes" reference still on my mind.

"Mummy," I asked, "do I have funny eyes?"

"Why," Mum answered, "did somebody say you did?"

"Sort of," I replied. "When I was at Pam's house today, she said that her mother said I have funny eyes and that you should get them fixed. What did she mean, Mummy?" I asked innocently. "Are my eyes funny? What does she mean I need to get them fixed? Pam said that her Mother said I looked ugly with funny eyes."

Mum's body stiffened. "No, Suellen," Mum said, "you do not have funny eyes. You just have to have a small operation on your eyes when you are ten years old. When you are ten, your eye muscles will be fully formed, and the doctors can then operate and fix your eye."

I looked at Mum with a puzzled expression. This was the first time I'd heard of any eye operation.

"You were born with a slight imperfection in your right eye," Mum explained. "I noticed it when you were three weeks old, in India. That's why we visit the eye specialist each year in Sydney and why you sit in the front row in school. This is why we don't play tennis and why we swim instead. When we go on leave next year, you will have your eyes operated on at the Sydney Eye Hospital. It's all been arranged. You remember the doctor you always see when we are in Sydney, Dr Johnstone? Well, he knows you, so he will be doing the operation."

She added, "Don't let your eyes worry you. If anybody says you have funny eyes, just ignore them. They know no better. They are being rude and ill-mannered, and you know how we feel about rude and ill-mannered people. Now," Mum dismissed me. "it's late. Please say goodnight to your father and go to bed."

Despite Mums air of indifference about my eyes, I could tell she was very angry.

"I expected better of Dorothy Russell," I heard Mum say to Dad. "Fancy her drawing attention to Suellen's eyes. Doesn't she know the child can't help it?" Mum paused to light a cigarette. "I'm going to phone her right now, and I am going to ask that woman to explain her comment. Does she think everybody is born perfect? How would she like it if I said her child had funny legs or something?"

"Yes," Dad replied, "the Russell woman was quite rude ... quite rude. Maybe she's jealous because Susie beat her daughter in the 100-metre running race at the sports carnival last week."

"Oh, for God's sake, Father," Mum exclaimed. "I don't care if Suellen beat her daughter or not. You don't run with your eyes."

Mum stubbed her cigarette in the ashtray and reach for the phone.

My imperfect eyes had never been an issue with me before. Ignorance is bliss, and my bliss had been shattered by an adult's ignorance. However, "There but for the grace of God go I." I could have been born with a *strabismus* in both my eyes and not just one.

On our next leave to Australia, I did have my funny eyes "fixed" at the Sydney Eye Hospital. My operation was a resounding success. My convalescence, however, was fraught with drama entirely of my own doing. But that, as you can well imagine, is another story.

I still today have the confidence my mother instilled in me as a child. I am stubborn and determined (another of my mother's traits) and often considered brash. When my life does not follow my planned route, and I feel hard done by, I remember Mum's words of wisdom.

"All things come to pass," she always said, "but never come to stay. Hold your head up and walk tall no matter what. For, when one door closes, another will open. This I promise you. I am your Mother, and I am telling you this, and you will see that I am right."

I believe my mother, for time and time again many things have come to pass. Many doors have been closed, and just as Mum said, a great many new and wondrous doors have been opened.

My mum passed away on October 9, 2010. I miss her so very much. I will never be able to talk with her again, never share her kitchen when she cooks, never swat the mossies in her garden or swim with her in the warm ocean waters—only, of course, in my memory. I am truly grateful, in mind, spirit, and body, for all she instilled in me. I miss the closeness we shared, especially in her swansong.

Rest in peace, Mum. You are always with me in mind and in spirit.

CHAPTER 4

My Dad

My dad's marriage to my mother was his second. Sadly, Dad's first wife left India after she and Dad divorced and took their children, a son and daughter, to live in England. The breakdown of their marriage was painful for all concerned and had far-reaching consequences.

In 1956, Mum, Dad, and I came to live in Australia. Dad did not see his son and daughter again for a great many years. He spoke often of the children, and even though he supported them financially and kept in contact by mail, I know Dad missed them terribly.

I knew from a very young age that I had step-siblings. Dad always shared their letters and cards with me, and he often kept me entertained with stories of their antics when they were young. Dad spent his life making up for what he had lost and often said he was most happy when I was growing up and lived at home.

Dad always rushed home from the office to be with me. He never missed a school speech night, school play, or school sports day and happily drove me (whenever he could) wherever I wanted to go. In fact, Dad indulged in my every whim. He was also often strangely absent when punishment was due, and it was Mum who, whenever I was naughty, came after me with wooden spoon in hand.

My dad was forty-one years old when I was born. He once told me I was his "second happiness" after a long time of sadness. Dad said his marriage to Mum was his first happiness. I believed him, and each and every day, my dad made me feel special.

I inherited Dad's olive skin and blue eyes. I also inherited his shorter than normal arms. If you believe Darwin's theory that all humans descended from an ape and apes have long arms, Dad proclaimed that he and I had evolved more, because our arms were shorter than normal arms.

I like Dad's explanation, and when I have to turn back the cuffs on my shirts and coats, I take heart in the fact that I have evolved. Dad was also a published author, so one can assume I have inherited his writing gene as well.

Like Mum, Dad had lived a life of prestige and luxury in South India, and the transition to being a working-class man in Australia and life as such was incomprehensible for him. Mum said Dad struggled daily when we lived in Australia. He often forgot which night was garbage-bin night, found the weekly lawn-mowing an arduous task, and even though he helped with other domestic chores, he was not very competent.

In later years, Dad developed some culinary skills. His "own" vegetarian and prawn curry was very popular with me.

Dad held a degree as a mechanical engineer, but he was mostly useless at any handyman tasks. On the odd occasion when he was required to fix this or that, he often hurt or cut himself in the process. As an example, one day Dad suspected our *haus boi* was helping himself to Dad's brandy and decided to fit a lock to our drinks cabinet door. All went well until Mum realised Dad had fitted the lock upside down.

Dad settled in to Rabaul immediately upon his arrival. He was suave and sophisticated, had impeccable English manners, and spoke with a cultured English voice. Dad possessed old-school charm and (certainly with all the ladies) was considered very handsome.

Within a few short weeks, Dad had joined a number of committees, associations, and clubs. He again was in familiar surroundings. As time progressed, Dad became a board member of Court Street Primary and Rabaul High Schools, a Rotarian, and was commodore of the Aquatic Club. He was also a fellow of the Zoological Society and a fellow of the Geographical Society, and he held the position of British Consul for East New Britain.

In 1982, Dad was recognised for his service to the community and business in Papua New Guinea with a Member of the British Empire medal. In later years, Dad also became an advisor to Prime Minister Sir Julius Chan.

As could be expected in a small town populated with social bureaucrats and small big business men, Dad was considered an enigma by some, and he only sought confidence from a very select few.

Dad was known not only for his business acumen but his community spirit as well. When he became general secretary of the Planters Association, he proposed the board offer a fully funded scholarship to three students from territory (or native) primary schools to attend Rabaul High School. The scholarships were much sought after.

Dad also decided that the Planters Association needed a company flag. He approached Rabaul High School and suggested that, by way of competition, the art students submit an appropriate design. Dad accepted the design from a young native girl, and her designed flag flew at Planters' for many years to come.

However, for all Dad's talents and letters after his name, there was something he couldn't do, something he just couldn't master, and that frustrated Dad immensely. From the family's point of view, Dad's frustration and subsequent actions caused many a moment of embarrassment.

Dad spoke the languages of North and South India and many of their dialects fluently. He could converse with maharajas in their palaces and haggle like a coolie in the markets and back streets of

Madras, but Dad, for the life of him, couldn't master Pidgin English, the universal language of Papua New Guinea.

At times, Dad really tried to speak Pidgin, but he often misinterpreted words and sentences. He became extremely frustrated and sometimes displayed irritation at the blank stares our native staff gave him whenever he engaged them in conversation.

At such times, Dad paced about, muttered under his breath, and grumbled loudly to anybody who cared to listen. Often, to Mum's horror, when Dad became really angry he lapsed into Tamil swear words. That, as you can imagine, made the situation even worse.

Dad often referred to Pidgin as "a damn stupid language." He complained bitterly to everybody, "Why can't these people understand me, for Pete's sake?"

Early one Saturday morning, Dad gently woke me. He had a pleading look on his face and carried a cup of tea for me his hand.

"Sorry to wake you, pet," he said as he placed the tea on my bedside table. "Your mother is not well this morning, so I'm not going to the office until later. I want to go to the *bung* and buy some eggs for breakfast. Would you like to come with me?"

"OK, Dad," I said, "I'll have a shower and get dressed. Just give me to ten minutes."

I knew the reason Dad had asked or my company. He needed help.

As Dad negotiated the *boi* trucks that lumbered along Malaguna Road, he and I discussed which fruits and vegetables we needed for the next few days. Mum was confined to bed after an operation and was unable to drive.

Ten minutes later, we arrived at the *bung*. My dad always spoke quietly and gently to everybody. He almost never raised his voice, so I was quite unprepared for the eruption that took place a few minutes later.

Dad parked the car in the dirt parking lot beside the long thatched huts that made up the *bung*. He took out our large *buka* basket and patted his shorts pocket.

"While we are here, pet," he said, "we will take our time and have a good look around for what we need. I have lots of change on me, that way we'll be right for a few days."

Dad and I made our way to the first stall. Dad took out his glasses from his top pocket and adjusted them on his nose.

"This woman has lovely tomatoes, and I can fry some for breakfast to have with our eggs," Dad stated.

I nodded and said that was a good idea.

We stopped in front of the tomato *mari*. Dad tapped his pocket, took out his hanky, and wiped his glasses. He adjusted his glasses on his nose, picked up a fat ripe tomato, and held it out towards her.

"Em ripe ... em got *baluse* inside?" Dad asked in "his" Pidgin.

As Dad waited for an answer, he turned the tomato over in his hands and checked for black spots.

Baluse is the Pidgin word for airplane. *Binatang* is the correct word for grub, bug, or insect. The *mari* looked at Dad and scratched her head. She frowned, rolled her wad of betel nut around in her mouth and grinned widely.

Dad stepped a little closer to the *mari* and jabbed at the tomato with his finger. He repeated his question, this time a little louder.

"Em got *baluse* inside?"

The *mari* stood up and pointed to the pile of tomatoes. She spoke rapidly in Pidgin and held up ten fingers.

Dad stared her in the face and asked his question again. This time Dad emphasized each word: "Em ...got ...*baluse* ...inside em, this tomato?"

The *mari* looked at Dad and then looked away. She hung her head in shyness and picked at a scab on her hairy leg.

"I know these confounded tomatoes are ten cents," Dad turned to me and said angrily, "but I am not buying them if they are full of grubs, for Pete's sake."

Dad picked up another tomato, thrust his hand towards the *mari*, and shouted, "You ...*mari* ...em got *baluse* inside, *baluse* ... em got *baluse* inside?"

Dad's raised voice attracted a host of *pikininis*. The *pikininis* clustered around us, pointed at Dad, and whispered behind their hands.

"Dad," I said embarrassed, "you have—"

'Be quiet, pet, please, I'll handle this. We don't want a riot on our hands. Sometimes these little *pikininis* become hysterical, especially if they think there is a show on. I know what I'm doing."

I stood back and folded my arms.

Dad looked about at the crowd. He waved his hand at the gaggle of *pikininis* to shoo them away. Irritated, Dad shouted his question again.

"Me want to know ...em got *baluse* inside?"

The *mari* grinned at Dad and looked away.

Dad glared at me and pointed to the *mari*. "Is this woman deaf?" he spluttered.

"Dad," I said, "the *mari* doesn't know what you mean. You are using the ..."

The *pikininis* and *mari* tittered. They looked at one another, covered their mouths with their hands, and tittered again. Like me, they were very embarrassed at the "show" going on.

Beads of perspiration formed on Dad's forehead and rolled down his cheek. He muttered under his breath, took off his glasses, and patted his shorts pocket. He took out his hanky and wiped his face.

I rolled my eyes and shook my head. "Dad," I said again, "the *mari* doesn't understand you. You are using the wr—"

Dad replaced his glasses and snorted loudly. "Pet, be quiet, please. I will handle this. I know what I'm doing."

The tomato *mari* pulled up her *laplap* and sat down behind her pile of tomatoes. She rustled in her *billum* and took out a new betel nut to chew. I could see the *mari* was clearly puzzled as to why this *masta* was asking her if her tomatoes were full of airplanes.

I stepped up to the *mari* and asked her in Pidgin if the tomatoes she was selling were free of grubs. She assured me they were. The *mari* stood up again, adjusted her *laplap*, and held out her hand for some money.

"These tomatoes are fine, Dad," I said. "There are no grubs in them, so you can pay the *mari*, and we will go and find the eggs."

Dad gave the *mari* a ten-cent piece and tipped the tomatoes into our basket.

"I don't know why these people can't understand me, pet," Dad said, shaking his head. "I just don't know."

Our basket filled rapidly with pineapple, big yellow bananas, and pawpaw. As time wore on, Dad became more and more irritated by the whole *bung* process.

Time and time again, Dad refused my assistance and continued to "shop" using his Pidgin. Time and time again, Dad's inquiries were met with blank stares.

"Gee, I'm hungry," Dad stated after half an hour or so. "I'm really looking forward to my fried eggs when we get home. I know we have some bacon in the fridge, so we fry that as well to have with our eggs."

I nodded and asked if we had nearly finished.

The egg *mari* looked up as we stopped at her stall. Dad put on his glasses again and peered at the eggs. He selected a nice brown egg and held it up to the light.

"Em fresh?' he asked the egg *mari*. "Em chicken lay this egg belong today?"

Here we go again, I thought. *Dad is hopeless. Why doesn't he just leave the talking to me?*

"The last time I bought eggs from this woman," Dad commented as he turned the egg over, "they had chickens in them, and I had to throw them all away before your mother caught on. I want to make sure these eggs were laid today and that they are fresh."

I nodded and sighed.

The black-stumpy-toothed egg *mari* smiled at Dad. She turned her head and spat a long stream of red *buai* juice on the floor. Dad frowned at the red stream and picked up another egg. He shook the egg vigorously near his ear and tapped his foot impatiently as he waited for her answer.

"Dad ...please ..." I begged.

"Yes, yes, pet, we are going home soon. I just want to buy some eggs for breakfast. Just be patient, there's a good pet. Why won't this woman answer me? Maybe she knows these eggs aren't fresh and is trying to diddle me. I'm just going to stand here until she tells me which ones are the fresh ones."

Dad wiped his brow again with his wet hanky and muttered under his breath.

I'd had enough. I was hungry, but Dad wasn't giving up. He wanted his eggs and that was that.

Dad pushed the egg into the *mari's* face and asked again, at the top of his voice, "Em this egg fresh? Em egg got chicken inside?"

The egg *mari* covered her mouth with her hand and giggled. She glanced over at her friends and laughed openly at Dad.

Dad's face turned purple. I thought it was time I intervened. I gently pushed Dad aside and asked the *mari* in Pidgin if her eggs were fresh. The *mari* assured me the eggs had been laid that morning.

We paid for the eggs and pushed our way through the throng back to the car.

After breakfast, Dad's temper had cooled somewhat.

"I don't know why these people don't understand me, pet," he said sheepishly. "I always have such trouble with this language. I didn't have any trouble in India. You just speak it so well. Will you teach me?"

I nodded and promised I would, but in my heart I knew the task was hopeless. I had tried on many occasions to teach Dad Pidgin, and each time, utterly frustrated, I had abandoned the exercise.

My dad always respected the fact that he lived in a house with Mum and I. He happily gave up his space in the bathroom cupboard to accommodate eyebrow tweezers and suchlike, and only complained if I used his Gillette razor to shave my legs.

Usually Dad showered and dressed first in the morning and came to breakfast all fresh. He smelled of Old Spice aftershave and always greeted me with a kiss on my forehead.

One morning, however, Dad was clearly out of sorts. I heard him asking Mum if she was going shopping that day, and if so, would she please buy some Tiger balm for his rash. The next morning when Dad sat down for breakfast, I noticed that an ugly red rash had appeared on his neck.

"I don't know why your mother has changed the talcum powder," Dad muttered under his breath. "That new powder makes me itchy. I have to keep putting on Tiger balm, and now it's burning."

Mum appeared at the dining room door. "What new powder, Father?" she said. "I haven't bought any new talcum powder. What are you talking about?"

"The one in the pink tin," explained Dad, scratching his neck for effect.

Mum looked puzzled. "What pink tin? Suellen, please get this blessed pink tin and show me what your father is talking about."

Before I could move, Dad jumped up. "I'll get it, I'll get it," he said. "Don't get excited."

Dad disappeared down the hall to the bathroom. He returned a few seconds later and handed Mum a pink plastic container.

'There!' he said, clearly pleased he had produced the goods. "That's the new powder."

"Oh, for goodness sake, Father," Mum cried, "that's not talcum powder, that's just a cleaning powder, to clean the bathroom with! It's in a new 'decorator' tin. I put it in the bathroom the other day."

Dad looked at the tin and frowned. "Oh, for Pete's sake ... well, why doesn't it say so? It looks like a powder tin. No wonder I've been scratching. All day yesterday, I scratched and scratched. I keep having to excuse myself and go to the men's room at the office. I was beginning to feel like one of the dogs. What happened to the powder tin?"

"It's there where it should be," Mum said crossly, shaking her head in disbelief, "on the shelf. Why don't you put on your glasses?"

Dad excused himself from the table to shower again, muttering about "new-fangled powder tins" all the way down the hall.

Dad and Mum had a very busy social calendar, and the two weeks before Christmas seemed to be the busiest of all. They were out most nights of the week at some "do" or other, and by Christmas Eve, Mum said if she had to eat any more party food, she'd be sick. Dad, though, seemed to enjoy the festivities.

We always held a big get-together at home on Christmas Day, usually attended by twenty or so single male plantation assistants. That was fun, but busy for Dad and Mum also. Mum always refused (except on the rarest of occasions) to socialise on Boxing Day. Mum maintained that she and Dad need to "charge their batteries," so she insisted the family have a quiet day—and "a quiet day" meant a picnic at the beach.

I remember one Boxing Day when we had decided to go to Ralabang, a copra plantation near Kokopo. About an hours' drive from town, Kokopo was the gateway to many of the plantations the family visited on a Sunday. Dad packed the picnic basket while Mum and I gathered our swimmers and towels and rounded up our dogs. We left the house just after breakfast.

Kokopo had a collection of small Chinese trade stores that sold (among other goodies) very excellent homemade bread. We often stopped for a short while at Kokopo and bought bread for lunch. It was a welcome relief after the long dusty trip from town, not only for us, but for our dogs as well. Our dogs always enjoyed a stop at

Kokopo; they ran about and sniffed and marked every bush and tree they could.

When I visited Rabaul in 2009, I was surprised to see Kokopo had become a thriving metropolis of businesses and shops. However when I was a child, Kokopo had just a few Chinese trade stores that hugged the waters' edge.

Kokopo, however, was steeped in history. In 1881, Queen Emma established her copra plantation Ralum at Kokopo. The plantation still produced copra—however, sadly, the Imperial Japanese air force bombed Queen Emma's original home, named Gunantambu, during World War II, and only the large cement steps remained.

The wide sweeping steps, once a feature in Queen Emma's lavish European-style home, descended almost to the water's edge in Blanche Bay. Sometimes when we stopped at Kokopo, we walked the short distance to what remained of Queen Emma's steps, stopped a while, and reflected on her life.

At that time, Queen Emma's final resting place (known to be somewhere on Ralum) had, for many years, remained a mystery. All that was left of her and her vast empire was a few broken steps.

Dad loved the story of Queen Emma and often remarked, as we sat on her steps, that Queen Emma's steps made a "mighty fine place for a rest."

The family loved going to Ralabang. It was secluded, unspoiled, and peaceful for all. Our picnic spot was shaded by coconut trees. The sand was white and the virgin coral reef at the water's edge hosted a plethora fish and sea creatures.

Mum and I are strong swimmers and avid snorkelers, and the coral reef at Ralabang offered an endless supply of fun. Dad was a poor swimmer and hardly ever joined Mum and me in the water. However, he did enjoy our picnics, and he happily sat on his banana chair in the shade and read his book while we snorkelled.

When it was lunchtime, Dad unpacked the picnic blanket, readied the food, stood on the beach, and waved madly for Mum and me to come in and eat.

As it was Boxing Day, our picnic basket was filled with leftover turkey, ham, and cheeses. Dad had also packed mangoes, bananas, and *kulaus*. The sweet water inside the young green coconuts quenched thirst better than water, and we had the fresh bread we'd bought that morning from the Chinese trade store at Kokopo.

Mum and I had snorkelled all morning, and our tummies now growled with hunger. We kept looking toward the beach for Dad's signal that lunch was ready, but Dad had his head down, intent on his book.

"Father is absorbed in his book," Mum commented. "Let's go in and eat."

We swam in, dumped our goggles and sandshoes in the shallows, and bolted up the beach.

"Where's lunch, Dad?" I yelled. "Mum and I are starving."

Dad looked sheepish and swung his legs off his banana chair.

"Well ...we only just have bread at the moment. I, um, accidentally left the picnic basket on the kitchen table at home. I thought I had put it in the car, but you see the phone rang ... and I thought somebody had put the basket in the car for me."

Mum and I looked at each other and groaned.

"I'm so sorry, pets," Dad apologised again, "but we can share the bread and ...."

Not only were we hungry, we were thirsty as well, and home was a hot and dusty hour's drive away. We threw our swimming gear in the back of the car, rounded up the dogs, and headed for Kokopo. At Kokopo, we stopped at a small roadside *bung* and bought some *kulaus*. Dad found a tap and cupped his hands under the water so the dogs could have a drink as well.

As we motored along the Kokopo Road to home, Dad tried to make conversation.

"Please don't be cross with me, my pets. When we get home, our lunch is all there ready. We can just have our picnic at the table. We don't have to do a thing, just eat. There's turkey and ham and lots of leftovers from Christmas day. Won't that be something?"

Dad was in coventry. Everybody, including the dogs, just ignored him. Poor Dad.

An hour later, we pulled into our driveway at home. Dad was eager to make amends.

"Sit down, sit down, my pets," he said. "There's no need to do a thing. I'll get the picnic basket and have everything ready in a jiffy."

Dad walked into the kitchen and looked around. The kitchen was as clean as a whistle—and as bare as Mother Hubbard's cupboard.

"Oh no, what the hell has happened here?" Dad groaned. "Where's the picnic basket, for Pete's sake? It's disappeared."

Dad's face crumbled. Beads of sweat formed on his brow as he searched frantically for the missing picnic food. He opened the fridge: no Christmas food. He opened the kitchen cupboards: no Christmas food there either. It seemed our picnic food had simply vanished into thin air.

Mum called loudly for our *haus boi* Joseph to come to the kitchen.

"Our picnic basket and food have disappeared," Dad moaned to Joseph. "I left the basket on the kitchen table, and now it's all gone— all our Christmas leftovers, and my ham ..."

Joseph scratched his head and looked stunned at such a silly question.

"I cleaned the kitchen," he replied. "You all went out in the car, and so I cleaned up the kitchen. I put all the old food in the bin."

Dad closed his eyes and shook his head. He sighed deeply. "Oh no," he muttered, "my ham ... you threw my ham in the bin? My turkey too?

Joseph nodded.

"Oh no, for Pete's sake," Dad groaned. "Show me the bin. I don't believe you."

Dad and Joseph trotted outside. Joseph lifted the lid of the garbage bin. As we lived in the tropics and it was very hot, the leftover Christmas food was, by now, a stinking mess.

Dad groaned in distress when he saw the food. He muttered a few choice words in Tamil and said to Mum, "I'm going to have a brandy. I know it is only afternoon, but I'm going to have one anyway, because I need it. I'm going to sit on the veranda with my brandy and smoke my pipe until I calm down."

Joseph had done his job well. He had thrown out *all* the food, washed the clean plates, and put away the basket.

Mum became fed up with Dad's grumbles about the loss of "his" Christmas leftovers. So the next weekend, she cooked a huge curry with all the trimmings.

"That will placate your father," Mum said to me. "You know how he loves his curry. It will stop him from whining to everybody about how Joseph threw out his ham. Everybody is sick of it."

I don't remember what we had for lunch that Boxing Day, but it certainly wasn't leftover turkey and ham. From that day on, before we left the house, I always checked that Dad had loaded the picnic basket into the car.

My Dad never wore pyjamas to bed. Ever since he was a boy in India, he'd slept in a *loungi*. Dad had bought his *loungis* with him from India, and (as you can well imagine) they were, by now, old, faded, and—because the *loungis* were washed every day—paper-thin. Much to Mum's disgust, Dad refused to throw any of his *loungis* out.

Dad often sat on our front veranda and read his book. Sometimes late at night or very early in the morning, I would catch Dad still dressed in his faded old *loungi*, head down, absorbed in his book.

"Excuse me, pet," he would say when he saw me (obviously embarrassed that I has caught him in his *loungi*), "but I'm just sitting here quietly reading. I'll go and change if you like."

Many years later, Dad lay near death in a hospital in Singapore. I had flown from Sydney to be with him. In ICU, Dad was clothed in hospital whites. He was still, pale, and small-looking. It unnerved me to see Dad in a hospital gown; indeed, the gown worried me more than the tubes and wires attached to him.

I knew Dad was very ill if he had allowed the hospital staff to dress him in anything but his *loungi*.

One morning, I went to the hospital early. My dad's bed was empty, all stripped—clean and empty. My heart thumped in my chest. I felt sick, and waves of nausea passed through my body. Where was my dad? Had he passed away in the night?

I flew down to the nurses' station and asked where Dad was.

"Your dad's improved," the nursing sister informed me, "so we moved him to the ward."

I raced down the corridor and into the ward. Dad was sitting up in bed. The hospital whites had been banished, and Dad was wearing his *loungi*. I knew then all would be well. And it was.

Dad seldom raised his voice, smacked me, or became angry. He preferred to teach me through his actions to have respect for others, to treat others as I wished to be treated, and to speak to others as I wished to be spoken to. At times, I fail …and when I do, I ask myself, "What would Dad think?"

Every day, Dad gave thanks that we were a together as a family. One day, he knew, everything would all change.

Dad wasn't perfect, but as a father, I couldn't have hoped for a better dad.

My dad passed away on August 11, 1986. I miss him every single day, with all my heart. I really do. I miss him because I can never speak with him again, never hear his funny stories. I miss the kiss he planted on my forehead every morning. I miss him everywhere, except of cause, in my memory. I was truly blessed to have him as my dad.

Rest in Peace, Dad.

CHAPTER 5

Our Beloved Animals

Sometimes I wonder if animals develop personalities that are particular to them, or do they take on a personality because they live with a certain family and are treated a certain way? Dogs and cats have always been an intricate part of me and, to a certain extent, have developed part of my personality as well. Mum told me that as a small child in India, I regularly invited our dogs Gunna, Raffle, Pooch, and Doodlebugs into my cot—and screamed when Leila, my Indian *ayah*, horrified I might "catch something," ousted them.

Mum said she was heartbroken at the loss of our dogs when she, Dad, and I left India for Australia. So when we left Australia to live in Rabaul, Mum made provision for our dog, Scamp, to join us. Poor Scampy endured five weeks aboard the ship *Soochow* before he arrived in Rabaul and rejoined our family.

When the *Soochow* docked, the captain informed us that Scamp had jumped overboard not long after the ship had arrived in Brisbane and was well on his way to the other side of the river until a pleasure craft (hailed by a crew member from the *Soochow*) plucked Scamp from the water and returned him to the ship. In the years that followed, our dogs Charlie and Dizzy and our cat Tansy also travelled to Rabaul by ship.

The family always had a population of dogs or cats that swelled and subsided with circumstance. Strays wandered in looking for a dry bed, a kind hand, or some love. We also minded pets for people who went on leave to Australia and never came back. Of all the cats and dogs that found their way to us, there are a few who shared our hearts.

Daisy Dog

Daisy was a heavily pregnant nervous stray that just appeared at our house one afternoon. Mum deduced that Scamp was the culprit responsible for Daisy's condition. Out of respect for Scamp, who was by now very dithery and grey, she decided to make a bed in the garden shed for Daisy and extended an invitation for her to stay with us for the duration of her confinement. Daisy wolfed the food Mum offered her and settled down in the garden shed for a well-earned rest.

When Daisy first arrived on our doorstep, Mum said that this was by far *the* ugliest dog she had ever seen. Daisy was short-legged and square-bodied, with a crooked snarling mouth filled with yellow stumpy teeth. The poor unfortunate dog was emaciated, potbellied by pregnancy, flea-bitten, and covered in matted fir and caked-on dirt.

In her past life, Daisy had been badly treated and viciously beaten, and as a result she was wary of humans. As a defence, Daisy had developed a cranky disposition and often displayed her nervousness with snarls and lip curls each time she was approached.

The family tried to befriend Daisy over the year or so she was with us. However, Daisy resisted our attempted kindness time and time again. Twice a day, though, Daisy emerged from the garden shed and woofed down the meal of tinned fish and boiled rice that Mum left at the door.

A few weeks after Daisy made her home in the garden shed, she gave birth to four or five puppies—none of which looked like Scamp.

As time wore on, Daisy led the pups outside and sat on her haunches, just out of my reach, and watched tentatively as I frolicked with the pups on the grass. Of all the pups Daisy produced, we favoured one in particular, a black and white boisterous male we named Bozo.

Early one morning, Mum noticed Daisy lying motionless on the grass in our front garden. As Mum approached her, Daisy whimpered and tried to stand. Horrified, Mum called loudly to me, "Look!" Mum pointed to Daisy. Sickened, Mum bent down to examine the poor creature. "Somebody has slashed Daisy with a bush knife!"

Daisy's wound gaped from her shoulder to the bottom of her rib cage.

"The poor thing is in terrible pain," Mum stated. "She can't stay here. We'll have to move her inside. Suellen, go and get Scampy's lead so I can muzzle Daisy, or she'll bite. And get me an old sheet from the linen cupboard so we can make a sling and carry her onto the front veranda."

Mum muzzled Daisy, and the two of us half-dragged, half-carried her up the front steps and onto the veranda.

"Oh dear, you poor dog," Mum whispered as we gently lowered Daisy.

Mum inspected Daisy's wound. The bush knife cut was deep and needed to be stitched. However, we did not have a veterinarian in Rabaul at that time, so as best she could, Mum swabbed Daisy's wound, puffed some antibiotic powder into it, and bound it with a strip of torn cotton bed sheet. We then moved Daisy onto a bed of old towels.

Over the next few days, Daisy's body raged with fever, and she became very ill. Twice a day, Mum cleaned the wound, puffed antibiotic power into it, and rebound it. Mum also told me it was vital Daisy take some food.

When we lived in India, Dad was the curator of the Madras Zoo. He and Mum often looked after sick and orphaned baby animals at home and found, through trial and error, that a large glass syringe (used to baste roast meat) was perfect to dribble or squirt liquid food into a sick animal's mouth.

By chance, we had an old baster on hand. Mum concocted a broth of chicken pieces, vegetables, and lots of garlic. She whizzed the broth in the blender and then fortified it by adding milk power. Twice a day, Mum and I painstakingly half dribbled, half squirted the broth into Daisy's mouth.

In time, Daisy's wound healed, and she grew stronger and stronger. One morning we found Daisy's bed on the veranda empty. Sometime during the night, Daisy had risen and walked outside—her first steps in nearly two weeks. We found she had returned to her old bed in the garden shed.

Daisy stayed with us for almost a year, and although the family treated her with kindness when she was ill, Daisy never allowed any of us to really befriend her.

Sadly, one day, Daisy disappeared. Dad made some enquiries around the neighbourhood as to her whereabouts and was told that her previous native owners had kidnapped her and taken her back to their village. Dad offered a substantial reward for Daisy's return, but to our distress, we never saw her again.

Bozo

Our dog Scamp was quite elderly, and his days of "guarding" us were long past. For the last month or so, Rabaul had experienced some civil unrest, and Dad thought it best we acquire another dog, as Dad said, "just in case."

When the subject of a new dog was tabled for discussion at dinner one evening, the family voted unanimously to keep Daisy's son Bozo. Bozo had developed into a strong and robust animal. As he matured, he grew to almost Great Dane size, dwarfing every other dog in the neighbourhood.

Bozo had a large, well-proportioned head, and he padded about on big soft feet. Unlike Scamp, whose coat was short-tufted and grey,

Bozo's coat was a thick, shaggy mass of black and white hair that curled over his back and down his haunches.

Unlike Daisy, who was nervous and aloof, Bozo possessed a happy disposition. Indeed, Bozo was everybody's pal. He loved children, trusted adults, and was pleased that he was loved and trusted in return.

The civil unrest in Rabaul had settled down, and I was allowed to visit friends after school again. Most afternoons, I jumped on my bike, joined my school friends, and roamed the neighbourhood at will.

Thanks to Bozo, just like the fabled Piped Piper, our group attracted children and other dogs alike. When I stopped and talked with friends, Bozo greeted everybody with a lick or sniffed about and marked his territory on a nearby tree, post, or bicycle wheel.

As Bozo matured into adulthood, he lost his devil-may-care attitude and became very protective of me and my group of friends. He lifted his lip and growled aggressively at any native who crossed our path.

At first I ignored Bozos newly acquired guard-dog attitude and simply told him to leave the natives alone. As time wore on, however, Bozo became more and more undisciplined. He veered from our group whenever I was out with my friends and, for no apparent reason, snarled and growled deeply at any native who happened to be nearby. If the native continued walking, Bozo ran after the native and nipped at his heals.

One afternoon, I found Bozo particularly unmanageable. He constantly ran off and refused to listen to my commands or adhere to my repeated calls of "Bozo, come here!" Unfortunately, an unsuspecting native man on walkabout ventured too close to me. With hackles raised, Bozo ran at the native man and bit him on his calf.

I don't know who was more surprised at the attack—the native, Bozo, or I.

The native man startled with fright, bent down, and examined his bleeding calf. Bozo emitted a low vicious growl.

"Bozo," I screamed, "stop it! Look what you've done. Get home, you naughty dog. Stop growling and get home now."

Bozo ignored my command and growled deeper.

"Be quiet Bozo," I shouted and pushed Bozo aside. I bent down and examined the native's calf. "I think I'd better tell my Mum," I said to my friends. "Bozo's bitten him badly. Mum's going to be cranky, and Bozo's going to get it."

"Yes," my friends agreed, "you'd better, or we'll all get in trouble."

When I arrived home with the limping, wounded native, Mum was not amused. She banished Bozo to the back veranda and, with cigarettes and coffee in hand, stood grim-faced on the front veranda.

"What on earth happened?" Mum asked as we stood on the bottom step. "Bozo has never bitten anybody before."

"I don't know, Mum," I replied and shrugged my shoulders. "Bozo just bit the *boi*, that's all. We were just riding our bikes, and Bozo just ran up and bit him."

"Did the native do anything to Bozo?" Mum asked. "Hit him or kick him or touch you or any of your friends?"

"No," I replied, "Bozo just bit him, that's all."

Mum sighed and shook her head. She beckoned the native to come closer and said in *her* Pidgin, "What did you do to my dog?"

The native man sat down on the front veranda steps. He pulled aside his *laplap*, whimpered loudly, and pointed to his bleeding wound.

"*Misis*," he said, "your big dog bit my leg. You put some medicine and bandage on it or I tell the *masta*."

Mum glared at the native man and told me to fetch a bottle of antiseptic, some cotton wool, and a bandage from the bathroom cabinet.

After Mum had dressed the Natives man's wound (Bozo had

inflicted four large punctures wounds), Mum gathered the blood-soaked cotton wool, capped the antiseptic bottle, and told the native to go.

The native man inspected the bandage and stood up. He held on to the veranda railing and gingerly tested his injured leg. He nodded and turned to Mum, held out his hand, and loudly spoke to Mum in Pidgin.

Mum shook her head and waved him away. The native man frowned and again addressed Mum in Pidgin.

A look of puzzlement crossed Mum's face. "What does this fellow want?" Mum asked me. "I can't understand him."

"Ten shillings, Mum," I replied. "He wants ten shillings because Bozo bit him, or he says he will tell Dad."

"What!" exclaimed Mum. "This fellow wants ten shillings just because Bozo bit him? What nonsense is this? Ten shillings or he'll tell your father? Father won't care. The man's a bloody crook! Tell him I'm not giving him ten shillings. Indeed. I ask you. Ten shillings!"

The wounded native man argued he wanted payment for Bozo's bite and would not leave until he had ten shillings. Mum finally agreed, gave him a ten shilling note, and told him loudly to go.

We escorted the native off our premises. However, Mum was worried.

"Just be careful with Bozo, please, when you ride your bike," she said to me. "I can't have him running around biting anybody else."

When Dad came home from the office, we told him of Bozo's biting incident.

Dad was surprised, to say the least. We had never had a dog who had bitten anybody before. As times in Rabaul were again unsettled, Dad asked me to keep Bozo at home until the situation *and* Bozo's behaviour improved.

In time, the civil unrest in Rabaul passed again. However, Bozo's bad behaviour continued. To family and friends, Bozo was a sweet and loving dog, but unfortunately his dislike for the native population grew. His attitude caused our family drama after drama.

Within weeks of what the family now referred to as "Bozo's biting incident," Bozo became almost uncontrollable outside the boundaries of our home. He completely disregarded any commands I gave him to stay by my side as I rode my bike. He ran off, with hackles raised, whenever he saw a native.

More often than not, Bozo caught his victims off guard, and before I could stop him, inflicted a nasty nip or two. Mum stocked the bathroom cabinet with bandages at home and always had a wad of ten shilling notes in her purse.

Mum was concerned about Bozo's uncontrolled behaviour and forbade me to take Bozo with me when I left the boundaries of our home. However, Bozo followed me anyway. As could be expected, Bozo came to attention of the local police.

Mum said her heart sank one afternoon when the police paddy wagon pulled into our driveway. She also told me she was acutely embarrassed when our very good friend Uncle Max Hayes stepped from the paddy wagon. Uncle Max was in full police uniform, complete with holstered pistol, notebook, and pen. Mum said she presumed then that Uncle Max had come on official police business about Bozo.

"Good afternoon, Max," Mum said in a somewhat guarded tone as Uncle Max stepped onto the veranda. "Are you looking for Betty? She …"

"Good afternoon, Poppy," boomed Uncle Max. "No, I am not looking for Betty. I have come to see you about your dog. I have received reports at the station that your dog has bitten a number of the local natives."

"Yes, Max," replied Mum, looking Uncle Max squarely in the eye. "I am fully aware of the unfortunate situation." Mum paused to light her cigarette. "But my dog is only protecting my daughter … and your children," Mum added.

"Yes, Poppy. However," Uncle Max replied curtly, "the natives have reported that your dog is vicious, and I cannot allow a vicious dog to roam the streets. It's too dangerous. I am here to officially warn you that if you do not stop the dog from biting the natives, the animal will be classed as a public nuisance and dealt with accordingly."

Mum bristled at Uncle Max's reference to Bozo as a public nuisance.

"My dog is not a public nuisance, Max, nor is the dog dangerous. My dog is only protecting the children, and what can I do? Bozo just follows the children on their bikes. I can't ...."

"Poppy," Uncle Max interrupted, "there have been a number of reports about the dog, and it is my duty to inform you that if you do not control the animal, the dog will have to be dealt with."

Mum knew she was on dangerous ground with Uncle Max. Mum also knew Uncle Max well. She decided to play him at his own game.

"Well, Max," Mum replied in a sarcastic tone, "far be it for me to stop you from doing your duty. You are quite welcome to take Bozo into custody. I will help you put the handcuffs on him if you wish. However, I can't guarantee your safety." A smile touched Mum face. "After all, my dog is soooo dangerous, he might bite you."

Uncle Max did not take kindly to Mum's comment about the handcuffs.

"Poppy," he replied in a stern tone, "this is no laughing matter. Do something about your dog, or I will have to charge you."

Mum stood up and walked towards the front door.

"It's no good charging *me*, Max," she said as she stepped onto the front veranda. "I didn't bite anybody's leg."

"Poppy," Uncle Max's face darkened. "this is your last warning. I am here to tell you officially, do something about your dog."

Uncle Max spun on his heels and, without a backward glance, strode purposefully towards the police paddy wagon.

Mum watched the paddy wagon disappear down the driveway.

She knew Uncle Max was right about Bozo. With a heavy heart, Mum lit another cigarette, walked inside, and reached for the phone.

Mum was good friends with Phyllis Skinner—the same Mrs. Skinner who Mum gave the fry pan to all those years ago. The Skinners owned Dolovat, a coco-producing planation about an hour's drive from town. Mrs. Skinner loved Bozo and often said that if Bozo became unmanageable in town, she would happily have him to Dolovat.

I wept openly on the day we took Bozo to Dolovat. I knelt before him, hugged and kissed his furry face, and tried to explain to him that he had to stay at Dolovat for his own safely. The Skinner family cherished and adored Bozo, and Dolovat provided plenty of land for Bozo to roam at will.

We visited the Skinners on a regular basis, and as time wore on, Bozo forgot his past life. Bozo loved the Skinners as much as they loved him, and for many years, Bozo reined supreme at Dolovat as king of his own castle.

Mum's Dog Charlie

Not long after the Skinner family adopted Bozo, our family left Rabaul for our annual leave in Australia. Most of the time, our house in Elanora Heights was tenanted, and Mum and Dad more often than not rented a house on Narrabeen Lakes for the month or so we were on leave.

However, this year our Elanora house was vacant, so Mum and Dad decided that we would stay in our house. It needed some maintenance and repairs, and the time we were in Australia was a good to time to attend to those tasks.

As we usually holidayed in Australia during the year, Mum insisted I attend school, and within a few days of our arrival, she enrolled me in the local primary school. Interestingly enough, many of the teachers at school thought I was the daughter of a missionary couple, as only missionaries lived in Papua New Guinea!

73

When I informed my teachers that non-missionary people also lived in PNG, my teachers expressed amazement and treated me like minor a celebrity. I must say, I enjoyed my celebrity status the whole time I was at school.

Elanora Heights Primary School was situated in bushland close to our home. For some reason, Dad was not comfortable with me walking alone through the bush to school, so most mornings he walked with me in the morning and waited by the quadrangle at the end of the school day to walk me home.

One afternoon, as I ran out from class, Dad walked quickly to meet me. "Hello, my pet," he greeted me, "guess what? Your mother and I went shopping today, and when you get home, there is something for you to see. So let's get a wriggle on, because your mother has been waiting all day to show you what it is."

As you can imagine, I was very intrigued as to what the "something for you to see" might be, but despite my excited questions, Dad refused to tell.

When we lived in India, Mum and Dad owned three cocker spaniels. Our dogs were bred primarily for retrieving snipe (a small game bird that lived in the paddy fields). However, as with all our animals, Gunna, Pooch, and Doodlebugs were also much-loved family members. It was heart-wrenching for Mum and Dad when they left our dogs behind in India, and they often expressed their wish for another cocker or two.

The "something for you to see" was in fact a six-week-old cocker spaniel puppy. The pup came from a well-known Sydney kennel and had an impressive lineage. Dad also casually mentioned (I think for Mums' benefit) that the pup had cost him "a whole month's salary"! Dad named our new pup Charles.

Charlie, as the family called him, was the cutest little thing I had ever seen. His coat was the colour of spun gold and soft as silk to touch. He had long ears, a gentle mouth, and big brown doe eyes.

As time passed, the family also discovered that Charlie possessed a real devil of a personality.

Mum loved Charlie with all her heart and spoilt him abominably. In fact, Charlie was allowed to do anything he liked, whenever he liked, without fear of *any* reprisal from Mum whatsoever. In return, Charlie loved Mum (and only Mum) unconditionally. He only tolerated Dad and me because we lived with Mum

If Mum went out in the car without Charlie, Charlie howled and yelped in protest, sulked by the front door, and ignored everybody else until Mum returned. He refused to sleep in his own little dog bed and took up residence on Mum's bed and the lounge furniture instead. He scratched doors if locked in or out, and he chewed socks, shoes, sheets, bedspreads, cigarettes, and matches. He ripped out newly planted shrubs and trees and tore big holes in the car upholstery. Completely unrepentant of any wrongdoing, he nipped and growled when chastised. In short, Charlie became the family brat.

One morning, the family decided to go out for the day to visit friends. Charlie was not invited. Annoyed at being left at home, he decided to amuse himself.

While we were away, Charlie completely demolished the inside of our home. He scratched and chewed all the newly erected Venetian blinds and curtains in every room except my bedroom; knowing how mischievous Charlie was, I had closed my door before I left. Charlie also clawed and gnawed a new lounge chair, chewed off all the buttons, and ripped up the cushions.

In the weeks we were in Sydney, my mild-mannered Dad lost his patience and became very annoyed at the havoc Charlie created. After he and Mum had replaced the blinds, curtains, and lounge cushions, Dad questioned Mum over her refusal to chastise (or allow anybody else chastise) Charlie.

"For Pete's sake," Dad said to Mum, "you have to start to discipline this puppy. He can't be allowed to carry on this way. He is ruining everything. It's come to the stage where we can't even go out now and—"

"Well," Mum cut Dad short, "Charlie is only a puppy, and puppies chew things. He is bound to grow out of it. Besides," she added, "it's been so long since I've had a cocker, and I don't have the heart to smack him. You smack him if it makes you feel any better."

Dad, of course, did not smack Charlie either. He just yelled and called Charlie "a naughty bad dog." Charlie didn't care. He just growled at Dad and ran and hid behind Mum.

As with all things cute, one tends to look past the misdemeanours of that person or in this case pet, and Dad and I grew love Charlie anyway.

Some weeks before, Dad had found a little stray kitten close to my school. Presumably, the kitten had been dumped, and my soft-hearted Mum decided to keep the little creature. We called the new kitten Tansy.

Our holiday drew to a close. Dad had been away from Rabaul for a month, and he returned first. Mum and I usually stayed in Australia for another few weeks. Just before we left Sydney, Mum booked Tansy and Charlie aboard the *MV Bulolo*. The *Bulolo* was on direct route to Rabaul, so Charlie and Tansy (unlike Scamp, who endured five weeks aboard the *Soochow*) would only be at sea for only a week or so.

On the day the *Bulolo* sailed, Mum kept me home from school. She needed my help to deliver Charlie and Tansy aboard the *Bulolo* by early afternoon. The *Bulolo* was moored at the overseas shipping terminal at Circular Quay, and as the Quay was about an hour's drive from home, Mum and I needed to start out early.

The morning turned into a comedy of errors that led to a fiasco of never-to-be-forgotten events. Our local vet recommended Mum sedate Charlie and Tansy before we started our journey and supplied Mum with a tablet for each animal. He advised Mum to give the tablet to the animals about an hour before we left home. Charlie swallowed his tablet, jumped on Mum's bed, and within a few minutes lapsed into quiet slumber.

Mum rolled Tansy's tablet in a ball of mince, and Tansy ate the mince without any fuss. However, as the sedative took affect, Tansy fought the effect of the drug. Terrified as to what had happened to her, Tansy screeched and howled in distress and, rather than sit quietly, dragged herself around the house in a half paralysed state.

As the time drew near for our departure, Mum put Tansy into our wicker laundry basket. The poor little cat was obviously very scared by the whole operation. She scratched at the basket frantically, hissed and spat when patted, and tried to claw her way out. Afraid that Tansy would escape the basket in the car, Mum bound the basket lid securely with some rope.

To calm her nerves, Mum guzzled a cup of strong black coffee and chain-smoked two cigarettes in a row. She threw Charlie's basket into the backseat of the car, picked up Tansy's basket, and placed it in the back seat as well.

Mum told me to sit in the back with Tansy and "talk to her." Mum quickly ran inside, picked up a very sleepy Charlie, and placed him on the front seat next to her.

Mum leapt into the drivers' seat and started the car. The motion of the car and the engine noise terrified Tansy. She yowled and screeched (in varied degrees of pitch) all the way to Circular Quay. The journey through the Sydney traffic was, to say the least, horrendous for all concerned.

Charlie and Tansy had to be cleared for travel by Australian quarantine before the animals boarded the *Bulolo*, so our local vet had made an appointment for us to attend a quarantine clinic on Bridge Street. Bridge Street was close to Circular Quay.

Mum parked the car at the Quay and decided it was best that we take a cab to Bridge Street. However, every cab Mum approached baulked at the sight of Charlie and Tansy. As time was of the essence Mum decided she and I would walk the animals to the clinic instead.

Charlie was still very sleepy, and he refused to walk at all; he took two steps and lay down on the pavement. As Charlie was almost fully grown, Mum found it difficult to carry him *and* his basket. Unfortunately, I was unable to help Mum, as I had Tansy in *her* basket

Mum and I now faced dilemma. We had to deliver the animals to the *Bulolo* by early afternoon, and now it was lunchtime.

Suddenly, Mum had an idea. She put Charlie in his basket, hoisted the basket on top of her head, and told me to do the same with Tansy's basket. Mum and I then set off to the Bridge Street clinic like two native women carrying water jars, with a drugged-asleep Cocker Spaniel and a drug-affected tabby cat that yowled nonstop.

The quarantine vet issued the necessary travel papers for Charlie and Tansy and, out of kindness, offered to drive us and the animals in his car back to the Quay. Mum said later that, when the vet offered a ride back to the Quay, she felt like falling on her knees and kissing his feet.

On board the *Bulolo*, Mum made herself known to the captain and asked to see the crew member assigned to look after Charlie and Tansy. The crew member, a jolly middle-aged cockney named Albert, befriended Charlie immediately. Mum explained that Charlie and Tansy were much loved and implored Albert to "please take care of them." Mum also advised Albert that Charlie's and Tansy's beds, blankets, brushes, and water and food bowls had been placed in a specially marked crate that was to be delivered to the ship that afternoon.

A few days later, Mum and I bade our Sydney friends goodbye for another year. As we boarded our aircraft at Sydney International Airport, my spirit soared. I would soon be home.

On the evening the *Bulolo* docked in Rabaul, the family gathered at the wharf and watched as the ship entered harbour. With excited anticipation, we debated aloud if Charlie and Tansy would remember us and wondered silently if they would like their new home.

Once the *Bulolo* docked, Albert led Charlie onto the deck. Charlie yelped and barked in excitement when he saw Mum, rushed straight up to her, and jumped into her arms. Mum burst into tears and cuddled and kissed Charlie all over. Albert disappeared and returned a short while later with Tansy.

Mum and Dad thanked Albert for his kindness to our animals, and as the *Bulolo* was in dock for a few days, invited Albert for dinner the next evening. When Albert visited, he informed Mum and Dad that Charlie's and Tansy's "luggage" never arrived aboard ship. He said the animals were a bit unsettled for the first few days. Charlie must have made his life a misery!

The next afternoon, however, the animals' luggage was delivered to Dad's office. Somebody had put the crate into the hold of the ship by mistake.

Tansy settled in very quickly with the rest of our menagerie, and Charlie soon claimed his place as top dog'. Dad and I noted that Charlie's behaviour hadn't changed one bit. In fact, Charlie's behaviour had become, if it was at all possible, far worse.

I guess animals and people alike are born with a particular personality and over time develop idiosyncrasies that set them apart from others. Goodness knows I have enough idiosyncrasies of my own. But of all the dogs the family owned when I was growing up, I remember Charlie as having a personality akin to a spoilt child and idiosyncrasies that, for a dog, at times baffled everybody.

Most times, Dad and I just ignored Charlie's brattish holier-than-thou attitude, however, when Mum wasn't around, we laughed openly about his doggy idiosyncrasies.

The moment Charlie arrived in Rabaul, he sought to re-establish his claim on Mum. Even before we had left the wharf, he exercised—with blatant belligerent indifference—one of his (or so he believed) many rights.

The *Bulolo* was the only ship docked at the wharf that evening. Dad had parked the car right in the middle of the wharf, and as we waved goodbye to Albert, Dad opened the back of the station wagon and called Charlie to jump in. Our dogs always travelled in the space behind the back seat; the family called this space the dog box.

Charlie looked at Dad, looked at the tailgate and the dog box, and looked away. Dad tapped the tailgate of the car and said, "Hop in, Charlie, and we'll take you home." But Charlie had other ideas. The dog box was *not* to his liking. Charlie looked at Dad with disdain, leapt onto the tailgate, bounced over the dog box and over the back seat, and landed on the front seat.

As Mum looked on, Charlie ignored Dad's repeated requests to get in the back. Dad sighed in resignation and muttered under his breath, "Oh, for Pete's sake, here we go again."

Mum eased herself into the front seat. Charlie yelped in excitement and clamoured onto her lap. He snuffed and licked Mum's face, and then pushed her aside and claimed the passenger window.

From then on, Charlie decided that the front seat of any car—be it Dad's office station wagon or Mum's VW—to be his rightful place, just so he could sit next to Mum. Only the brave attempted to move him.

Most of the time, Dad was infuriated by Charlie's blatant refusal to sit in the dog box, especially if we had been for a swim and Charlie's coat was wet and full of sand.

'Oh! For Pete's sake," Dad often lamented to me when Mum wasn't around, "why can't Charles sit in the dog box like a normal dog? Why does he *always* have to sit in the front and shake wet sand over everything?"

"Because he's spoilt and Mum lets him, Dad," I replied. "That's why."

One evening, Charlie behaved very badly. For the next a few days, Mum attempted, in a half-hearted way, to instil some discipline into her dog. Suffice to say, Mum failed miserably.

The family had been asked out for dinner, and Charlie was not invited. Dad insisted Charlie be locked on the front veranda. As we drove off in the car, Charlie howled in distress.

Mum was uncomfortable all evening and nervously smoked cigarette after cigarette. At the earliest opportunity, Mum pleaded a headache and asked Dad to take her home. Dad was not amused; however, ever the gentleman, he made the necessary excuses and we said our goodbyes.

As we stepped onto the front veranda at home, we noted that Charlie had entertained himself in our absence. A disaster of epic proportions lay before us.

He had chewed the cane lounge and shredded the cushions. Long strands of white kapok littered the floor. He had scratched at the books and magazines that had been left on the coffee table, and shredded paper lay everywhere. As a final defiant gesture, Charlie had jumped in and out of the veranda fish pond and smashed all the water lilies.

Dad fumed when he saw what Charlie had done. Too angry to speak, he just looked at the mess and muttered, "Oh, for Pete's sake,' under his breath. He swung around and glared at Mum.

Mum reached into her bag for a cigarette. She looked past Dad and said in a stiff voice, "Well, it's your fault; you should *not* have insisted Charlie stay at home. He must have been lonely. He's only a puppy," she added. Mum flicked on her lighter, lit her cigarette, and drew deeply. "What do you expect from a puppy?"

"The confounded dog is not a puppy," Dad replied angrily. "He's—" Suddenly Dad stopped mid-sentence. "Oh no, for Pete's sake," he muttered as he bent down and picked up a piece of white plastic. "The beastly dog has chewed my banana chair. Look!" Dad waved the piece of white plastic under Mum's nose. "I use that banana chair to sit on at the beach, and now he's chewed that too. What am I going to going to lie on from now on, for Pete's sake?"

Mum picked Charlie up and tucked him under her arm. "He's

only a puppy," she said quietly, stroking his head, "and puppies chew things."

"Puppy indeed," Dad spat. "Well, that's just fine and dandy. Why don't you give your 'puppy' one of your best evening frocks and let him bloody well chew that. With a bit of luck, your 'puppy' will choke on the frock, *and* we will all get some peace."

Dad stormed off towards the drinks cabinet. He stopped in front of the cabinet, reached for his brandy decanter, and poured a generous amount of Napoleon brandy into his brandy balloon.

The next day, Mum bought Dad a brand new banana chair—a blue one because blue was Dads' favourite colour. However, out of spite Dad refused to lie on his new blue chair; when questioned as to why he wasn't using it, he said that he found the chair "uncomfortable."

Even though Charlie was naughty, he radiated a very loveable Dennis the Menace attitude, and most of the time Dad and I found it impossible to stay mad at him for any length of time.

Charlie was a spaniel, and he loved water, any water. He loved sea water, rainwater, muddy water, green slimy water, and storm-drain water. As long as Charlie could swim in the water or roll in the water, Charlie was in his element.

The family loved the fact Charlie that loved the water. However, Charlie often engaged in a "water activity" that irritated Dad immensely.

Mum loved ponds and water lilies and had positioned a large round submerged concrete pond near our *hauswin* in the front garden. The pond was filled with water lilies and (to keep the mosquito larvae at bay) housed a number of small native fish. The lily pads covered most of the surface of the pond, and when the lilies flowered, the pond overflowed with sunshine-yellow flower heads.

Unfortunately our pond attracted the cane toads as well, and sometimes the pond water swirled with toads and toad eggs. Charlie considered the toads as playmates, and when the fancy took him, he played in the pond.

He jumped at the toads, chased after them, splashed around, and generally turned our pond into a muddy mess of smashed and broken water lilies.

Every time Dad heard the tell-tale splash as Charlie jumped into the pond, dad stopped what he was doing, flew down the front veranda steps, and brandished his hockey stick at Charlie.

Dad never ever whacked Charlie with the hockey stick; the hockey stick was just an idle threat, and Charlie knew that. Charlie therefore considered the whole fiasco a game.

"Get out of the lily pond, you damn confounded dog!" Dad yelled. "Get out now, for Pete's sake! Get out! You're breaking all the lilies. I'll give you a touch of my hockey stick if I catch you in that pond again. Now get out, you damn naughty dog."

As soon as Charlie saw Dad charge across the lawn, Charlie leapt out of the pond and ran around Dad's legs. Just as Dad bent to whack Charlie with his hockey stick, Charlie yelped in excitement, scooted out of Dad's way, ran around the lily pond a few times, bolted up the veranda steps, and bounced around the veranda furniture.

As soon as Dad stepped onto the veranda, the naughty dog ran and hid behind Mum.

Charlie's (sometimes) daily frolic in the lily pond turned into a battle of wills between my dad and Mum's dog.

"That damn dog jumps into the pond just to get my back up, for Pete's sake," Dad often said, "and the damn dog knows it too. He thinks he is smarter than me, but he's not. He's just a damn dog, for mercy sake."

I found Dad and Charlie's antics hilariously funny, although I was careful not to laugh when Dad was around.

Most of our leisure time was spent in and around water. Mum and I either snorkelled a coral reef or, in the wet season when the ocean was rough, journeyed to one of the many inland rivers and rode the rapids on old tyre tubes. I had great fun, and Charlie did too.

On the weekdays, after Dad came home from the office, he

often drove Mum and me to Pila Pila for a swim. Pila (as the family called it) was a nice drive from home and offered deep water, a sandy bottom, and no coral—perfect for an afternoon cool-off.

As dusk fell very quickly in Rabaul, we were organized and ready to leave home as soon as Dad had finished his afternoon cup of tea. Most times, Mum and I enjoyed (what Mum called) a "really good swim" before we headed home for our showers and dinner.

Charlie's first swim at Pila was a memorable one. The family discovered Charlie had an amazing talent: he swam underwater just like a seal. In fact, in the months that followed, I was delighted (more than delighted, I would say) that Charlie swam just as well underwater as he did on the surface.

Mum found a large stick at the water's edge, and as Charlie loved to play fetch, Mum threw the stick far into the water. Charlie splashed into the water and dog paddled towards the stick. As Charlie reached the stick, the stick sank to the bottom.

Charlie looked around and yelped in frustration—his stick had vanished. He put his head underwater, kicked his back legs hard, and disappeared from view. He surfaced a few seconds later with the stick in his mouth. Charlie shook the water from his ears and swam back towards Mum.

We say that the good Lord works in mysterious ways and the fact that Charlie held his breath quite well underwater proved a bonus for me: I outsmarted Charlie whenever we swam at Pila and (for an hour or so) had Mum to myself.

Charlie constantly vied for Mum's attention, and even when we swam, he never strayed far from her side. Most times, Dad and I just tagged along behind Charlie and Mum, and when Charlie nipped and growled at us if ventured to close to Mum, we just ignored him. However, at Pila, Charlie soon realised I cared little for his bad attitude. He quickly learned his limitations as a dog and grudgingly accepted Dad's company on the beach or amused himself elsewhere instead.

For many years, whenever we swam at Pila, I always played water games with Mum, and Charlie's continued dominance of Mum's time and affection irritated me no end. Quite by accident, I discovered a method to rid myself of the pesky dog and for a short while enjoyed a spot of mischief. I was delighted and amused to discover that my plan worked beautifully, and oh! was revenge sweet.

The high tide mark at Pila was always littered with driftwood of all shapes and sizes. Charlie often dragged the driftwood around the beach or carried it into the water for a game of fetch.

Most times, I enjoyed myself as Mum and I bobbed around the surface and played with Charlie. We threw the stick back and forth, back and forth between us until our arms ached. However, Charlie never knew when enough was enough; he wanted to play all the time. Sometimes I just wanted to play games with Mum, and Charlie objected to that.

It was late afternoon, and the water at Pila was slick like glass. The high tide had littered the beach with sea debris, and after Dad parked the car, Charlie dragged a piece of old wooden plank to the water's edge. The plank was smooth-edged and encrusted with small barnacles and seaweed. Charlie looked back at us and wagged his little tail. He wanted a game of fetch.

"That wood is too long to throw, Charlie," I said. "Go and find another bit, and I'll throw that for you instead." Charlie looked at me, looked at the plank, and barked again. "That wood is too big, Charlie," I said again. "Find another piece that's smaller."

I waded into the water and, with lazy strokes, swam away.

Charlie barked again, closed his mouth around the end of the plank, and dragged it into the water. Charlie's little legs pumped hard as he swam after me. I grabbed the end the plank and, in lazy circles, towed Charlie around.

After a few minutes, the plank became waterlogged at Charlie's end. Time after time, Charlie ducked his head under the water, grabbed his end of the plank, and surfaced the plank again.

Eventually, though, Charlie grew tired. I saw he was out of breath. Suddenly I had an idea. I was sick of towing Charlie around and wanted to play with Mum. I took a big breath, duck-dived with my end of the plank, and held the plank hard against the sea floor.

Charlie dived again, closed his mouth around the plank end, and tried to lift the plank from the sea bottom. Out of breath, Charlie surfaced, took a breath, duck-dived again, and tried to surface his plank.

I too was out of breath. I hoped Charlie would abandon his plank and either find another piece of driftwood to play with or leave me alone. I surfaced, took a breath, duck-dived again, and held the plank hard on the sandy bottom.

Charlie duck-dived and surfaced again and again. He grew more and more tired with each dive; his little lungs were no match for mine. He abandoned his plank, yelped in frustration, and dog paddled back towards the beach.

From then on, whenever Charlie annoyed me at Pila, I played my underwater tug-of-war game.

Mum, of course, chastised me. "You are cruel to my dog," she said. "He is no match for you in the water, and he just wants to play."

I took little notice of Mum's words. I just wanted some time with Mum in the water, without Charlie and his pesky personality.

When Charlie was about two years old, he was killed by a speeding car. We buried him near the lily pond in the front garden.

My mother was inconsolable at her loss, and sobbed and sobbed. Her grief was so severe, she carried it with her for a long time.

The memory of Charlie stayed with the family for many years. We did not speak of our loss, but rather remembered him as the funniest dog we had ever owned. For a long long time, a memento of Charlie hung on our lounge room wall.

The family had gone to Nonga for an afternoon swim. It was the wet season, and the sea was littered with debris. Charlie dragged a large palm frond out of the water and up the beach. Tangled in the waterlogged frond was a long piece of driftwood shaped like a snake. We took the "snake" home, and after the "snake" had dried, Dad hammered two red thumbtacks in its head and we hung it (along with our other Rabaul carvings) on our lounge room wall.

Charlie's snake hung on Mum's lounge room wall in Australia until she passed away, and now, almost fifty years after Charlie dragged this snake up the beach at Nonga, the snake (along with my Rabaul carvings and memorabilia) adorns *my* hallway.

I left Rabaul not long after Charlie died for my first year of boarding school in Australia. The days that led to my departure were busy, and my Mother addressed my school list like a zombie.

On the morning of my departure to Australia, Mum and Dad took me to the airport. After I had checked in my luggage, we adjourned to the airport lounge.

As the announcer called my flight, my mother said goodbye, kissed my cheek, and turned away. She was still so very grief-stricken at Charlie's death. Dad walked with me across the grassy airstrip that led to the aircraft steps. At the bottom of the steps, he put his arm around my shoulders.

"Pet," he said, "you are now going away to school just like I had to when I was a boy. I had to leave India to go to school in England. When you come home again, you'll be a big girl, and we'll have a new cocker puppy, so don't be sad anymore. I will look after your mother."

A few months after we lost Charlie, Dad contacted the kennel in Sydney where Charlie was born and enquired about a new pup. I was in boarding school when Charlie's half-brother arrived in Rabaul. He too travelled to Rabaul aboard the *Bulolo*.

Dad, for some reason, always named our animals, and when the new pup arrived, Dad called him Benjamin Disraeli.

Mokey and Mother's Pet

Not long after we first arrived in Rabaul, one of Mum's friends gave us a black and white kitten. Unfortunately, the kitten was attacked by our neighbours' dog and subsequently died as a result of his injuries.

Suffice to say, Mum was furious. She marched next door, ticked off the owner of the dog, and banned the dog from ever entering our yard again. The dog, of course, completely ignored Mum's warning and shortly after trotted over.

As I approached the dog and shooed it off, the dog ran at me and nipped my inner thigh. When Dad came home from the office that afternoon, he paid our neighbours a friendly visit and politely suggested they find the dog a new home, which they did.

Dad (ever precious) made it known about town that we had lost our kitten and enquired if anybody had a kitten that needed a loving home.

Soon after, we received word the Joyceys (who owned Vimmy Plantation) had a litter of kittens that needed homes. Mrs. Joycey offered a kitten to Mum.

Vimmy Plantation was situated at Kokopo, so the family made plans to visit the Joyceys for lunch the following Sunday. When we arrived, Mrs. Joycey led us into her kitchen and pointed to a box in the corner. Inside the box, all huddled together, lay a litter of grey kittens.

Mrs. Joycey told Mum the kittens were Russian blues. Mum's heart melted at the sight of the grey balls of fluff, and we came home with a little female.

Mum called our new grey kitten Smokey. For some reason or other, over the next few days, the family dropped the "S," and our new kitten just became "Mokey."

"Mother's Pet" was a poor neglected tortoiseshell-coloured puss that actually belonged to our next-door neighbours' *haus boi*. Dad named the little cat Mother's Pet because Mum used to shoo the half-starved puss away from our dog's dinner every night.

However, Mom's soft heart was no match for Mother's Pet's advanced state of emaciation, and so Mum placed food out for the little puss as well. Not surprisingly, Mother's Pet half-adopted us. The name was such a mouthful to say that the family just called her MP.

One day, Mum mentioned that she thought MP looked a little fatter than usual. Upon closer inspection, Mum discovered that MP was pregnant. A few days later, a somewhat thinner MP appeared again for her daily feed. Mum noted that as soon as MP had finished her rice and fish, she disappeared under the house. When Mum crawled after her to investigate, Mum discovered that poor MP had given birth to three little ones in the dirt beside our water tank.

Mum called for a cardboard box and some old towels, and everybody rallied around and ferried MP and her new babies upstairs and onto the veranda. From that day on, MP became part of our family.

The tomcat that had "tomcatted" with MP also had his wicked way with Mokey, and a few days after the birth of MP's kittens, as Mum was preparing lunch for some friends, Mokey went into labour.

Mokey was not amused by the discomfort of her labour and wanted company. She refused to lie in her birthing box, which Mum had placed in my bedroom, and get on with it; instead, Mokey dragged herself around the kitchen after Mum and yowled in pain at each contraction. When Mum and her guests sat down for lunch, Mokey dragged herself into the dining room. Mum apologised to her guests and asked if they objected to Mokey's birthing box being in the dining room.

Mokey finally gave birth to a tiny, tiny, seemingly half-dead kitten. Mokey took a long hard look at her offspring, hissed loudly, and promptly slapped the poor little thing.

"Oh dear," said Mum, "I wonder what's the matter with Mokey? It appears she's rejected her kitten."

Mum picked up the kitten and wiped it with a clean rag. She then commented that for a newborn, the kitten had an unusually large head. However, large head or not, the kitten was alive (albeit only just), and in its weakened state, if the kitten was to live, it needed milk from its mother.

Mum placed the kitten near Mokey's teat again. Mokey stiffened. She hissed in annoyance, spat at the kitten, hissed loudly again, and dragged herself to the other side of the box.

"Oh dear," Mum said again. "Mokey, for goodness sake, whatever on earth is the matter? Your baby will die if you keep carrying on like this."

Mum picked up the kitten again and gently placed it on Mokey's teat.

Mokey twitched the tip of her tail in anger and inched herself further down the box. She hissed like a cornered snake and, with claws extended, slapped at Mum's hand.

"Oh dear," Mum said. "What are we going to do if Mokey won't accept her kitten? The kitten will die."

Mokey narrowed her eyes and hissed again. Mum picked up Mokey's box and put the box in my bedroom.

"I have guests," Mum said to me. "I'll deal with Mokey later."

When Dad came home from the office and saw Mokey's new baby kitten, he promptly called the kitten Nicholas, after the Russian Tsar Nicholas III. Mum was impressed with the name Nicholas (as the new kitten was half Russian blue); however, Mum also pointed out that Tsar Nicholas III had died violently at a young age, so maybe the name Nicholas for Mokey's still-weak little baby was a bad omen.

Dad nodded. "However," he grinned, "the reason I thought Nicholas was a good name was, not because of the new kitten's Russian connection, but because of Tsar Nicholas's head."

Mum looked at Dad with a puzzled expression. "What on earth are you talking about, Father?" Mum asked.

"Well," Dad continued with a smirk, "Tsar Nicholas had a large head compared to his body, and this new kitten has a big head as well.

So I think Nicholas is a very apt name. Don't you think so, Suzie?" Dad looked at and me and winked.

"Oh for goodness sake, Father." Mum rolled her eyes in disgust. "I don't know how you can make such a silly observation. Tsar Nicholas did not have a big head, it was of normal size. Don't be so silly. I'll get a picture and show you."

Mum ran off and returned a short time later with an encyclopaedia She thumbed through the pages and found a picture of the late tsar and tsarina of Russia.

"There," Mum stated as she pointed to the tsar. "The tsar's head is normal."

Dad winked at me again and replied, "Oh, all right, darling, if you say so."

Big head or small, Mum and I liked the name Nicholas, and so we christened the new baby kitten "Nicholas, Tsar of Rabaul."

Mokey still hissed and spat at Nicholas and refused to allow the kitten to suckle from her. As the day wore on, Nicholas grew weaker and weaker. Mum said she doubted Nicholas would survive the night.

However, Mother Nature stepped in and relieved Mokey of her motherly responsibilities.

When Mum went to check on Mokey and Nicholas the next morning, she discovered that Nicholas had disappeared.

"Oh no," Mum thought, "Mokey has taken Nicholas somewhere."

However, as she walked past MP's box, MP meowed loudly. Sometime during the night, MP had jumped into Mokey's box and kidnapped Nicholas. Nicholas looked content, and his tummy was fat and round and tight as a drum. He'd obviously had a good feed. From that moment on, Nicholas became part of MP's litter, and the kitten never went hungry again.

When MP's kittens were six weeks old, Mum found homes for all of them except Nicholas. As Nicholas was, as Dad put it, "a touch soft in the head," we decided to keep him.

Shortly after, the town tomcat came tomcatting again, and MP once more fell pregnant.

"Oh no," lamented Mum as MP grew fatter and fatter. "Here we go again. I hope we won't have a repeat performance and all the drama we had the last time these cats had babies. I suppose Mokey's pregnant too."

Interestingly enough, even though Mokey lived to a ripe old age, she rejected all further "male advances" and never fell pregnant again. As for MP, Mum took her off to the vet as soon as her second litter were old enough to be housed and MP was de-sexed.

When the tom came a-calling again, all he encountered were two old maids who hissed and slapped him whenever he came near!

Many years later, my daughter Leanne asked me to mind her little cat Billie for a few days. The "few days" lasted twenty-two years. Billie had many of MP's traits. She was small, loving, a good cat mother, and loved all the animals who shared our home. I often wondered if Billie was MP reincarnated. My family was grief-stricken when Billie finally passed away. Billie, along with many other "family members," now rests peacefully in my garden.

Nicolas

Under MP's watchful eye, Nicholas (who always seemed to have his face in her tummy suckling) thrived. Even though Nicholas was only few days younger than MP's own litter, Nicholas grew at a much faster rate and in no time at all was twice their size.

Over time, Mum again found homes for MP's babies, and Nicholas enjoyed the fact that he now had MP all to himself. However, over the next weeks, Nicholas developed a habit, the sight of which Dad found most distasteful.

Nicholas was now almost half-grown and still suckled from MP. Dad, found that disgusting. Whenever Dad saw Nicholas attached to MP, Dad dragged Nicholas off, scolded him severely, and threw him outside. Not that Nicholas cared. Nicholas just marched straight back inside and jumped into MP's box.

As the weeks passed, the family realized that Nicholas just didn't look as "normal" as our other cats. In fact, Nicholas's head, once too large for his kitten-body, had (seemingly) failed to grow very much and was now too small for his adult-body.

At maturity, Nicholas's head was only about the size of a small mandarin. Dad, with his quirky sense of humour (and much to Mum's annoyance), renamed Nicholas "Pinhead."

Nicholas grew into a much loved and spoilt puss. He led an utterly charmed existence, blissfully unaware that the attention lavished on him was not because he was a good-looking puss but because family and friends felt sorry for him.

Thanks to Mum, Nicholas was privy to an endless supply of food treats: milk, fish (tinned and fresh), meat (raw and cooked), and cheese. I remember Dad was none too pleased one evening when he opened the fridge and found his favourite blue-veined cheese missing. Nicholas loved blue-veined. Mum, who loathed blue-veined cheese, later admitted to Dad that Nicholas was "hungry" so she gave Pinhead Dad's cheese. In fact, each time Nicholas sauntered past the fridge and meowed loudly, Mum loaded his plate. Consequently, Nicholas was quite chubby—or to put it more bluntly, Pinhead was just plain fat.

Nicholas also detested exercise. In reality, he walked very little at all. He just lounged around the house, and when he was hungry, he stood near the fridge and meowed loudly.

There was a time, however, when Nicholas decided to accompany Mum as she walked in the garden. Unfortunately, Nicholas's "walk" turned into Nicholas's "run," and that was the end of any exercise as far as Nicholas was concerned.

Mum kept a few beehives at the bottom end of the garden, and every so often donned suitable attire and smoked the bees into submission. When all was quiet, Mum collected the honey.

One day, Nicholas followed Mum down to the hives. Mum noted that as she approached the hives, the bees seemed agitated. Just as Mum applied the smoker, a group of guard bees buzzed Nicholas and stung him right on the tip of his sticking-up-in-the-air tail! Nicholas squealed in pain, leapt into the air, and ran for his life.

Nicholas's yowl scared the daylights out of Mum. She jumped in fright, knocked against the hive, and dropped the smoker. The bees, cranky at being disturbed, buzzed Mum in anger. In view of her current circumstance, Mum abandoned her idea to collect the honey and left the bees to settle again.

From that day on, Nicholas never ever ventured near the beehives again.

Nicholas lived for many years and never really changed from his kittenish ways. He remained a happy, fat, not-quite-right-in-the-head pussycat that always seemed to be around whenever you happened to open the fridge.

Benjamin Disraeli

I was at boarding school when our new cocker spaniel puppy arrived in Rabaul. Dad, called our new pup Benjamin Disraeli. Very soon, Benjamin Disraeli became just Dizzy.

Dizzy was Charlie's half-brother, and even though the pups shared the same blood, the similarities ended there. From the very start, Dizzy was a family dog—happy in the company of each family member individually or all the family together. Dizzy took kindly to our many friends who frequented our home and loved our native staff as well.

Dizzy was almost fully grown when I came home for my August school holidays, and within a day or two he realized that I was part of his family as well. Dad usually woke me each morning with a cup of tea, and when Dad placed the tea on my bedside table, Dizzy bounded into my bedroom, jumped on my bed, and greeted me with a lick on my face.

I was very happy that Dizzy accepted me into his family "pack" so readily and was quite surprised to find that he was content with just being a dog within a human world. In other words, Dizzy knew his place in the pecking order of our family. As a whole, his acceptance of that fact made a world of difference. This is not to say that Dad or I loved Dizzy any less than we loved Charlie—we didn't—but Dizzy loved all of his human family *equally,* and that made our day-to-day lives a lot more pleasant.

Dizzy possessed a really inquisitive attitude to all beetles and insects—and like any hot and steamy tropical location, Rabaul teemed with all manner of creepy crawlies. Indeed, as far as insects and beetles were concerned, Rabaul was full of the weird and the wonderful.

We were lucky that the insects and beetles were all quite friendly, and none was considered dangerous or poisonous. There was a certain type of beetle, however, that commanded a healthy respect whenever one happened to cross its path: the *Oryctes rhinoceros* (we just called the beetle a rhino beetle or copra beetle). To our horror, Dizzy loved to play with rhino beetles.

The rhino beetle is a formidable creature. An adult rhino beetle has an oval body topped by a squarish head. It can measure up to six centimetres in length, and it has a hard black shell and barbed legs. The beetle also has a large pair of horns or pincers that jut from its jaw, and when angered, the beetle hisses just like a snake.

Like it's namesake the rhinoceros, the rhino beetle is easily riled if disturbed, and often uses its horns as a defence. Suffice to say, the rhino beetle reined king over all the creepy crawlies that lived in Rabaul.

I was home from boarding school one evening when Dizzy had a very, very close encounter of the beetle kind.

It was the wet season and had rained heavily that afternoon, and although the sky had cleared somewhat, the horizon was still thick with storm clouds. The air had cooled, and as usual after a heavy bout of rain, the insects were out and about.

The family had finished dinner and one by one had drifted away to find something to read or something to do. I had made my way onto the front veranda, and with a book under my arm curled up on the cane lounge to read. Dizzy padded in and flopped himself on the floor at my feet.

He sighed deeply, rolled onto his tummy, and spread his back legs frog-like out behind him. Within a few minutes, his eyes closed, and he dropped off to sleep ... or so I thought.

All of a sudden, a large rhino beetle flew over the veranda railing and landed with a loud thud close to the water fountain. I heard the noise, put my book aside, and looked up. I suspected the thud-noise was a rhino beetle.

Dizzy also heard the thud. He opened his eyes and focused his attention on the beetle as it crawled towards Mum's potted orchid.

The events that transpired over the next few minutes turned our veranda into a wrestling ring—complete with a hyped-up-audience that yelled loudly—and very nearly sent my poor dad into a cardiac arrest.

As soon as Dizzy saw the beetle, he sprang to his feet. He charged past me, knocked over a small coffee table, and stopped within a centimetre of the beetle. The beetle turned, faced Dizzy, and hissed loudly. Dizzy dropped on all fours and growled softly. Unafraid, the beetle opened its long pincers, waved them about madly, and hissed back at Dizzy even louder.

Annoyed by the crashing-hissing-growling noises, I flung my book down and stood up. "Dizzy," I said crossly, "come here. Leave the beetle alone. Come. Leave it or it will nip you."

Mum and Dad, alerted by the noise, stepped onto the veranda.

"Is something the matter pet?" Dad said. "I heard a loud bang."

"It's Dizzy," I replied. "He knocked over the coffee table. He's after that rhino beetle that's near Mum's orchid. We'd better get him away from it, Dad, or the beetle will nip him. The beetle's already mad."

"Yes, yes," said Dad. "I can hear it hissing. We can't have it bite Dizzy, for Pete's sake. Those things have a nasty nip."

As Dad approached the beetle, Dizzy sprang to his feet and snapped at the insect. The beetle spread its wings and launched its heavy body into the air. Dizzy jumped to catch the beetle and missed.

The beetle collided with Dizzy's long fanned-out ear. The startled beetle hissed and hissed in anger as it hooked its barbed legs in the hair under Dizzy's ear. Dizzy squealed and shook his head violently. The beetle hissed and hissed like crazy and latched on even tighter.

Dizzy yelped in anguish and shook his head violently from side to side. Dizzy was panic-stricken. He was unable to shake the beetle free. He bolted through the veranda door and into the lounge room.

Dizzy lapped the lounge room twice, careered off the bookcase, ran under the dining table, and knocked over three dining-room chairs. As Dad dived under the dining table to catch him, Dizzy ran into the kitchen.

The kitchen erupted into a melee of noise. Dad shouted at Dizzy to stop, Dizzy squealed with panic, and the angered rhino beetle hissed and hissed.

Dizzy, followed closely by Dad, shot though the kitchen door and ran into the hallway that led to the veranda.

I screamed like a cheerleader egging on a favourite football player. "Catch him, Dad. Catch him. Get him before the beetle bites his ear. Quick, catch him!"

In a mighty effort, Dad lunged and crashed tackled Dizzy. He gripped Dizzy by the back of his neck and pinned him to the floor, but poor Dizzy was frightened. He misunderstood Dad's intentions, squealed in distress and struggled violently to break free.

In the meantime, the rhino beetle became even more irate. It hissed and hissed like a cornered snake …and the stress was all too much for Mum. She covered her ears and turned away.

"For God' sake, Father, do something!" Mum screamed. "Get that thing off Dizzy. I can't bear it. The poor little dog is so frightened. Do something, I beg of you."

"For Pete's sake, I'm trying," shouted Dad. It was the one and only time I heard my father raise his voice to my mother. "I'm trying, goddamn it, for Pete's sake, but Dizzy won't hold still, and I can't get the damn beetle off with one hand. If I let Dizzy go, he will bolt again. If you hold the dog, for Pete's sake, I can then see the damn beetle and get it off!"

My mother, for once, did as she was told. She bent down, grabbed Dizzy's back legs and held them still. Dizzy struggled violently and tried to get up, he shook his head from side to side and yelped as the beetle hissed again.

"For Pete's sake," Dad shouted, "will somebody hold his front legs."

I bent down and pinned Dizzy's front legs to the floor. Dad relaxed his grip on Dizzy and very carefully lifted Dizzy's ear.

'Oh, for pity's sake," Dad muttered. "What a mess."

The rhino beetle had endured its roller coaster ride under Dizzy's ear and had embedded its barbed legs deeper and deeper into Dizzy's long under-ear hair. The beetle was now almost completely entwined, with only its head *and* nippers visible—and the beetle was mad, very very mad.

My dad was not scared of many things, but an irate rhino beetle that nipped inflicted a nasty wound, and Dad for once was nervous. Each time Dad attempted to pluck the beetle from Dizzy's under-ear, the beetle twisted its head around, waved its nippers, hissed loudly, and tried to nip Dads fingers.

It was a seemingly no-win situation between Dizzy, the beetle, and Dad. Poor Dizzy, poor beetle, and poor Dad. Dizzy yelped each time the beetle hissed, the beetle hissed each time Dizzy yelped, and my dear old Dad yelped and cursed each time the beetle tried to nip him.

In sheer desperation, Dad hit the beetle with the back of his hand. Mum squealed and hurled a barrage of abuse at Dad.

"Don't kill it! Don't kill it! You'll kill it. Stop that. Stop. Stop. You'll kill it. You'll kill it!"

"For Pete's sake," yelled Dad, "*you* stop it. I won't kill it. These things are as tough as old boots. I won't kill it. How else am I to get the damn thing off? The thing is trying to nip me, for pity's sake."

Dad's backhanded swipe had half-dislodged the beetle. Dizzy shook his head, and the beetle dropped to the floor. Free at last, the beetle hissed again, spread its wings, and flew off into the night.

Dad emitted a long sigh, drew his hanky from his pocket, and wiped his face.

"Phew," he groaned, "that was an effort. I hope the damn dog has learned his lesson. For Pete's sake, don't let him go near those damn confounded things again, please Susie." As if it was my fault! "I can't go through that again.'

Dad struggled to his feet and stuffed his hanky back into his shorts pocket.

"I need a brandy," he muttered, "or I won't be able to sleep tonight after all that excitement."

"And I'll have a scotch, please," Mum added in a small voice. "A stiff one."

When Dizzy was a young dog, I found a pattern in a magazine for a child's toy. The toy (the magazine called it a "gonk") was a swimming-frog-shaped bag filled with sand or raw rice.

I decided to sew a gonk for myself and disappeared into Mums sewing room. I immerged a few hours later with a purple (I couldn't find any green material) raw-rice-filled gonk.

Alas, Dizzy fell madly in love with my purple gonk. One morning, he jumped on my bed and claimed the gonk as his own. From that day on, whenever Dizzy was at home, his precious often slobbery gonk dangled from his mouth. Come night-time, Dizzy refused to go to sleep without it.

Over the years, I sewed lots of gonks for Dizzy—red ones, yellow ones, blue ones, and even the odd green one as well.

Since we did not have television in Rabaul, the family developed ways and means to entertain ourselves in the evenings. We played Scrabble or mah-jong, listened to the radio, played records, chatted among ourselves, or just settled down with homework or a good book. Whatever the chosen situation, unless Mum and Dad entertained, the unspoken rule in the house was that the evenings were "quiet time."

Most times, Dizzy happily abided by our "quiet time" rule and fell asleep with his beloved gonk tucked under his chin. However, sometimes Dizzy misplaced his gonk. Come bedtime, he drove everybody mad as he looked for it.

One evening after dinner, Dad settled down on the veranda settee to read his book. He was tired and complained of a sore tail bone (the injury was a result of a boyhood fall). Dizzy leapt on the settee, pawed Dad's arm, and whimpered. Dad patted Dizzy's head and opened his book. Dizzy whimpered, jumped off the settee, and wandered off. He returned a few minuted later, jumped up on settee, and whimpered again. Dizzy had lost his gonk.

"For Pete's sake," Dad muttered under his breath, "what is wrong with that damn dog? He's mooching around from room to room with his claws going screech, screech on the floor, and I can't concentrate on my book."

"He's lost his gonk, Dad," I said. "You know he can't sleep without it."

"Well, for Pete's sake, help him find it, can't you? So we can all get some peace. I can't stand his screech-screech claws on the floor. Ask your mother. She may know where the damn gonk is. For Pete's sake, all I ask is for some peace in the evening, and my tail bone is sore. I do not want to come home to a damn circus."

I must admit I wasn't too interested in finding Dizzy's gonk, and after a half-hearted quick look-around, I came back to Dad.

"I can't find it, Dad. Dizzy must have dropped it somewhere."

Dad jumped up from the settee. He winced in pain and threw down his book.

"Oh, for Pete's sake," he groaned, "I just want some peace and quiet. My back is sore, and I've just taken my tablet. Where has the wretched dog put it then? Go and look in the bedrooms or something."

Rather than wait for help, Dad stomped off.

After a fruitless search in the house, Dad and I finally found Dizzy's gonk in the garden. We'd had rain that day, and the rice-filled gonk was wet .The rice had swelled, and I knew that in a few days, Dizzy's precious toy would reek of mould.

"Oh, for mercy's sake," Dad muttered as he picked up the gonk. "The damn thing's all wet. Dizzy can't have that, it will drip everywhere."

It was too late for me to sew Dizzy a new gonk that night, so Dad (after some persuasion) surrendered an old sock. I filled Dad's sock with some raw rice and tied a knot in the top.

Dizzy eyed his new gonk with interest, he was not quite sure at to what the sock was supposed to be *or* do. He sniffed at the sock-gonk and whined loudly.

"Oh go on, you silly dog," Dad said, irritated by the whole process, "that's the best we can do at the moment, pick it up and go to sleep, or I'll dong you on the head with the damn thing and *make* you go to sleep. I just want some peace and quiet so I can read my book."

Dizzy took Dad's hint of a "head dong" quite literally. He picked up his new sock-gonk and disappeared to find a cool spot. When I went to bed half an hour later, I found Dizzy fast asleep on the veranda, his chin resting on his new sock-gonk.

Dizzy lived with us for many happy years. One day, when Mum was on leave in Australia, Dizzy fell ill. Dad took Dizzy to the new local Rabaul vet, and the vet injected Dizzy with an antibiotic. Dizzy reacted adversely to the medication and died a short while later. My heartbroken Dad buried Dizzy, with his precious gonk, next to Charlie near the lily pond in the front garden.

CHAPTER 6

Ruth

I was about twelve years old when I first became aware of death. Up until then, I knew that people died. When they died, I knew they went away and didn't come back. But I didn't know, *really* know, of anybody who had gone away and had not returned.

Dad's mum Ivy Ellen (known to everybody as Granny) died on Christmas Eve the year before I was born. Mum and Dad named me after her, and Granny was the only person I knew of who had actually passed away.

When I was a child, I did not class our family as religious, although Dad and I attended church quite regularly. On the first Sunday of each month, our church held a family service, and Dad and I usually attended the service together. Mum held her own beliefs about God and the universe and did not attend church. Mum said she believed in a higher entity that encompassed all religions, not just Christians. Dad and I respected Mum's beliefs.

Regardless of creed or profession of faith, all ministers of religion and their families were well known in our small community. Indeed, clergy and townsfolk mixed freely with one another. As a family, we regarded the Catholic priests as personal friends, visited many of the

Seven Day Adventist mission stations, and were regularly welcomed in the homes of many others.

On my first day at Court Street Primary "A" School, Mum walked me to my new classroom and presented me to my new teacher, Mrs. Ross. As Mum walked away, I sobbed and sobbed. It was my first day at my new school, and I was quite overwhelmed by yet another change in my life. Mrs. Ross took me by the hand and led me into my new classroom.

There were only about fifteen or so children in the class—small by the standards of today—and as Mrs. Ross and I paused in front of the blackboard, a young girl raised her arm.

"Yes, Ruth," Mrs. Ross said.

The young girl stood up.

"There's a spare seat at my desk, Mrs. Ross," the girl said. "She can sit next to me."

Mrs. Ross nodded, and I made my way between the rows of desks. As I pulled out my chair and sat down, the girl smiled at me.

"My name is Ruth Haley," she said. "What's yours?"

Before I could reply, she added, "You're new here, aren't you?"

I nodded.

"Well, I'll show you where everything is," the girl stated, "at play lunch."

I nodded again and smiled weakly. I warmed to the girl at once. All of a sudden, my fears settled and my tears dried.

At play lunch, Ruth took me under her wing. She led me around the school and pointed out the girls' toilets, the drinking taps, and the play area. Ruth noted that I was dressed in a skirt and blouse, and she said she would ask her mother if she could lend me one of her school uniforms until I got mine. Ruth also told me that her real name was Andrea, but everybody called her by her middle name, Ruth.

"If you call me Andrea," she stated, "I won't know you are talking to me, because I'm used to Ruth. Everybody calls me Ruth, so you just call me Ruth too. Not Andrea."

I nodded my head and smiled to myself. If Ruth wanted me to call her Ruth and not Andrea, that was fine by me. I understood completely. I also had an attitude about my name. I did not answer if anybody called me Sue instead of Suellen. I still carry that attitude today.

At lunch, Ruth led me to a big fig tree that grew close to our classroom. She sat down under the tree, patted the ground beside her, and opened her lunch box. As we nibbled our sandwiches, Ruth told me her father was a priest and that they owned their own church.

"What church do you go to?" she asked between mouthfuls. Ruth just naturally assumed that I attended a church.

"I don't know," I replied, and I shrugged my shoulders. "I used to go to Sunday school when we lived in Sydney, but I don't know if it had a church."

Ruth bit into her sandwich and frowned. "Well, Sunday school *is* church," she informed me, "a children's church. I go to Sunday school, and then I go to Daddy's church, so I go twice on the same day. All my friends go to church," she added, "so if you don't know which church you go to, you can come to *my* Sunday school and then you can come with me to Daddy's church."

Ruth smiled. The question of which church I attended was settled.

Ruth and I were friends now, so I was more than happy to comply with her wishes. I found out later that I did go to the same church as Ruth anyway. Ruth's father was our Anglican minister, and our family are Anglicans.

My new friend Ruth was unpretentious and self-confident. She was a robust girl who brimmed with well-being. Her skin was clean, her eyes blue and bright, and her pale golden hair was dead straight, cut into a pageboy style. Ruth possessed a happy disposition, and she giggled at everything. She was mischievous and at times serious, and she held an inner peace, a strong faith in God, and a knowing destiny seldom seen in one so young.

I learnt early in our friendship to leave Ruth in charge of all "God" things, and as a child, I was suitably impressed that Ruth knew all about how God worked and how things would be in the heaven. I was happy for her to lead me on my path to enlightenment; I trusted her with all my heart.

'My daddy's a priest," Ruth often stated with pride, "and my daddy knows all about God and heaven. Daddy told me that when I die, I'll go straight to heaven. Besides, God likes priests, because priests do God's work. God likes priests' children too," she added, "so I'll be all right."

Ruth often assured me that she would go to heaven one day; there was never any doubt in her mind.

Our scripture classes were always held after play lunch on Wednesdays. One Wednesday morning, I was most surprised when Ruth me steered towards the third grade classroom. When questioned as to where we were going (our Anglican scripture class was held in our classroom), Ruth informed me that we were going to sit with the Catholics.

"Why?" I asked.

"Because," Ruth said, "I want to make sure that the other priests are teaching what they are supposed to teach about God and not telling any lies. Next week we will go to the Methodist scripture, and then we'll go to the Baptist scripture. If they are telling lies about God, I'll tell Daddy and they'll get into trouble."

I paused a moment, I unsure if we'd be allowed into a Catholic scripture class.

"Come on," said Ruth as she tugged on my arm. "Father Frankie is there already, and he's waiting to start. Hurry up or we'll be late."

I nodded and followed Ruth into the classroom. After all, who was I to question Ruth? Ruth was an expert on God—born to it, so to speak. Certainly Ruth knew better than I if the other ministers were "telling lies about God."

Ruth and I were a team, and I was happy to tag along.

From then on, whenever we fancied, Ruth and I sat with the other
Scripture classes. Nobody seemed to mind. In fact, the other ministers
greeted Ruth with a smile and a wave whenever we entered their
classroom.

Every so often, however, just for a break, Ruth and I stayed in
our own classroom and listened to Father Haley as he quietly spoke
of the love of God.

Ruth and her family lived in the rectory, the official residence for
our Anglican priest and his family. The rectory was situated on the
grounds of our very modest, very small wooden Anglican church.

A very large, very impressive white marble Catholic church
stood not far away, in the convent of Our Lady of the Sacred Heart.
The convent was situated on Balanataman Street, the same street on
which I lived.

As Ruth and I lived within walking distance of each other, we
played together most afternoons after school. We played the usual
New Guinea kid games, sorted through our shell collections, or
swapped stamps. We swam in the local pool, rode around on our
bikes, or frolicked with our dogs. There were also times when Ruth
and I did nothing. We just sat under the tree at home and, as children
do, talked of school, family, and friends.

Sometimes, as Ruth and I flitted between the rectory and my
home, we stopped and sat for a few moments in either the Anglican
or Catholic church. More often than not, we were drawn to the
Catholic church, for the Catholic church held more secrets.

One afternoon, Ruth and I were walking through the convent
grounds on our way to the rectory. As we neared the Catholic
church, Ruth broke her stride and paused.

"Let's go inside the church," she said, "and see if we can catch
anybody coming out of confession."

"Confession?" I asked, puzzled. "What's that?"

"Well, the Catholics have confession and we don't," Ruth
informed me. She turned to face me, for she felt this was important

and that I should take note. She took on her *I know all about God* voice and lent close to me.

'The Catholics have confession to confess their sins," she told me. "They tell the priest all the wrong things they have done, and then the priest forgives them."

"What sort of wrong things?" I asked, puzzled.

"Bad things ... sins. Like telling lies and stealing things," Ruth replied. "The devil makes them do it, so it's not their fault. But they have to tell the priest all their sins anyway, and that's called confession. The devil is really evil, and the Catholics get tempted by the devil all the time, you know, and so they have to go to confession. At confession," Ruth looked me square in the face to make sure I listened carefully. "They get the priest to bless them with holy water. The devil hates holy water," she added, "and then the priest forgives them. After that, they can go to heaven when they die and not hell."

I looked at Ruth and frowned. I was confused about the Catholics and their confession. My mind leapt into overdrive. I knew lots of Catholics; indeed, some of Mum and Dad's best friends were Catholics. The Campbells, for example, were Catholics, and they weren't bad; they didn't lie and steal. On the other hand, I *had* heard Auntie Dot talk to Mum of "going to confession," so now I was worried.

I also wanted to know what else the Catholics classed as a "sin," and did we Anglicans have the same sins as the Catholics?

Ruth tapped my arm and broke into my thoughts. "Come on," she said as she tilted her head towards the church, "let's go inside and see if there is anybody we know doing their confession. We'd better hurry before it's too late."

I nodded my head and grinned mischievously. I decided to quiz Ruth later about the Catholics and their sins. I was curious, yet eager to see if we'd caught anybody at confession.

The foyer of the Catholic church was empty and very quiet. A long wooden table shrouded in a white embroidered cloth stood against the sidewall. The table held neat piles of prayer books, religious leaflets, and small boxes of coloured rosary beads. A sturdy heavy-based plinth stood in an alcove by the door. The plinth was topped with a large marble font filled with water. Ruth made straight for the font, dipped her fingers into the crystal water, crossed herself twice, and peered inside the church.

"Nobody yet," she said in a hushed tone.

Ruth pointed to the font and whispered, "That's the holy water I told you about. You have to cross yourself with it before you go inside."

"What for?" I asked. "You told me it was for the priests to bless the bad Catholics with so they can go to heaven."

A look of exasperation passed over Ruth's face. She shook her head and raised her eyes.

"You have to cross yourself too," she stated in a voice that suggested I was too stupid for words, "to keep the devil away, remember. Look, we're in the Catholic church now and ..." Ruth leaned close to my ear and whispered, "the devil comes here sometimes. The Catholics have a really really bad evil devil, and he makes you do bad things. You have to cross yourself with holy water. It comes from the Holy Land and the priests bless it to make it *more* holy because the devil hates anything that's holy. The nuns put the holy water near the door so everybody can cross themselves before they go inside. That way the devil can't get them."

Ruth looked me square in the face. "Listen," she said, "Daddy told me the devil makes you do things you don't want to do, evil things, and then you go to hell and become one of his slaves. So you'd better cross yourself, or the devil will get you."

A wave of panic swept over me. My heart started to pound so hard my chest hurt. I was scared—dead scared. I grabbed Ruth's hand and tugged hard. I wanted to bolt. I wanted to run as fast as I could away from this Catholic church and its evil devil. What if Ruth was wrong and their holy water didn't work?

Ruth plunged our hands into the font. "Hurry up and cross yourself," she said, "before it's too late."

I crossed myself until the front of my T-shirt dripped with holy water. Obviously I had misunderstood Ruth about the sacred water. I didn't want to go to hell, and I certainly *did not* want the devil to make me his slave.

My voice quivered as I asked Ruth if the devil knew that we were Anglicans and not Catholics. Maybe he didn't, and that frightened me even more.

Ruth rolled her eyes again. "Stop being a scaredy-cat," she said, "of course he does. My daddy's a priest, remember?"

The fact that Father Haley knew me and that I was an Anglican quelled my fears ... somewhat. I knew that, if the need arose, Father Hayley would put in a good word for me, so I was safe. Suddenly I felt sorry for the Catholics, especially our friends.

"Come on," said Ruth, "let's go, or confession will be over and we might miss somebody."

I nodded my head and, just for good measure, crossed myself again. I'd heard enough devil talk for one day anyway. Besides, I felt we'd stayed by the font far too long. I was half convinced that the devil had heard Ruth as she discussed his evil ways and now skulked nearby, pitchfork in hand, ready to pounce and drag us both off to hell.

A cloak of cool air enveloped Ruth and I as we stepped inside the church. It was deserted except for a cluster of white-veiled nuns seated in the front two pews. The sisters of Our Lady of The Sacred Heart knelt, heads bowed, in silent mid-afternoon prayer.

We tiptoed over to a pew and sat down. Ruth pointed to a row of closed wooden doors. "That's where everybody goes to confession," she whispered.

I looked over at the doors. I really didn't care too much if we saw anybody or not. My mind was still on the Catholic devil. Ruth's tale of slaves and sins and a devil that made you do things frightened me more than anything in the whole world. I did not want the devil to get me, and I wondered if I had crossed myself correctly—or indeed if I'd crossed myself *enough* to keep him at bay.

I had never been inside our Catholic church before and felt quite overwhelmed by it all. The marble dome seemed to touch the sky, the marble altar seemed a mile long, and everywhere you looked, statues sat atop carved marble plinths.

The walls were filled with stained glass life-sized pictures of Jesus and His disciples; Mary and Joseph in the manger; and Mary Magdalene, her face distorted by grief as she wept at Christ's crucifixion.

A dark and foreboding picture of a cloven-hoofed Satan with pitchfork in hand, placed appropriately near the confessionals, terrified me to the very core. I tried not to look at the beast's angular twisted face, but I felt my eyes drawn to him again and again. Was I being tempted? I was terrified now that if I misbehaved, I'd go straight to hell, and goodness knows what Satan did to his captured slaves.

I quickly averted my eyes and inched closer to Ruth. Deep inside, I clung to the knowledge that, because of Ruth's connection with God, I was safe from the evil kidnapper. I was glad she was with me.

Ruth and I sat in silence on the hard pews and stared at the closed doors. After a few minutes, my fear abated somewhat, and I looked around. The inside of this house of God was certainly impressive. I was curious to know how the Catholics afforded to build such a big church and even more curious as to where the money came from to buy all the marble statues, pictures, and plaques that adorned the interior.

I decided to ask Ruth. She pressed her lips together and frowned. "Ah well, you see," she replied after some thought, "the Catholic fathers and nuns collect money. They visit all the native villages every week, and they collect money from everybody there to pay for everything."

"That's mean," I said, wondering aloud if any of *our* native house staff were Catholics.

"Our church has lots of money too," Ruth informed me, "but Daddy doesn't waste the money on building a big church or buying pictures and things. Daddy gives the money to the poor people instead, so they can buy food and clothes."

The Anglican religion grew in my estimation. I vowed to ask *my* daddy for more money for the collection plate the next time we went to church so that *Ruth's* daddy could help the "poor people" to buy food and clothes.

As the minutes ticked by, Ruth and I waited and waited to catch somebody as they came out of confession. But the wooden doors in front of us remained closed.

In the weeks to come, Ruth and I returned to the Catholic church whenever the fancy took us. We sat on the hard pews, swung our legs, and nudged and whispered to one another each time we heard the echo of footsteps behind us. Even though we witnessed the confessional doors open and close once or twice, we never ever saw anybody we knew.

Secretly, though, Ruth and I were pleased that we never caught anybody we knew at the confessional doors. After all, as we discussed on a number of occasions, *we* certainly did not want to be associated with anybody (friend or not) who had succumbed to temptation by the Catholic devil and had to confess to a priest in order to go to heaven.

Ruth always assured me that we Anglicans were never tempted by the devil, and that's why we didn't have confession. That sounded reasonable to me. Ruth also assured me that when Anglicans died, they automatically ascended to Heaven to sit on the right hand of God. Phew, what a relief!

The frightful life-sized picture of Satan that hung in the Catholic church when I was a child soon became an object of ridicule for me. In fact, I became quite brazen in my contempt. As soon as I entered the church, I marched straight up the picture, thrust my thumbs into my ears, waggled my fingers, laughed in his face, and stuck out my tongue. Sometimes, when Ruth wandered off, I even kicked the evil one in his shins and hissed, "Get back to Hell where you belong!"

One day at school, Ruth told me that she and her family were soon to go south on leave. "On Saturday," she said, "we're going to catch the plane to Sydney, and Daddy said we'll be away for a whole month."

"Leave" was a word we used for annual holidays. Most of the Rabaul folk took their leave in Australia.

"See you when I get back," Ruth said a few days later.

"OK," I nodded, "see you when you get back."

A few days later, I was surprised to see Dad enter my classroom. He whispered to my teacher Mr. Booth and asked if I might be excused from school for the rest of the afternoon. I noticed that Dad's face was full of sadness as he put his arm around my shoulders and propelled me towards the car.

"We will just go and sit in the church grounds, my pet," he said, "under the big tree where it is cool. I have something to tell you."

"What's wrong, Daddy?" I asked.

"I'll tell you when we get there, pet," Dad replied and patted my arm.

Dad was strangely silent as we drove down Mango Avenue. He sighed deeply and turned left into Malaguna Road. At the large fig tree that marked the boundary of the Anglican church, Dad eased the car off the road. He stopped the car under the tree and pulled on the handbrake.

Dad lit a cigarette, inhaled deeply, sighed again, and turned to face me.

"Pet," he said quietly, "I have something to tell you. There was a terrible accident yesterday. It's your friend Ruth and her sister, Lesley. They were run over by a car in Sydney, and an ambulance had to take them both to hospital. The new minister phoned me at the office this morning. Father Haley phoned him and asked him to let everybody know. I'm afraid both the girls were hurt very badly, and the doctors had to operate on them. Little Ruth was especially hurt; she has very bad head injuries."

He went on, "Everybody is very worried. The new minister said that Ruth is in intensive care, and as far as we know she is still hasn't woken up yet after her accident. Lesley was also hurt very badly, but not as badly as Ruth, and she's in intensive care too. Father and Mrs. Haley are both at the hospital with the girls."

The news of Ruth and Lesley's accident stunned me into silence. I had never heard of anybody being run over by a car before. I looked at Dad and frowned. A million questions rattled through me. What did he mean Ruth had "head injuries"? What sort of car had run over the girls? Was the car a big one? Was the car going very fast? And why was she still asleep if the car had run over her yesterday?

Ruth was my best friend. Just knowing she'd been hurt made me feel sick inside. I asked Dad if Ruth would be all right. I was too scared to ask him anything else.

"Of course she will all right, pet," Dad replied and patted my leg. "Of course she will be, and Lesley too. They'll both be all right. You'll see. I'm sorry I can't tell you more," Dad continued, "but you and I will go to church on Sunday, and we'll pray for your friend and Lesley to get better soon so they can come home. Maybe the new minister will have more news by then. I'm sure Father and Mrs. Haley will keep in touch."

I tried to imagine what it was like for Ruth and Lesley, but I couldn't. I had no conception of fear or pain. I'd never heard the siren of an ambulance let alone been in one, and I'd only been in a hospital once in my life, when I was seven years old and had my tonsils out. I didn't like the hospital one little bit.

Even though I didn't really understand the graveness of Ruth and Lesley's accident, I remember how frightened I felt inside.

At dinner that evening, Mum expressed sorrow at the news of the girls' plight. Mum said she felt frustrated by the lack of information and wondered aloud if the Sydney hospital would speak to her if she phoned and asked about the girls. Mum also said she could only imagine the anguish and heartache felt by the Haley family at that time.

Mr. Willcock, our school principal, held a full assembly at school the next morning. There were some children who had not heard the sad news. The assembly was attended by many of the ministers of other faiths and we all prayed for a quick recovery and safe return of Ruth and Lesley.

In the weeks to come, Father Haley periodically phoned our minister with news of Ruth's and Lesley's progress, but phone calls to and from Australia were expensive, and thus their conversations were hurried and limited. However as the weeks rolled by, we learned that Lesley's injuries had responded well to treatment, and she was becoming stronger and stronger each day. Alas, Ruth had sustained terrible head injuries, and her condition remained serious for a long, long time.

I still went to church with Dad on Sundays, although with some reluctance. I resented the new minister and didn't like his sermons. I missed Ruth's whispered explanations of the Holy Scripture, and I missed her strong clear voice as she sang the hymns we knew so well. I missed her at school, too. In class I stared at her clean empty desk, and day after day sat under the fig tree and ate my lunch alone.

One afternoon many months later, I was surprised to see Dad at our school gates. Dad's *draivaboi* Robin always collected me from school, so it was unusual to see Dad at the gate and not Robin.

"Hello, my pet," Dad said with a smile as I ran up to him. "I have some good news, so I thought I would pick you up myself this afternoon and take you home. Father Haley is coming home today, and Mrs. Haley and the girls will be home in a few weeks' time. Lesley is out of hospital now, and Ruth will be out soon too. So everybody is OK. Isn't that wonderful news? What say you and I go to church on Sunday, I'm sure Father Haley will have more news for us then."

A warm inner glow filled me when I saw the familiar white-cloaked Father Haley at church that Sunday. Ruth's Dad was home, and that meant Ruth would be home soon too.

Father Haley greeted his flock after an absence of many months. He thanked us all for our prayers and kindness, and he was honest and open as he shared his fears and the pain he and his family had endured the last few months.

As we knelt to pray, Father Haley asked God to bring his family home soon.

As my family sat at dinner a few weeks later, Dad told us Father Haley had called him at the office that afternoon. "Mrs. Haley and the girls will be home soon," Dad informed us. "In fact, they are coming home on the *Bulolo*, and the ship left Sydney today."

"Oh, that's wonderful news," Mum exclaimed. "We should celebrate their homecoming."

"You'll have your friend home soon, Susie," Dad smiled, "and won't that be good. You have missed her, haven't you?"

I nodded and smiled. I *was* glad Ruth would be home soon. I *had* missed her company, more than anybody would ever know. Soon though, everything would be back to normal, or so I thought.

The very next week, Dad took me to meet the *Bulolo*. Even though the wharf was only ten minutes' drive from home, Dad and I left the house an hour early so we could (as Dad told me) "park the car in a good spot."

The ship was to dock in the early evening, and as Dad and I waited, the wharf slowly filled with people. It seemed everybody had the same idea, for within half an hour, there were people and cars everywhere. The wharf *and* foreshore were jam-packed with friends waiting to welcome the Haleys home.

As Dad and I waited, I saw lots and lots of people I knew. I saw kids from school and teachers as well—Mr. Booth and Mr. Willcock were there—plus faces I'd seen in town (people Mum and Dad nodded to) and friends I'd seen at church and other functions we had attended. There were familiar faces everywhere.

The Catholic clergy were amongst the welcomers. Father Frankie, the head Catholic priest, long black rosary beads slung from his waist, smiled at me as he glided past. The Sacred Heart nuns, hands hidden in their habits, clustered serenely to one side.

As the *Bulolo* entered Simpson Harbour, the captain announced the vessel's arrival with two long hoots from the ships horn. A wave of happiness swept over me. I put my hand in Dad's and smiled up at him. I felt as if today was the first day of school holidays.

As the ship drew closer and closer, a surge of excitement vibrated through the impatient crowd. Everybody was charged with emotion. Some of our own had been away for far too long, and now they were home.

I scanned the ships railing as she docked. I could see Mrs. Haley and Lesley, but I couldn't see Ruth. Suddenly, a small figure in a yellow headscarf waved and waved.

"There's your friend, Susie," Dad said and pointed. "Look, there's Ruth. Wave to her, so she can see us."

I stared hard at the yellow-headed figure. Dad was wrong. That girl wasn't Ruth. That girl seemed small and thin. That girl certainly wasn't *my* best friend Ruth.

The gangplank hit the wharf with a bang. The yellow-headed girl flew down the ramp and flung herself into Father Haley's arms.

"Daddy, Daddy!" she cried, completely unaware of the crowd. "We're home."

The wharf erupted in noise. Everybody cheered and shouted in greeting. The gangplank swayed as a mass of welcomers clambered to greet Mrs. Haley and Lesley. Ruth was home.

I knew Ruth had been sick, but her appearance shocked me. Her face, once innocent and childlike, told of pain and heartache.

Her cheeks, once sun-kissed and plump, were hollow and pale. Her eyes, once vibrant and filled with mischief, were now distant, and I averted mine. As Ruth clung to Father Haley, I noticed the flesh on her limbs had melted away. Her arms were reed thin, and her legs resembled the stick figures she and I drew in class.

No wonder I thought Ruth was somebody else.

It had been many months since Ruth and I had seen each other, and all of sudden I felt shy. I am sure she did too.

"Are you better?" I asked.

"Yes, thank you," Ruth replied, "and my hair is growing now. Mummy bought me lots of scarves to wear, and ..."

I nodded and tried not to stare at her scarf.

"Will you be at school soon?" I enquired.

Ruth bobbed her head. "Yes. Mummy said as soon as I have seen the doctor and he says it's OK."

I nodded again and clung to Dad's hand.

Dad and I fell in with the crowd as we walked the Haley family to their car. As Father Haley drove off, everybody waved and whistled.

"Ruth is very skinny, Dad," I said as we made our way back to our car.

"Yes, pet," Dad said as he put his arm around my shoulders. "After all, she has been very sick. But she is home now, and she'll soon be as good as new. You'll see."

Ruth returned to school soon after, but for the morning lessons only. This time Ruth was dressed in a skirt and blouse and *I* was in my school uniform. I asked Ruth if she would like to borrow one of my uniforms to wear.

"No thank you," Ruth replied. "Mummy is making me some new ones. They just aren't finished yet."

Every play lunch Ruth and I made our way to the big fig tree near our classroom and sat under the thick tangled branches. We didn't play hopscotch or turn the skipping rope, we just shared our play lunch and sat quietly until the bell rang and we returned to class.

Ruth never spoke to me of her accident, and I didn't ask. I wonder now if Ruth really understood the consequences of her accident; perhaps not. I felt, though, that she accepted, unquestionably, the fate that had befallen her.

At times, I sensed that Ruth felt older than me—wiser, perhaps, from having known pain. At other times, I sensed that Ruth envied my innocence and craved to forget. Sometimes I sensed that Ruth felt neither—she felt the same as before, only she knew she wasn't.

Quite obviously Ruth had changed. Her accident had traumatized her both physically and mentally. Saddest of all, Ruth's accident had shattered her innocence and robbed her of her carefree attitude to everything and everybody.

Oddly enough, Ruth and I never ever spoke of God again. We never visited the Catholic church after school or spoke of the Catholic devil. We never spied on the other ministers or swapped scripture classes.

I still attended church with Dad and saw Ruth there, but Ruth and I did not sit together as we had done in the past. Ruth sat with her family in the front pew, and I sat with Dad in the middle pew. After the service, Ruth went home.

Ruth and I were still best friends; we both knew that. We just had to be patient together and wait for her to get better. And when she did get better, everything would be as it was before. I was convinced of that.

At Christmas time, my family and I went on annual leave to Sydney and only returned to Rabaul a week or so before the new school term resumed.

On my first day back at school, everybody assembled in their new classes on the school quadrangle. I looked around for Ruth and saw her in our old class line. I waved, and she beckoned me over.

"I have to stay here," she said.

"Why?" I asked, puzzled.

"Because I missed lots of school last year," she said, "when I was sick. So I have to stay in my old class."

"That's OK," I shrugged. "I had to repeat grade two."

"Well, we can still play together," I added.

Ruth shook her head. "The doctor said that I can't play very much. I'm still not allowed hopscotch or play skipping. But," she said with a grin, "I can play jacks, if you want to."

Ruth jangled in her pocket and drew out some coloured plastic knuckles.

"What are they?" I asked.

"Jacks," Ruth replied. "The nurses taught me to play when I was in hospital. They're good fun, look."

Ruth squatted in the dirt, threw the jacks into the air, and caught them on the back of her hand.

"See," she laughed, "they're easy."

I looked at Ruth and frowned. I wasn't sure about this new game she called "jacks."

Mr. Willcock called for everybody to assemble in his or her new class line.

"See you under the tree at play lunch," I said to Ruth as I scooted off.

In the weeks I had been away, Ruth's health and well-being had improved greatly. Her hair had grown enough for her to discard the scarf she had worn for so long. Ruth's hair was beautiful; light brown now (rather than a pale Nordic blond it was the year before) and all soft and fluffy and flyaway, like a new baby's. Her arms and legs were lean rather than stick thin, and her cheeks were plump and sun-kissed. Ruth smiled more readily now, and at times she even giggled.

Although I could see Ruth was better—much better than before I'd left—the tropical heat seemed to bother her. She fanned herself constantly to stay cool and often complained that she was hot.

Every play lunch, Ruth and I met under the fig tree and played jacks or marbles. Ruth's doctor ordered that she rest in the afternoon, so more often than not, Ruth went home for lunch and did not return to school until the next day.

One day at play lunch, Ruth seemed restless. She fanned herself constantly to stay cool. She seemed flustered and said she felt sick and wanted to go home.

I walked with Ruth to the headmaster's office. Ruth asked Mr. Willcock to phone the rectory so she could go home. Ten minutes later, Father Haley pulled up outside the school gates. He hustled Ruth into the car and drove off at high speed.

The next morning, I waited under the fig tree, but Ruth wasn't at school. When Dad came home from work that afternoon, he told me that Ruth was in Nonga Hospital. The next day, Mum phoned the hospital and asked how Ruth was. The sister on duty told Mum Ruth was "comfortable" but not allowed any visitors.

Over the next two days, Ruth's condition deteriorated. On February 16, 1965, Andrea Ruth Haley, or "Ruth" as her family and friends knew her, passed away. Ruth's family was with her when she died.

As soon as Dad heard the news about Ruth, he collected me from school. Dad silenced my questions and drove me straight home. He then took me into the garden and told me my best friend had died.

Mum, Dad, and I gathered as a family in our sorrow. We stayed quietly at home until late in the afternoon, and as the sun set we drove to our little grassy airstrip so our dogs could have a run. As we made our way through the streets of the town centre, I noticed the flags at half-mast.

"Are the flags at a half-mast because of Ruth?" I asked Mum.

"Yes," Mum replied quietly, "as a mark of respect for her. How terrible for Father and Mrs. Haley. How terrible for everybody."

After dinner that evening, we tuned into our local radio station. After the news, the station announcer called for a minute's silence in remembrance of Ruth. People from far and wide had phoned the station and expressed sympathy for the Haley family. This is how it was for our small community; we had lost one of our most precious gifts, a small child, and the town mourned.

As we lived in the tropics, Ruth's funeral was held the next day. I don't remember if Ruth's service was in the morning or in the afternoon, but I do remember that after breakfast, Dad sorted me out.

"Come and sit with me on the front veranda, Susie," he said. "I have something to tell you. Pet," he said, "I know how sad you feel because at one time, I felt very sad too. You know, Granny died on Christmas Eve, the year before you were born. Everybody was so upset we didn't have a Christmas that year. We buried all her presents with her."

I looked at Dad and nodded. I'd heard Dad's story many times before.

"You will always remember Ruth, pet," he added. "Do you know why?"

I shook my head.

My Dad never missed an opportunity to tell a story. "When I was a boy in India, I had a best friend called Joe. One day Joe was run over and killed by an elephant, a rogue elephant. Joe's mother very upset, and so was I. Even though Joe died a long long time ago, I still remember him to this very day."

"Were you and Joe best friends, Daddy?" I asked.

"Yes, pet," Dad nodded, "best friends. Just like you and Ruth."

I put on my best blue dress for Ruth's service and my good black patent-leather party shoes. Mum picked flowers from our garden, and when I entered our church, I placed the flowers near Ruth's coffin.

As Mum and Dad sat down in our middle pew, I squeezed myself between them. I noticed that our little Anglican church was overflowing with Ruth friends.

Father Haley and Father Frankie (our much-loved and respected Catholic priest) stood quietly at the altar together with another white-cloaked clergyman. It was Father Dean Rowney, our Anglican priest from Lae, who conducted Ruth's' service.

I do not remember much about the service at all, but I do remember that I kept my eyes firmly fixed on Ruth's coffin and tried to imagine her asleep inside. I did not really believe I would never see her again.

As we said goodbye to Ruth that sad day, tears flowed from the whole of Rabaul. And when Ruth's coffin left our church, we, her school friends, lined the pathway as a guard of honour.

After Ruth's service, Dad and I followed Ruth's flower-laden car to our local cemetery, a small clearing at the base of South Daughter Mountain. Only a few people had gathered there to say a last goodbye. As Ruth's coffin disappeared from view, I watched as Father Haley prayed and threw a handful of dirt into Ruth's grave. I felt overwhelmed by sadness. As he stood alone quietly in his sorrow, I wanted to go to him, to ask him, to *tell* him, to please ask God to bring Ruth back.

Later that afternoon, as I sat quietly by myself on the front veranda, I felt, for the very first time in my young life, the deep incomprehensible emotion people call *sorrow*. I did not cry or sob or wonder why Ruth had died. My emotion was much quieter than that. I felt a physical pain deep inside me—pain, numbness, and confusion and those feelings hurt.

The day after Ruth passed away, Father Frankie held a requiem mass for Ruth in the Catholic Church. I chose not to attend the Mass. However, I do remember that when the Mass had finished, Balanatanum Street, Malaguna Road, and the convent that surrounded the church was filled with people—not just Catholics, but people of all faiths. It was a poignant reminder of Ruth's passing and a testament to the bond our small community shared.

The adults who were around me at the time of Ruth's death said that I was too young to realise what had happened, and that was a blessing. Adults are funny people, for it was *they* who didn't understand. I had lost my friend, my first true friend. I certainly knew what had happened. I knew Ruth was gone, but I also knew with absolute certainty where Ruth had gone to. I also knew that one day I would see her again. Ruth and I had discussed that fact often enough.

I still carry the memory of Ruth in my heart. I still think of our Anglican church, the Catholic church, and yes, even the Catholic devil. And I still remember vividly the happy days we had together as children in a place lost in time.

Not so long ago, I came across an old school autograph book. On one of the pages, Ruth had written in big bold letters: "Roses are red and violets are blue. You are my best friend and that's true. Love Ruth Haley."

Rest forever with God, Ruthie. I hope you have remembered to keep a seat for me.

The last time I was home, I visited the Catholic Church. As I stood in the foyer, I noticed the marble font had gone. A small wooden table and a white ceramic bowl stood in its place. As I dipped my fingers into the holy water, I smiled; it had been many years since I had crossed myself. My eyes grew misty as an overwhelming feeling of nostalgia swept through me.

In my mind, I saw Ruth, my best childhood friend. I saw her at school, at church, skipping, swimming, and playing jacks … and in my mind, I heard her tell me, very clearly, not to be afraid ever, because we are Anglicans, and Anglicans are not tempted by the Catholic devil. I crossed myself again, just for good measure.

The church was empty of worshipers, and I noticed the inside had changed. The marble altar had been replaced by a wooden one, the statues and stained glass windows had gone, and the front pews were empty of nuns. Like all buildings in Rabaul at that time, a fine layer of volcanic ash covered every surface.

I strode over to the alcove beside the confessional doors. The picture of Satan had vanished; the space was empty. All of a sudden,

I felt cheated. This is *not* how it is supposed to be. The last time Ruth and I saw him, he was lurking next to the confessional doors, pitchfork in hand, ready to pounce on some poor Catholic who had sinned. *Damn*, I thought, *damn, damn damn*. For old times' sake, I just wanted to kick his shins and tell him to continue to stay the hell away from me and mine, and to remind him that Ruth was watching him and *if* he slipped up ever, mark my words, Ruth would get him for sure, and he'd be history. Of that I was certain.

My story of Ruth was first published in 1996. Before publication, I contacted the Haley family and asked their permission to share my memories of Ruth. After publication, Father Haley, who was then an assistant bishop of the Anglican Catholic Church in Australia, wrote me a beautiful letter. In part, his letter said *"we feel you have captured in writing something which only another child could experience and we could only sense."*

How true …

CHAPTER 7

Our Friends

We did not have television in Rabaul when I was a child, and as a result, I sought entertainment elsewhere. I swam every day, collected seashells and stamps, rode my bike, and played with my school friends.

Even though we were fairly isolated, we still kept abreast of world events. Mum and Dad tuned into the ABC or BBC every night, and the Australian newspapers were delivered by air every Saturday morning.

The lack of television protected me from the everyday horrors of murder and mayhem so often seen on TV today. I lived in an untouched paradise in the true sense of the word. The only trouble I heard of came from faraway places, and the only violence I encountered was a slap on the bottom from my parents. One-parent families were non-existent, drugs were a word that had no meaning, and only adults drank alcohol and smoked tobacco.

Is it any wonder that so many of the children who spent their formative years in Papua New Guinea have been accused of being spoilt, blasé to the point of ignorance in their attitude, and maladjusted? And why so many of us, when we meet, speak only of our "spoilt and maladjusted" youth?

For many years in Rabaul, we shared our lives with three wonderful families: the Dixons, the Hayeses, and the Campbells. Here are some of the happy times we enjoyed together on our little island in the Pacific Ocean.

The Dixon Family

Leigh, James, and Paul Dixon, like me, were New Guinea kids through and through. The only life we knew was of sunshine and fun. We lived with the whims of nature every day, and without a second thought, took for granted the natural abundance and splendour of our island paradise.

We giggled and jigged along with the ever-present *gurias* and barely glanced at the roadside signs that read "Danger! Unexploded Bombs." (The bombs were a legacy of World War II.) We wrinkled our noses when Tavurvur Volcano belched sulphur fumes, and passed over tiger cowries (*Cypraea tigris*) as big as a man's hand when we snorkelled. We feasted on mangoes, ate paw-paw for breakfast, and rather than lollies, sucked on Chinese chilli-soaked ginger pieces instead. In our innocence, we assumed the rest of the world lived as we did.

It was Christmas, and the family had joined the Dixons to celebrate this special day in their home on Namanula Hill. Auntie Kathyann had provided a lavish traditional feast on Christmas day, and when we had finished stuffing our faces, she banished all children outside.

"Now, children," she addressed us, "we adults wish to partake of our Christmas fare in peace and quiet. You have all finished your lunch now, and you will go outside and play with your new toys and not return until called. Is that understood, all of you? I don't care if you kill each other, you will stay outside until summoned."

We all nodded and scooted outside.

Paul Dixon was a cute-as-a button two-year-old with a shock of curly blond hair and a vocabulary of only one word: "baa." Some months earlier, Paul had accidently swallowed some of his grandmother's heart pills, and the effect of the medication had left him with a temporary speech impediment. Rather than hinder his cheeky personality, Paul's impediment enhanced his animated view of everything and everybody and endeared him to all.

That year, Santa had given Jamie a new toy train. The train was fine and smart looking, with a brightly coloured engine and eight carriages. The train was also powered by the very latest technology: mentholated spirits.

Young Paul was very taken with Jamie's new train and wanted the train for himself. Paul threw aside his new Christmas toys and pestered his elder brother all morning to play with the train. Time and time again he tugged on Jamie's hand, pointed to the train, and yelled, "baaaa, baaa," and a much louder "baaaaaa!" when ignored.

After lunch, Jamie gave in to Paulie's loud baaaas, and the two brothers struck a bargain. Paul could play with Jamie's train for a short time, if Paul stopped being a pest and never asked for the train again. Paul, at two years old, agreed.

As the afternoon progressed, Paul sat quietly on the veranda and "baa-toot-tooted" everybody with Jamie's train. As the time passed, Paul became thirsty. Mindful of his mother's warning to stay outside, Paul unscrewed the cap of the fuel tank on the train engine and drank the mentholated spirits.

The mentholated spirits burnt Paul's mouth in an instant. He gagged and spat on the ground, vaulted off the veranda and ran up to Jamie.

"Baa, baa," Paul croaked as he tugged on Jamie's arm. "Baaa … baaaaa."

Santa had been very generous with gifts that year and had given Leigh a plastic toy army. The army consisted of soldiers and assorted army vehicles. Leigh and Jamie had "dug in" the army around some broken coral rocks, and the boys were annoyed at being disturbed. The "enemy" was near, and their soldiers were in danger.

"Oh, what's wrong, Paul?" Jamie said crossly. "Rack off. The Japs are close. Rack off or you'll give us away."

Paul coughed and spat in the dirt.

"Baa!" he wailed loudly and pointed at the train.

"What do you want? If the train's empty, too bad. I'm not filling it. You're a pest. Now just rack off and wait for Dad."

"Baaa ...baaaa baaaaaa," Paul wailed as he stamped his little bare feet.

I emerged from under the shade of the mango tree and walked over to Jamie.

"I think there is something wrong with Paulie's mouth," I said. "I think he's drunk the stuff in your train."

Paul started to cry and spat on the ground again.

"Baa," he coughed, and wiped his palms over his tongue.

Leigh looked up at me and frowned. He stood up and brushed the dirt from his shorts.

"Did you drink the stuff in Jamie's train?" he shouted at Paul. "Did you?"

Paul sniffed and spat on the ground again.

"Because if you did," Leigh shook Paul by the arm, "you're going to get it. Show me the train. If you've drunk that metho, you're in big trouble."

Paul shook his head and then nodded. He gagged and baaaad louder.

Leigh put his face close to Paul's and sniffed Paul's breath. He frowned and screwed up his face.

"Phew, Paul, you stink," he said. 'You did drink the train metho didn't you? Well, you're going to die, 'cos Dad said the metho's poisonous and it'll kill you. You're stupid for drinking it, and Dad's going to get you now ... and so is Mum. Somebody better tell them that Paul's going to die ... or *we'll* get it too."

"Paul's drunk the train metho," Leigh said to Jamie and I, "and Dad said it's poisonous, so we had better tell somebody or Paul'll die."

Given the situation, it *was* important that "somebody" tell the adults what Paul had done. However, when an adult "laid down the law," we children abided by that law, without a second thought. Auntie Kathyann's warning was foremost in our minds, and all of us were scared of the consequences if we disturbed the adults at lunch.

"Look, we'll all go inside together," announced Leigh. "They can't get mad if Paul's going to die, can they? Come on."

We mounted the steps and stood on the veranda by the dining room door. Leigh pushed Paul to the front and whispered loudly to him to "go inside and tell Dad."

Paul ran through the door and up to Uncle Bob.

Uncle Bob enjoyed fine food. Indeed, his reputation was unsurpassed among our friends. Mum said that Uncle Bob had a "cast-iron gut" and "would eat anything," so when the Christmas turkey came out of the oven, nobody was surprised when Uncle Bob placed the turkey neck and gizzard on his plate.

Paul stood by Uncle Bobs' chair. A strangled "baaa" passed his lips.

Uncle Bob threw Paul a disdainful look and placed the remains of the turkey neck on his plate. He washed his fingers in the crystal finger bowl and wiped his hands on his damask serviette.

"Yes, Paul," he said dryly. "Do you require something?"

"Baa," said Paul as he pointed to his mouth and stuck out his tongue.

Uncle Bob frowned.

Paul screwed up his face, thrust his fingers in his mouth, and clawed at his tongue. He heaved and spat on the floor at Uncle Bob's feet.

Uncle Bob drew in a sharp breath and turned away.

"Kathyann," he said, "your son has just spat on the floor."

"Baaa baaa baaa!" yelled Paul even louder.

"Oh, for goodness sake, Paul, what is the matter?" Uncle Bob shouted. "Can't you see I'm having my lunch? Kathyann, ask him what he wants, can't you?"

Auntie Kathyann laid her knife and fork on her plate. She looked from adult to child. "Robert," she said crossly, "I am having my lunch. Paul, what is the matter? I told you to stay outside until called."

"We think Paulie drank the metho," Jamie yelled from the veranda. "He must have been thirsty, and *you* said we had to stay outside."

"What metho?" Auntie Kathyann asked.

"My *train* metho," Jamie yelled loudly.

Auntie Kathyann jumped up from the table and grabbed Paul by the shoulders. She shook him hard and shouted, "Paul, did you drink the metho in the train? Did you?"

"Baaaa," nodded Paul.

"Oh my goodness," Auntie Kathyann whispered. "Robert get the car."

Uncle Bob and Auntie Kathyann whisked Paul off to Namanula Hospital.

Luckily, the mentholated spirits had little effect on Paul, and all he suffered from was an upset tummy. By the time Uncle Bob and Auntie Kathyann returned from the hospital, Jamie's new Christmas train had been banished to a top cupboard, and Paul spent the rest of Christmas afternoon in a pampered haze of milkshakes and boiled lollies.

Some time ago, Uncle Bob told me the saga of the train continued. Jamie came to him a few weeks later and complained that his train wouldn't run properly. Upon close inspection, Uncle Bob found that the mentholated spirits used to drive the train had been replaced with whiskey: Uncle Bob's whiskey. Uncle Bob suspected their *haus boi* Balus had drunk the metho. When Uncle Bob confronted Balus, Balus confessed. He had indeed drunk most of the metho and replaced the metho with whiskey. Balus was subsequently dismissed.

For a number of years, the Dixons accompanied our family on

our usual Sunday picnic. We were always happy to see them, and when the two families joined together, we became a jumble of chaos and laughter.

The Hollands and Dixons shared cars, goodies for lunch, and beach towels. Auntie Kathyann also loved Chinese salty plums and always had a bag of the treats stashed nearby. Auntie Kathyann was very generous with her salty plums and distributed them freely every time we children came near her.

Uncle Bob was an enthusiastic collector of seashells, and there was always animated banter between the two families as to who had the better shell collection.

The Dixon boys, like me, were very strong swimmers, and they enjoyed snorkelling the coral reefs that dotted the coastline of Rabaul just as much as Mum and I did.

I remember this day particularly well.

It was mid-Sunday afternoon and the two families had been at Nordup since early morning. After lunch, Mum, Uncle Bob, the boys, and I picked up our goggles and sandshoes and headed once again for the reef.

Auntie Kathyann and Dad had spread a beach towel under the shade of the coconut trees and settled down for a chat. Like Dad, Auntie Kathyann rarely swam. The Dixons had recently been blessed with a new baby daughter, Awan, who after her feed had fallen asleep in her *buka* basket on the sand. Paul, who was still too young to snorkel, amused himself with some nearby hermit crabs.

As the late afternoon approached, the waterlogged Holland and Dixon reef explorers drifted slowly towards the shallower water. Leigh and I had left the main party and lagged behind. The sea was calm and slick like glass, and as we all were totally at home in the water, our absence passed unnoticed.

Suddenly, Jamie ran from the water and up the beach.

'Leigh's drowned Suellen!" he screamed to Auntie Kathyann and

Dad. "I tried to get her up but I couldn't. Leigh's standing on her underwater and she can't breathe."

Dad jumped up and ran to the waters' edge. He automatically counted heads. One was missing. As Dad shaded his eyes against the afternoon sun, he saw Leigh way out in the distance. Although Dad knew the water was deep (it was high tide), Leigh was standing up. As Dad looked on, Leigh wobbled from side to side, lost his balance, flayed his arms about, balanced, and stood up again.

The colour drained from Dad's face. He knew instinctively something was wrong.

"Bob … Poppy … get Susie … get Susie …Bob!" Dad screamed at the top of his lungs.

Dad waved arms frantically to attract attention and ran into the shallow water. As Dad couldn't swim, he was powerless to do anything.

Uncle Bob lifted his face from the water and looked toward the beach.

"Bob!" Dad shouted through cupped hands. "Leigh's standing on Suellen. She's underwater and can't get up." Dad pointed to the outer reef. "They're over there. Get her up, Bob, quick! Get her up, or she'll drown."

Uncle Bob spun around and saw Leigh in the distance. With adrenalin-powered strokes, Uncle Bob reached Leigh within seconds. He duck-dived between Leigh's legs and saw my motionless body pinned under Leigh's feet. Uncle Bob grabbed me by my arm, pulled hard, and pushed me towards the surface. As my head broke the water, I heaved, coughed, and heaved again.

"What is going on?" screamed Uncle Bob as he pushed Leigh out of the way. "Get back to the beach now, you little fool."

Uncle Bob took hold of me and towed me back towards the shore. As Uncle Bob and I drew near, Dad ran up the beach and fetched my beach towel. Everybody gathered around as Dad draped the towel over my shoulders.

"There there, pet," he said, "you're OK now. Thank you, Bob," Dad added. "That was a lucky escape, wasn't it?"

I coughed and rubbed my face with my towel. I turned to Leigh and stared hard into his eyes.

"I couldn't get up, you stupid idiot!" I shouted. "I only said you could stand on me for a little while. It wasn't my fault you were tired. You nearly drowned me! I'm never going swimming with you again."

I hiccuped, stormed off, and sat in the car.

Later on, Uncle Bob gave Leigh a severe tongue lashing about water safety. Needless to say, the very next Sunday, all was forgotten, and Leigh and I paired again and snorkelled off into the distance.

Many years ago, Mum and I visited Uncle Bob and Auntie Kathyann in their home in Benora Point. As we spoke of our shell-collecting days, Uncle Bob gave me part of his shell collection. Uncle Bob's shells now share a space with my shells in my glass-topped table on my back veranda.

The Swedish ambassador planned a visit to Rabaul, and Auntie Kathyann had decided to host a small cocktail party in his honour. Apart from the Planters Annual Dinner, Auntie Kathyann's party was *the* social event of the year, and the invitations were very much sought-after. However, the invitations were only offered to the heads of departments and their wives, bank managers and their wives, and one two professionals—a *very* select gathering indeed.

Mum and Dad decided that I, for the benefit of "experience and education," should be introduced to the Swedish ambassador. Mum informed me that I would accompany her and Dad to Auntie Kathyann's party and that I should consider said meeting with the ambassador a "privilege."

There were, however, strings attached to that privilege.

On the afternoon of the party, Mum issued me a stern warning: bad or impolite behaviour would be dealt with promptly and severely, and after the initial introductions to the ambassador, I was to say goodnight, leave the immediate area, and stay out of sight for rest of the evening.

Auntie Kathyann had excelled herself in every aspect to ensure Mr. Ambassador felt welcome and comfortable that evening. Her staff had worked tirelessly all day. Her large garden had been clipped and manicured to perfection. Bamboo poles topped with a cloth bag soaked in mosquito repellent, ready to be lit at dusk, lined the drive and surrounding area and the large mango tree under which most of the guests would sit had been strung with low-slung kerosene lanterns. Cane chairs had been scrubbed clean and placed in intimate circles, white damask tablecloths had been starched and ironed, and the silver was polished and crystal glasses washed.

Auntie Kathyann had also given a great deal of thought to the party menu and ordered Russian caviar, smoked salmon, and pumpernickel. Suffice to say, only the very best of Australian wine, French champagne, and spirits would be offered.

By nine o'clock, the ambassadors' welcome party was in full swing. Auntie Kathyann's *haus bois*, dressed in their white starched *laplaps*, hovered silently and offered delicious little treats on silver trays. Cocktails, Pimms No. 1, Johnny Walker (Black Label naturally) whiskey, laughter, and conversation flowed endlessly as the social elite of Rabaul clambered to impress our distinguished guest.

Auntie Kathyann was pleased the evening had, so far, progressed without a mishap. However, the Dixon boys and I were bored—very *very* bored—and we were somewhat miffed as well. We children had been introduced to the Swedish ambassador when he had first arrived at the party and had been smartly dismissed a few minutes later. We were bitterly disappointed in His Excellency. He certainly wasn't what we expected, and now we felt sorely ripped off.

The adults had touted Mr. Ambassador's importance so much that we had likened him to the British royal family, and were stunned when he arrived in a normal car, was dressed in a normal white shirt and trousers, and was, of all things, *bare-headed*. Where was his jewelled crown? We wondered. And didn't all royals wear a long cape and carry a sceptre?

As we discussed the absence of Mr. Ambassador's crown, cape, and sceptre, Jamie suggested his crown and or his cape might be under guard in a special locked box, and that Mr. Ambassador might wear them later. If that was the case, we children were determined to be around to witness the event.

A large frangipani tree was situated on the perimeter of the garden, and the tree was a perfect vantage point for us to observe Mr. Ambassador. The tree had wide spreading branches, so we could all sit comfortably under the tree and still see the party guests. Apart from that, the tree was situated on a direct route from the kitchen to the party, and as the *haus bois'* passed us with trays laden with yummy treats, we freely helped ourselves to whatever was on offer.

From time to time, Dad glanced over in our direction, just to make sure we behaved ourselves. Once or twice he caught us as we stared and whispered at Mr. Ambassador and, annoyed, motioned at us with his hand to clear off. We could see by Dad's face that he was not amused. Finally, Dad strode over and in no uncertain terms told us to "bugger off, quick smart." Dad reminded us that it was rude to stare and that Mr. Ambassador did not "appreciate rude children."

Somewhat affronted by Dad's remark about rude children, we lapsed in to silence.

The mosquitos had also taken refuge under the frangipani tree. The buzzing little blighters settled on our bare arms and legs and nearly sucked us dry (I guess the mossies were hungry too). However, mosquitos or not, we were determined to stay exactly where we were, just in case Mr. Ambassador's cape, crown, and sceptre *did* appear.

As time wore on, we became even more bored. We were sick of waiting for something to happen and decided Mr. Ambassador was a fake.

"I know where there is something buried," Jamie stated with

authority after a while. "It looks like a grave. I bet it's an old Jap body. The Japs always buried their bodies with their swords and guns and things; I bet the stuff's still there. Who wants to go and dig it up?"

Paul squashed a mossie and wiped the blood from his leg.

"Baa!" he volunteered.

The fact that there was and old Japanese grave nearby fired our curiosity. The Japanese had occupied Rabaul during World War II, and it was quite possible that indeed, there just might be an old war grave nearby.

After we discussed the grave and likely contents thereof, we decided that Jamie and Paul would go and dig up the grave, and the rest of us would stay under the tree—just in case we were wrong about Mr. Ambassador and he might finally bring out his crown, cape, or sceptre. If the grave contained anything of interest, the boys would bring the souvenirs back to us before they showed anybody else. Jamie and Paul grinned with anticipation and disappeared into the darkness.

The mission was a success, and the bounty hunters ventured forth to bestow their buried treasure on the honoured guest. Those attending Mr. Ambassador's welcome party were unaware that two small boys had invaded their select gathering. The boys slipped into the circle of light and scanned the sea of merry faces. Paul fixed his eyes on the centre of attention and pushed his way through the enraptured audience. The crowd parted without a murmur.

Paul stopped in front of Mr. Ambassador. "Baa!" he said and ever so gently placed his "treasure" in Mr. Ambassador's lap.

Mr. Ambassador looked down at his lap. He frowned and looked back at Paul.

Paul drew himself to his full height. "Baa!" he grinned.

A smile touched Mr. Ambassador's lips. "Tank you," he said. "And vot do ve have here?"

The boys had indeed found some "treasure." Not World War II treasure, though. A once-treasured and now very dead cat!

The party guests stepped back as the putrid stench of the rotting carcass permeated the night air.

Uncle Bob jumped up from his seat and ran over to Mr. Ambassador. He grabbed the dead cat by the tail and raced to the edge of the garden. He lifted the carcass high above his head and swung his arm in a circle. The cat's tail snapped off with a crack, and the carcass sailed through the air and landed in the bushes below. Uncle Bob looked at his outstretched arm; the cat's tail protruded from his clenched fist. He flung the tail over the edge and strode purposely back to party.

Mr. Ambassador stood up and brushed the dirt from his starched white trousers. He bent over, ruffled Paulie's blond curls, and roared with laughter. "Tank you, young man," he said, "tank you. In all my travels, I have never received such an unusual gift."

"Baa!" grinned Paul.

Jamie looked at Uncle Bob. In spite of Mr. Ambassador's kind remarks, Jamie knew he and Paul were in for a tongue-lashing. Jamie grabbed Paul's arm, and they bolted towards the frangipani tree. The boys vaulted up the trunk and scrambled along an outstretched limb. Leigh and I bolted too, just in case Uncle Bob confused one of us with one of them.

"Mr. Ambassador," Auntie Kathyann began, "I sincerely do apologise ..."

Mr. Ambassador roared with laughter again. "Oh, please, please, not to worry, Mrs. Dixon. Please. Children vill be children ... and I tell you someting, after zee war, everybody, including me, also looked for tings that were left behind by our enemy."

Just last week, Andrew and I visited Auntie Kathyann, Awan, and Awan's husband, Robert, in country New South Wales.

Over lunch, I asked Auntie Kathyann if she remembered Mr. Ambassador's party.

"Of course I remember," she replied, "as if it was yesterday. That incident with Paul and the cat really turned the party around. It broke the ice, and everybody settled down and enjoyed themselves. I can still see Bob standing at the bottom of our garden with the cat's tail in his hand. The ambassador was such a nice man and so jovial. We had such a wacko time. The party went on till the wee small hours, until there was nothing left to eat and nothing left to drink. I really don't know how I got through the next day," Auntie Kathyann added. "I had such a headache."

It had been many years since I had seen Auntie Kathyann, and over fifty years since I had last seen Awan. We enjoyed a magical two days, reminisced about our times in Rabaul, and remembered with love those we had lost.

When the Swedish ambassador retired from his official duties, he visited Rabaul again. When Mum and Dad heard he was in town, Mum invited him for dinner. Mr. Ambassador—his actual name escapes me—was a relaxed, jovial gentleman who spent the greater part of the evening in conversation with me. He told me he was a grandfather and had grandchildren similar in age to me. "Now that I am retired," he said, "I am able to enjoy their company more often than before."

He also me I was lucky to live in such a beautiful country, have warm weather all year round, and most importantly, have the freedom to do whatever I wished without the constraints of *too* much parental influence!

In those lazy and carefree days, the mischief and fun was enjoyed not only by the Dixon children and me but by the adults as well. Not so long ago, after lunch one day, Uncle Bob laughed loudly as he related this anecdote to me.

Rabaul Trading Co. employed a Greek gentleman named Con. I remember Con was very fat, had skinny white legs, and sported black slicked-down hair. Con told everybody that he had a wife, "Elena," in Greece, and that Elena was very beautiful. Alas, nobody believed him.

As you can well imagine, we were all surprised when one day

Elena arrived in Rabaul—and even *more* surprised that she was indeed very beautiful. Unfortunately, Elena didn't like Rabaul, and she left soon after without so much as a by-your-leave.

Con was devastated when Elena left and subsequently took to "the drink." Not the usual Johnny Walker that most people enjoyed, but his own homemade liquor: a concoction of aniseed oil and gin. Con called his homemade liquor ouzo.

One day Dad and Uncle Bob decided to "distil" some of their own ouzo. Armed with a few bottles at a picnic one Sunday, Dad and Uncle Bob sampled the home-distilled ouzo all day. The hangover that ensued, for both of them, had painful results. Dad was violently ill the next day and was unable to go to the office. Uncle Bob suffered the same consequences.

When I reminded Mum of the incident, she said, "Oh yes, that was dreadful. I remember Bob and your father making Con's bloody ouzo and getting sick. I had to phone Fathers' office and tell lies that day. I had to tell Father's secretary that Father had an upset stomach. I couldn't possibly tell her that your father was hung-over from making his own moonshine, now could I? Your father and I had a bloody great fight over it. I was most embarrassed. Kathyann was furious with Bob too. She also had to ring Bob's secretary and also tell big fat lies."

The Holland and Dixon families enjoyed many fun-filled and joyous years in Rabaul, and shared a friendship so strong and fulfilling that it extended even when Uncle Bob joined the Food and Agricultural Organization of the United Nations in 1963. For many years, Uncle Bob and Auntie Kathyann corresponded with my family from many parts of the world—Ecuador, Venezuela, Samoa, Nepal and Indonesia. Uncle Bob retired from the UN in 1981, and he and Auntie Kathyann settled in Australia.

I was visiting my mother when, one morning, Auntie Kathyann phoned to tell us that Uncle Bob had passed away the evening before. His death was sudden and unexpected.

Mum and I spent the day in quiet reflection. Mum sobbed at the loss of a true and cherished friend.

"Kathyann and Bob were such good friends," Mum said. "I loved them, I really did, and I miss them. I miss them both."

Mum chose not to attend Uncle Bob's service. "I just couldn't bear it," she said, "and Kathyann will understand.."

I too was greatly saddened by Uncle Bob's passing. I would never be able to talk with him again, never be able to laugh and reminisce about the times our families shared on a little island in the middle of the Pacific Ocean. Except, of cause, in my memory.

Robert Gilder Dixon 5/9/1916 – 12/8/2004

Rest in peace, Uncle Bob

The Hayes Family

After we had been in Rabaul a few years, the Hayes family joined our circle of friends. Uncle Max was a commissioned officer of the Royal Papua New Guinea Constabulary. He was also the official police photographer for the Rabaul police station, and as the station in Rabaul was always busy, Uncle Max carried out other normal police duties as well. Auntie Betty was a Queen's appointed nursing sister who specialised in ophthalmic nursing, and she had been appointed to a senior nursing position at the (native) Nonga Base Hospital. Uncle Max and Auntie Betty had two young daughters: Suzanne, who was a little younger than I, and a toddler, Vanessa. Vanessa was born in Rabaul at the primitive European Hospital on Namanula Hill.

Uncle Max was a tough and stern police officer. He frightened the wits out of everybody in town, and largely due to his dedicated efforts, our town remained virtually crime-free. Uncle Max insisted the police station operate strictly to rules and regulations, and he never deviated from those rules for anything or anybody. He even booked Auntie Betty (much to her annoyance and everybody else's mirth) whenever she parked illegally or exceeded the speed limit. Uncle Max also "arrested" Suzanne one day and escorted her to the police station, photographed her, and "charged" her for not eating her dinner.

Auntie Betty was a wonderfully placid woman with an infectious throaty laugh. When off duty from the hospital, she devoted her time to the local Girl Guide Association (of which I was a member), collected seashells and stamps, and—much to our amusement—tried her hardest to outwit Uncle Max.

The Hayes family lived in Biak Street, a few streets away from us, and as we enjoyed their company, we saw them often.

One afternoon, Auntie Betty dropped by our house for a coffee and chat with Mum.

"Poppy," she said as she eased herself into one of our lounge chairs, "my *haus boi* Buut told me the other day that he was a cannibal when he was a *pikinini*. I want to know what it was like being a cannibal and ..." Auntie Betty stirred her coffee and added hesitantly, "if Buut liked eating human flesh."

It is a documented fact that, many years ago, cannibalism took place in Papua New Guinea—not only on the mainland but on the surrounding Islands as well. The practice of eating human flesh was regarded as ritualistic. If a family member had passed away or a tribe had been victorious in battle, the natives believed that if the deceased were eaten (either whole or part thereof), those who engaged in the act assumed the departed spirit and strength and therefore become more powerful.

Understandably, the early missionaries actively discouraged cannibalism and valiantly endeavoured to stop this abhorrent practice.

Our family knew of a few *Lapun* natives who admitted that they had, at one time, tasted human flesh, although (for obvious reasons) the subject was rarely discussed at the dinner table. However, our very dear friend Auntie Betty had a sharp and enquiring mind, and cannibalism was only one of the many topics she sought reference and discussion on.

Auntie Betty's interest in Buut being a child cannibal took Mum completely by surprise. Mum remembered thinking at that time, "Just like Betty to wonder about such a thing!" However, out of respect for her friend, Mum chose not to question or judge Auntie Betty's curiosity.

"Well, Betty," Mum suggested, "if you *really* want to know the ins and outs of cannibalism, why don't you simply just *ask* Buut!"

Auntie Betty sighed deeply at Mum's suggestion. "I did, I did, Poppy, the other day, but Buut wants a bottle of whiskey as payment for the information, and you know Max. If he finds out, he will be very angry. I bought the whiskey, and ...' her voice trailed off.

"Well, Betty," Mum added, "you are quite welcome to bring Buut here to the house when Max is at the station. You can ask Buut in privacy then to your heart's content, without fear of Max finding out. Maybe that will satisfy your curiosity. Just let me know when and—"

"Oh, Poppy, thank you!" Auntie Betty interrupted. "I was hoping you would offer. Fancy, a cannibal in our midst!"

Auntie Betty stubbed her cigarette in the ashtray and stood up. A smirk touched her face as she said goodbye to Mum and left.

It was imperative that the meeting between Auntie Betty, Buut, and Mum be kept a secret from Uncle Max. It was illegal for the native population to consume alcohol, and Mum and Auntie Betty knew that. They faced dire consequences if Uncle Max found out.

After many cloak-and-dagger phone calls, a day when Uncle Max was *on* duty at the police station and Auntie Betty was *off* duty at Nonga Hospital was finally arranged.

Everything had been prepared as per Auntie Betty's instructions that hot and steamy morning. Promptly at 9 a.m., Auntie Betty's noisy old blue VW roared up the driveway and screeched to a halt in our carport. As Mum heard the sound of Auntie Betty's car, she walked onto the veranda.

"Hello, Poppy," said Auntie Betty, her eyes shining with anticipation as she strode up the veranda steps. "Buut has agreed to tell all today. Haven't you, Buut? Is the coast clear?"

"Good morning, Betty," Mum replied. "Yes, there is nobody here, and everything is ready for you."

"Buut," Auntie Betty said breathlessly, "come on. Poppy … now …let's get started. Where are we all going to sit?"

Buut was a sumu–sized native from Namantanai in New Ireland. In earlier days, the native tribes of New Ireland and New Britain were considered warlike and were well known for their internecine warfare. The Namantanais' were also very much feared for their ardent cannibalism.

Buut's face split into a wide grin as he lumbered up the veranda steps and mumbled a shy good morning to Mum. Clutched tightly to his bare chest was a bottle of Red Label Johnny Walker whiskey. Buut looked at Auntie Betty and patted his precious bottle. He was ready and eager to tell his story.

Mum returned Buut's greeting and led the way to the back dining room. Earlier that morning, Mum had placed some glasses on the dining table, along with a large alabaster ashtray and matching table cigarette lighter.

Auntie Betty pushed Buut into a chair and poured a generous portion of whiskey into a nearby glass. She flopped down and slid the glass over to Buut.

"Poppy," Auntie Betty said with a low throaty laugh. "Isn't this exciting?"

Auntie Betty lit a cigarette and inhaled deeply. She reached for Buut's Johnny Walker and filled her own glass.

"Right," she said. "Let's begin. Buut, remember a long time ago when you were a *pikinini*, you told me you ate some human flesh. Is that true or *gaiman?*'

Buut nodded his head and said yes, it was true that when he was a very small child he had eaten human flesh.

Buut lifted his glass of whiskey to his lips, drained the glass in three noisy gulps, and settled back into his chair. After some thought, he grappled in his *laplap* pocket and placed a wad of native tobacco and a half sheet of newspaper on the table in front of him. He selected a thick strand of tobacco and rolled the sticky wad into a strip of torn newspaper.

"Was this human flesh nice?" Auntie Betty whispered. "Did it taste good?"

Buut reached across the table and picked up the table lighter. He flicked the lighter, held the flame to his long thin newspaper cigarette, and inhaled deeply. He shrugged his shoulders and ran his hands over his woolly hair.

"*Misis*," he said, "some of it was good. Some parts I did not like. They were too tough."

Auntie Betty raised her eyebrows and looked over at Mum.

"Tough? How tough, Buut?" Auntie Betty asked. "Well, that's interesting, isn't it, Poppy? So what parts were tough, Buut? Was the leg tough, or the arm tough? You tell me."

Buut shrugged again and grinned. He slid his empty glass towards Auntie Betty, indicated for her to fill the glass again, and sucked deeply on his cigarette.

"*Misis*," he said as he reached for his glass, "I will tell—"

"Well, what about the top part of the leg?" Auntie Betty cut him off midsentence. "Or the top part of the arm? Surely that couldn't be tough. What do you mean *tough*, Buut? Do you mean tough like *bulmakau*, or what?"

"*Misis*, I will tell you—"

"Buut," Auntie Betty interrupted again. "what about—"

"Betty, for God's sake!" Mum leant across the table and tapped Auntie Betty's arm. "Let the man speak. Give him a chance to talk. There is no hurry. We have all day."

Buut looked over at Mum, picked up his glass tumbler, and drank noisily. He wiped his mouth with the back of his hand, turned down his mouth, and shrugged again.

"Yes, *Misis*, I tell you—leg and arm, some parts were tough."

Auntie Betty slid the bottle of Johnny Walker towards Buut and indicated with her hand for him to fill both glasses again.

"Buut, I can certainly understand you say some parts were tough, but even so, I want to know more. I want to know what part you liked best … and," Auntie Betty continued, "what parts you didn't like. Was the human flesh nice anyway … even the tough bits?"

Buut filled both glasses with whiskey. He looked at the tip of his newspaper cigarette and snorted. He reached for the table lighter again, lit his cigarette, and sucked deeply. The pungent smoke swirled around Buut's face as he leaned back in his chair and frowned.

"*Misis*, suppose you …"

"Well, what about the bottom then?" Auntie Betty asked in an exasperated tone. "You know," Auntie Betty stood and patted her ample behind, "what about the bottom? Is that tough? Tell me that. You're not telling me very much, and you said you would, so you'd better, or I'll have my whiskey back. That bottle came out of my housekeeping money."

Aunty Betty's "cannibal cross-examination" morning had progressed too slowly for her liking, and she was frustrated by the lack of information. Buut seemed reluctant to say anything other than human flesh was "tough."

Buut hiccuped and pinched the end of his glowing cigarette. He tucked the half-smoked cigarette behind his ear and coughed loudly.

"Yes, *Misis*," he nodded. Buut turned down his mouth and snorted, "the bottom is tough too." Buut shrugged his shoulders, grinned, and hiccuped again. "*Misis*, suppose you …"

"OK, Buut," Auntie Betty sighed, "drink up. Now what about the other bits, you know, the bits inside?"

Buut nodded, lifted his glass, and drank noisily.

"Have you eaten any of that?" Auntie Betty pressed on.

"Yes, *Misis*, I have also eaten some of the insides … and I didn't like that either."

Aunty Betty pounded Buut with more and more questions until finally Buut's syllables ran into each other and his words become more and more slurred with each answer. As the contents of the whiskey bottle fell, Buut's eyes fluttered closed. His head dropped forward and rested gently on his big chest.

Auntie Betty sighed and shifted into a more comfortable position in her chair. She looked over at Mum and helped herself to another glass of Buut's whiskey.

"Well, Poppy," she said, "I suppose all things said and done, I've learnt two things this morning. One, obviously, Buut has eaten just about every part of the human body, and two, he says he didn't particularly like any of it, it was all very tough. I wonder if that is true, or is he just saying that?"

Auntie Betty lit another cigarette and topped Buut's glass with more whiskey. She drew deeply on her cigarette and lapsed into thought.

"Maybe the victims were just skinny old missionaries, Betty," Mum laughed. "You know, all sinew and no fat. You know what they were like, the poor buggers, half-starved and half-dead with Malaria. Who'd want to eat them anyway?"

"Yes, Poppy," Auntie Betty sighed at Mums comment, "maybe you are right. Perhaps they were all sinew and no fat. With everything they had to go through, no wonder they were half-dead."

"*Misis, Misis.*" Buut stirred and raised his head from his chest. He reached for his glass, lifted the glass to his lips, and gulped noisily. His eyes glazed over, and a fat tear slid down his round face. "*Misis,*" he slurred, "when I was a small child, many years ago, in my home village, I tasted every part of the human body, and," Buut placed his hands on the table, "I'll tell you which is the best part to eat." He slapped his big soft yellow palm. "This part, the palm of your hand, that's the best. It is very tasty …very soft and juicy! And I liked this part too," he added. Buut scraped back his chair, thrust his big feet in the air, and prodded at his hard cracked soles. "This part!"

With a smug grin on his face, Buut hiccuped again and massaged between his toes to reinforce his point.

Auntie Betty and Mum looked at each other. Stunned into silence, Mum shook her head in disbelief and reached for another cigarette.

"There you are, Betty," Mum shivered. "You have your answers. Your *haus boi* Buut *has* eaten human flesh, even if he was only a child-cannibal. And for future reference, if you are going to eat a human, the palm of your hand and the sole of your foot are the best parts. If I were you …"

"*Misis* …" Buut looked up again and indicated to Aunty Betty to refill his glass. The whiskey had loosened his tongue. "*Misis* … I will tell you what happens."

Mum told me later that Buut was "very matter of fact" as he then explained the gruesome process used to prepare a human for eating. Mum and Auntie Betty listened intently as Buut told of his cannibalism.

With morbid revulsion, Mum asked Buut if he'd eaten native people or white people.

Buut replied that he was just a small child and didn't remember whether the flesh he'd devoured had been black or white; he'd just simply eaten it. That was all!

Mum stood up. She was thoroughly disgusted.

"Betty," she said, "I *really* have had enough for one day." Mum looked at her watch, made reference to the time, and suggested she make some coffee. Buut needed to be in a sober state before Uncle Max returned home from the police station.

After numerous cups of Mum's strong black brew, Auntie Betty and Mum pushed a very drunk Buut into Aunty Betty's VW. Aunty Betty thanked Mum again, revved the engine, and roared off home.

Mum told me later that she was revolted by Buut's tale and was chilled to the bone by the whole episode. "Only Betty," Mum added, "would want to know about such things."

That night as the family settled down to dinner, we heard a car backfire as it screeched to a halt under our carport.

"Sounds like Betty," Dad said. "I bet Max got wind of Buut and the whiskey."

Dad was right. Buut's loud drunken singing had alerted Uncle Max, and Uncle Max had threatened to dismiss Buut for being drunk on duty. Aunty Betty had confessed to her part in the incident, and Uncle Max was extremely annoyed. Auntie Betty, Suzanne, and Vanessa stayed with us for a few days until Uncle Max cooled off; the family was not surprised Uncle Max found out "who did what, where, and when"—after all, Uncle Max was well skilled in the art of cross-examination.

Dad, as usual, saw the funny side of the whole thing and gave Buut a new name. From that day on, Buut was known to all as "Buut the Cannibal King." When the Hayes's left Rabaul a few years later, Buut became our *haus boi*. We found him to be a very jolly and efficient fellow, except for one small thing. Buut insisted on laying the table with the knife on the left and the fork on the right, and that irritated Dad immensely.

Uncle Max was a member of the New Britain Historical Society. As Rabaul is rich in both cultural and geographical history, the society was very fortunate and grateful to have him as a member. Uncle Max was (and still is today) a very talented and enthusiastic photographer. His expertise with his cameras was (and still is) very much in demand.

Our families shared a mutual interest in one of Rabaul's earliest pioneers. This mutual interest ignited a search to find a lost burial site; most people used the pidgin word *matmat* for cemetery or burial ground. For a number of years, the lost *matmat* was a topic of discussion for many of the townsfolk. However, the rampant tropical jungle had reclaimed the *matmat* site, and although we knew the *matmat* was situated on a plantation at Kokopo, the exact location of the *matmat* was a mystery.

The *matmat* belonged to a Samoan-American girl called Emma Kolbe. In the nineteenth century, Emma had built a vast commercial empire throughout the Western Pacific. Emma's astute business acumen, determined will, and colourful life is a well-documented, if not sometimes misconstrued, tale.

Emma Eliza Coe was born in Apia, Western Samoa, in 1850. After the loss of her family fortunes in 1878, Emma left Apia. By 1879, she and her second "husband" had established a native trade post at Mioko in the Duke of York Islands. The "Duke of Yorks" (as the islands were known) is a small cluster of islands situated in the St. Georges Channel, midway between New Ireland and New Britain.

In 1882, Emma bought some land—for a reputed few axes and a handful of coloured red beads—on Blanch Bay on the Gazelle Peninsula of New Britain Island. Emma planted coconuts on her land and established a copra plantation. Emma named her plantation Ralum. The European market clamoured for the copra produced at Ralum, and as Ralum produced more and more of the dried smoked coconut, the sales brought Emma great wealth. She built Gunantambu, a magnificent European-style house that overlooked Blanch Bay, erected offices, and opened trade stores.

Over the next few years, she summoned her seventeen brothers and sisters from Apia and resettled them on her vast estate. Emma's business, wealth, and reputation grew and grew over the next two decades, and she became the wealthiest woman in the South Pacific. Thus, she was known by all as Queen Emma.

In 1892, Queen Emma's lover, Captain Agostino Stalio, was killed by natives on the Faed Islands; Emma was said to be devastated. She created a private *matmat* on a hilltop overlooking Blanch Bay at Ralum and erected an elaborate monument in the captain's memory. Captain Stalios's monument carried a very unique inscription.

On July 19, 1913, Paul Kobe, Queen Emma's husband, died in Monte Carlo as a result of a car accident. Less than forty hours later, on July 21, Emma—who was ill with diabetes—also passed away.

It is documented fact that the bodies of Emma and Paul Kobe were dispatched to Hamburg and cremated, with their ashes returned to Ralum a short while later. The ashes were then interned in large ceramic urn and positioned on a cement slab. The slab lay within arm's reach of Captain Agostino Stalios's monument.

In January 1942, the Japanese Imperial Air Force bombed Rabaul and the surrounding areas. The bombing continued for two solid weeks. The aftermath left the Gazelle Peninsula, the township of Rabaul, and the settlement at Ralum, including Gunantambu, in ruins. All that remains of Queen Emma's original Ralum are a few coconut palms and part of the elaborate terraced steps that once fronted Gunantambu.

The tropical jungle consumed most of Ralum over the next decade and a half, and as a result of misplaced and or destroyed records, the exact location of Queen Emma's *matmat* remained a mystery.

In 1955, Queen Emma's *matmat* was located not far from the ruins of Gunantambu. A work party was sent from Rabaul, and the *matmat* and surrounding area were cleared of *kunai* grass and smashed debris. Unfortunately, interest in the *matmat* waned, and the rampant tropical jungle once again reclaimed the site.

Queen Emma was our most famous pioneer, and it was a shame her *matmat* had disappeared again. For some time, rumour abounded though the historical society grapevine that somebody had stumbled across a clue as to the precise location of Queen Emma's *matmat* on Ralum, although nobody quite knew who that "somebody" was.

Uncle Max was always one to follow a rumour, especially if there happened to be a mystery involved. His interest aroused, he decided to make some discreet inquiries of his own. Armed with a few sketchy facts, he pinpointed a likely location.

One Saturday afternoon, Uncle Max organized a search of the likely area. He enlisted the help of his family, a couple of *polis bois*, and Mum and I. Dad declined to help with the search and stated that he was "too busy at the office"—a likely story, as Dad never went to the office on a Saturday afternoon. Later, Dad confessed he thought it highly unlikely we would find anything "historical" at all.

Uncle Max decided we would take two vehicles: the Hayes family and the *polis bois* would ride in the police paddy wagon, and Mum and I would take Dads' office car.

We set off along the Kokopo Road. Half an hour later, we veered off the main road and bounced on to the dirt track that led to the Ralum Plantation. The track into Ralum was steep, full of potholes, and in parts overgrown with razor-sharp *kunai* grass. Uncle Max halted the police paddy wagon alongside a small clearing and alighted from the vehicle. We saw that the *kunai* in the clearing had recently been slashed. The dead *kunai* indicated that somebody else had been there just recently.

I must say at this point that *I* didn't particularly want to be there. I'd rather we were swimming at Ralum beach, not bush-bashing as it were, and I said so to Mum. The task at hand daunted me. The vegetation ahead was choked with tangled vines, bamboo, and pockets of *kunai*. Whoever had been there before had abandoned the effort, for beyond the clearing, the jungle looked largely undisturbed. Mum noted my grumbled misgivings and promised me a swim later. Her promise lightened my mood somewhat, and I joined Uncle Max beside the paddy wagon.

"Everybody gather round." Uncle Max cleared his throat and addressed us in his best police voice. "It is a documented fact that many years ago, the woman known as Queen Emma, along with some of her family and friends, were buried in a private cemetery on this plantation. You all know who Queen Emma was, don't you?"

I nodded, even though I had no idea who Queen Emma was.

151

"Well, over the years, Queen Emma's cemetery has been lost, and we are here to find it today."

I nodded again.

"I have it on good authority," Uncle Max continued, "that the missing cemetery is located not far from where we stand now, and I have some information at hand that may assist us in finding it."

We all nodded again. Uncle Max flipped open his notebook—Uncle Max was never without his notebook—and cleared his throat again.

"We are looking for a large cement slab with an indentation in the middle—a large headstone bearing the name "Captain Agostino Stalio," a large stone angel with folded wings, and any other various crosses or headstones that may bear witness to the fact that we are in the vicinity of a cemetery."

"Oh, isn't this exciting, everybody!" Auntie Betty exclaimed and clapped her hands. "A treasure hunt!"

Uncle Max had equipped the *polis bois* with large police-issue bush knives, and for the next hour or so the *polis bois* slashed and chopped at the jungle vegetation. The rest of us cleared the chopped debris, stacked it out of the way, and cleared and stacked some more. The air was humid and still, and before long our clothes dripped with perspiration and stuck to our bodies like wet newspaper. The slashed *kunai* grass was sharp and cut deeply into our arms and bare legs.

Auntie Betty busied herself with first aid to all and applied gentian violet and sticking plaster whenever it was needed. When we whinged and carried on about Uncle Max's wild goose chase, she applauded our efforts and promised us fame and fortune after we had found the missing *matmat*.

After some time, Suzanne joined the circle of wounded around Auntie Betty. She limped painfully and complained of a stubbed toe.

"I stubbed my toe on this big thing in the *kunai* grass," Suzanne said, "a stone thing, and it hurt. The thing is big—" Suzanne spread her arms wide "—and I can't move it."

Suzanne's "big stone thing" aroused Mum's interest. She called to Uncle Max that Suzanne had found something that needed to be investigated. Uncle Max called a halt to all activity, and with renewed enthusiasm, we all followed Suzanne as she limped towards a part of uncleared jungle.

Suzannes "big stone thing" was in fact a large angel carved in marble. The angel had toppled from its base and fallen, face down, into the *kunai* grass. Two marble blocks topped with a slightly askew marble plinth stood next to the angel. The blocks were covered in dirt, and the plinth was overrun with vines. With eager hands and a sense of elation, we pulled the vines from the plinth. Mum brushed away the dirt, and a faded inscription came to light. It read:

> In loving memory of Captain Agostino Stalio, who was shot by the natives of the Faed Islands while bravely assisting the imperial Judge to arrest the King and his son for the Massacre of John Coe. Born at Dalmatia, 1854. Died at Faed Islands, 2nd September, 1892.
>
> Oh for the touch of a vanished hand and the sound of a voice that is still.
>
> This stone is erected as a mark of esteem by his Many friends in the Bismarck Archipelago.'

"Oh my God," whispered Mum, "we are standing in Queen Emma's *matmat*. Queen Emma's missing *matmat*. We've found it. We've finally located it. After all this time, it has finally come to light again. Isn't that wonderful! Good on you, Suzanne."

And yes, good on Suzanne, for *she* had *really* found Queens Emma's missing *matmat*.

The *polis bois* cleared the debris from Captain Agostino's *matmat*. Alas, the marble angel was too heavy for them to position back on top of the plinth, so we stood the angel on the ground next to the grave.

Now that we had found Captain Stalio's final resting place,

Emma and Paul Kolbe's had to be close by. With bush knives in hand, the *polis bois* slashed the *kunai* around the captains' gravesite. In due course, we found many graves and smashed marble headstones, but most intriguing of all was a large flat concrete slab. The slab was unmarked except for large indentation in the middle. We knew, however, that this flat slab of concrete had at one time held the urn that contained the ashes of Queen Emma and Paul Kolbe. The urn, of course, had long ago disappeared.

Uncle Max informed me just recently that the ashes of Queen Emma and Paul Kolbe were interred in South Head Cemetery in Sydney NSW.

When I returned to Rabaul in 2013, I was elated to discover Queen Emmas' private *matmat* is still accessible on Ralum. As I walked amongst the gravestones, I found the angel that once looked over the grave of Captain Agostino Stalio. The angel stood on the ground (just where we had left her all those years ago) next to the plinth it once adorned. Situated not far away, a plain unmarked cement slab lay hidden in the razor-sharp *kunai*.

Just recently, I happened to find some old photographs. Thanks to Uncle Max and his inescapable appetite to capture events on film, my memory of the day we found Queen Emma's *matmat* lingers still.

Uncle Max attended most of our school events, sports days, and birthday parties. As a child, I cringed whenever he came near, because just when we least expected it, Uncle Max would boom in his best police voice, "Suzanne, Vanessa, Suellen … look at the camera."

The Hayeses left Rabaul in 1966. Uncle Max was posted to Bougainville, and Auntie Betty and the girls went to Australia. In 1967, the whole family enjoyed a nine-month holiday in Europe. Upon their return, Uncle Max resumed his police duties on the New Guinea mainland—in Kainantu, Goroko, Lae, and finally the police headquarters at Konedobu in Port Moresby. After many years of dedicated service in PNG, Uncle Max returned to Australia in 1974.

He then worked as a court official until he retired in 1992. Uncle Max is also Korean War veteran.

Just recently, Andrew and I visited Uncle Max in Melbourne. It had been many years since I had seen him. Although the years had softened him, he was just as I remembered him—a fine, upstanding, sharp-witted, astute policeman through and through. We enjoyed two days with Uncle Max, and as we leafed through his many scrapbooks and photo albums, we revisited those halcyon days our families shared in Rabaul.

On June 23, 1998, Vanessa phoned me close to midnight and told me news I did not want to hear: Auntie Betty had just passed away. She passed peacefully and quietly in her sleep, just as she would have wanted to.

Betty Rose Hayes (nee Bach) S.R.N. O.N.D.
22 January 1925 – 23 June 1998.

My mothers' voice sounded small and tired when I spoke to her a few minutes later. I asked Mum if she wished me to accompany her to Auntie Betty's service. "No, Suellen," Mum whispered, "I'm not going to Betty's service. I couldn't bear it."

My mother had lost her dearest friend. Mum sent a small posy instead and a plain white card, which read simply, appropriately, 'Goodbye Old Friend, Till We Meet Again."

I was greatly saddened by Auntie Bettys passing—saddened because I would never be able to speak with her again and never again hear throaty laugh … except, of cause, in my memory.

Rest in peace, Auntie Betty.

I still keep contact with Uncle Max to this day; indeed, we talk often of Papua New Guinea, as he is a wealth of knowledge. I am touched by Uncle Max's continued interest in my family and eternally grateful for his beautiful photographs that captured so many of my precious childhood memories.

Thank you so very much, Uncle Max, for everything.

The Campbell Family

The Campbell family arrived in Rabaul from Samurai (a tiny settlement on the very southern tip of the New Guinea mainland) aboard the good ship *Bulolo*.

The *Bulolo* was the flagship of the Burns Philp fleet and an illustrious ship in her time. It is also rumoured that Winston Churchill and President Roosevelt once held a war meeting aboard the *Bulolo* in the mid-Atlantic.

The *Bulolo* docked at many of the small New Guinea townships on her round trip between Australia and Papua New Guinea; indeed, she provided a vital link between the two countries. The ship's safe arrival was a blessed event all round, as she often conveyed passengers home from leave in Australia and sailed again with folk who were due leave in Australia. Apart from that, the ship supplied our grocery stores with necessary goods (and for those folk so inclined, a traditional Sunday roast) as well as electrical items, stationery, cosmetics, spare parts for this and that, boxes of special-ordered what-nots, packages, and mail.

As soon as the ship docked, Auntie Dot and Uncle Peter made their way to Burns Philp, one of only two department stores in town. Auntie Dot needed some provisions for her new home, and as Uncle Peter was to assume his new position as the Rabaul Burns Philp accountant, their visit to the store was an opportunity for Uncle Peter to introduce himself to his new staff.

At that time, Mum worked in the cosmetic come chemist department at BP's. (everybody just called Burns Philp B.P.'s). Auntie Dot walked up to the counter and asked for some baby items for her five-week-old daughter, Emily. As Mum and Auntie Dot chatted, baby Emily stirred in her *buka* basket. Aunty Dot lifted the basket onto the counter.

"Oh my goodness," Mum commented, "what a tiny baby. Was she born prematurely?"

"Oh no," Auntie Dot laughed, "everybody says that. Emily is

actually a full-term baby—just small, that's all. Just small, and she's fine. She's a really good baby, too."

For some reason, Mum was worried about Auntie Dot's tiny tiny baby, so that night Mum persuaded Dad to accompany her to the Campbells' for a quick visit. As the Campbells were new in town, Mum offered to help with anything they needed, at any time. From that day on, a firm friendship developed between the two families.

Michael, the eldest of the Campbell children, was just four years old when first introduced to our family. Over the years, we spent many happy hours with Michael, and as a result gained a small understanding of the unique innocence (and at times trials and tribulations) of a child born with Down's syndrome.

One evening, after a hurried dinner, Mum told me to gather my pillow and toothbrush. "We are going to the Campbells tonight," Mum said as she and Dad herded our dogs and I into the car, "because Michael is sick in Nonga Hospital. He's having an emergency operation tonight, and your father and I want to be there if Dot and Peter need any help."

Young Mickey was unable to understand when his tummy was full and consequently had an appetite that rivalled a fully grown man. Unfortunately, Mickey also had an appetite for a number of non-food items.

One morning, Auntie Dot discovered that Mickey had vomited and decided to take him to our local doctor. An X-ray showed a large obstruction in Mickey's intestine, and the doctor ordered immediate surgery. Mickey now lay gravely ill in Nonga Hospital.

Under normal circumstances, any person who required major surgery was referred to a hospital in Australia. However, as Mickeys' situation was an emergency, a decision was made to operate on him in Rabaul.

Aunty Dot's eyes were red and swollen as she greeted us in her kitchen. She and Uncle Peter were concerned over the decision to have Mickey operated on in Rabaul. Nonga Hospital was ill-equipped, with neither the qualified staff nor the appropriate equipment needed for such an operation.

However, Mickey was lucky. A prominent English surgeon was on an exchange-education program at our hospital. The surgeon was only in town for a few weeks, and when he heard of Mickeys' plight, he offered to perform Mickey's operation. Mickey was very ill, and the English surgeon was concerned.

The surgeon told Dot and Peter to "go home and pray" while he prepared his theatre and briefed his medical staff. Time was of the essence if little Mickey was to (as he informed Dot and Peter) "come through the night." As you can imagine, this news worried all concerned.

The fact that Mickey had been born with Down's Syndrome mattered little to our family. He was accepted into our lives unconditionally, just as any other child would be. We knew the meaning of his funny little grunts and noises. We dismissed his temper tantrums as "Mickey behaviour" and ignored his need to pinch food from our plates. All in all, Mickey just did what any other Rabaul child did. He swam like a fish and ran like the wind. He fought and squabbled with his siblings, and he was cheeky to his parents. When Mickey was naughty, he was punished just like the rest of us.

My dad was especially fond of Mickey, and Mickey loved Dad as well. Mickey often attached himself to Dad whenever we saw the Campbell family, and Dad didn't mind one bit. Dad always greeted Mickey with "Hello, little fellow," and often said that Mickey "always attacked life with gusto," whatever that meant.

The night that Mickey awaited his operation, the adults fussed little about rules and early nights for children. We children were allowed to drag our pillows into the lounge room and spread out on the floor. As we huddled together, stories of Mickey's antics peppered our conversation. Desperate for news, we who loved Mickey waited in suspended animation. As the night wore on, adults and children alike struggled to drive the feeling of dread from our heavy hearts.

Finally, sometime past midnight, the phone shrilled. Uncle Peter jumped at the noise, sprinted across the room, and snatched the phone from the cradle.

"Peter Campbell," he answered in a voice rasped by cigarettes.

Uncle Peter listened, nodded, and listened again.

"Thank you, doctor," he replied. "Thank you very much. Yes, my wife and I will leave now."

"Michael is out of surgery and in intensive care," Uncle Peter said, delivering the good news we had all prayed for.. "The doctor said he is stable for now and that Dot and I can see him now if we wish. The doctor also said that he has several mementos from Mickey 'op' that we can have. I wonder what he means by 'several mementos'?"

The next day, after Aunty Dot had visited Mickey in hospital, she dropped by our house and gave us an update on Mickey's condition. As Mum seated Auntie Dot on the veranda, Auntie Dot reached into her bag and placed a large coffee bottle full of bits and pieces on the coffee table.

"The doctors found these things inside Michael," she said as she tipped the contents of the coffee bottle onto the table.

"Oh my goodness, Dot!" Mum said, shaking her head in disbelief.

The surgical team had recovered thirty-two separate items from Mickey's tummy, intestine, and bowel—a treasure chest of objects, in fact.

They included one of Uncle Peter's 24-carat-gold cufflinks (Uncle Peter had accused Auntie Dot of losing his cufflink); one or two golf tees; a sprinkling of little red golf-ball markers; fruit seeds; a small unbroken torch bulb; buttons; a few small gold safety pins; and a bucket load of watermelon pips. Most of these items were embedded in odd-shaped watermelon-pip-spiky balls of undigested Chinese chewing gum.

As Aunty Dot remarked to us, it was a real miracle that Mickey had survived.

Mickey enjoyed the fuss and attention lavished on him as he convalesced, and in a few weeks he had made a complete recovery.

For many months to come, Mickey happily lifted his T-shirt on command and grunted softly as he pointed his little finger at his tummy scar and told the story, in his own funny way, of his big operation.

Only a few years separated Michael and his younger brother, Matthew, and the time had arrived for the boys to start kindergarten.

Auntie Dot and Uncle Peter had decided that their sons would commence their early childhood education on the same day. Matthew was to attend the kindergarten of Our Lady of the Sacred Heart (OLSH) and Mickey, because of his special needs, would attend the smaller Mater Dei kindergarten.

Aunty Dot took Mickey and Matthew to BP's—where the store offered a very necessary staff discount—and purchased the boys' respective uniforms, school shoes, and socks.

At 8 a.m. sharp on the first day of kindergarten, Auntie Dot presented Matthew for enrolment at OLSH. The Mother Superior oversaw all new enrolments in her kindergarten, and as Aunty Dot waited in line, Mother Superior glared at her through narrowed eyes. Mickey also waited in line, dressed very smartly in his new Mater Dei uniform.

As Auntie Dot stepped up to the office desk, Mother Superior stood up. She folded her hands inside her white habit and looked Mickey up and down. She was not amused. In a clipped tone, she informed Auntie Dot that Matthew could only attend "her" kindergarten if Mickey *also* attended.

Aunty Dot was dumbstruck. She tried to explain to Mother Superior that Mickey had special needs, and as the Mater Dei kindergarten was much smaller than OLSH, Mickey was better suited to Mater Dei. The Mother Superior, however, was indignant at any suggestion that a rival kindergarten could provide better early education for Mickey. She stood firm by her decision: no Mickey, no Matthew.

Heartbroken, Auntie Dot and the boys returned home. Later in the morning, Aunty Dot phoned Mum and told Mum of the events that had happened that morning. Mum was outraged when she heard that the Mother Superior of OLSH had refused to enrol Matthew without Mickey.

"Oh! Good God, Dot," Mum growled, "that's preposterous. What right has a nun, Mother Superior or not, to tell *you* what kindergarten your sons can and cannot attend? That is ridiculous. I'll phone Cyril now at the office and tell him to do something. He can phone Father Frankie (the head Catholic priest and a cherished family friend) and report this Mother Superior. I'll ring you back in a minute."

Mum slammed down the phone, picked up the handset again, and dialled Dad's office number. She related the story to Dad and in no uncertain terms instructed Dad to "fix" the matter of the Campbell boys "quick smart."

Goodness knows what strings my Dad pulled—a large donation to the OLSH kindergarten, perhaps? But the Mother Superior relented. That afternoon, Matthew was accepted for enrolment at OLSH kindergarten and Mickey at the Mater Dei kindergarten.

When Mickey was about six years old, the Campbell family left Rabaul to settle in Australia. Auntie Dot enrolled Mickey in a school that very expertly administered to his special needs. The school taught him to talk, read a little, and write his name.

Mickey enjoyed a full and happy life, and as an adult lived in a home with a carer and three other friends. Mickey always remained very much a part of the Campbell family; he visited home every second weekend and was always included in family occasions.

The Campbell family settled in Brisbane (QLD) and for a number of years kept close ties with my family. On occasion, I stopped in

Brisbane on my way to see Mum, and more often than not I caught up with the Campbell family as well.

Mickey passed away on June 26, 1997. The news of his passing filled me with an overwhelming flood of sadness and nostalgia, for the Mickey I knew and for the times our families shared in Rabaul.

One afternoon, as I passed through the gates of my primary school, I saw Uncle Peter. He waved frantically and beckoned me over.

"Susie," he said, "your Mum has asked me to pick you up and take you out Nonga Hospital. Your dad has taken a turn—malaria, we think. Your Mum called me at BP's and asked me take you to the hospital. Dot is with her at Nonga."

Dad was in hospital for a number of days, and during that time, the Campbell family took me under their wing. They fed me, looked after our dogs and cats, and every evening ferried me to and from the hospital to see Dad. Every single morning, Auntie Dot visited her Catholic church, lit a candle, and prayed for Dad's recovery.

I usually look forward to my birthday. However, a week before I was to celebrate, Uncle Peter phoned me. With choked emotion, he told me that Aunty Dot had passed away the day before. Aunty Dot's death was sudden and completely unexpected.

Auntie Dot passed away a year, almost to the day, after Mickey. She and Michael now rest side by side.

A few days later, I arranged to fly to Brisbane to attend Auntie Dot's service. My heart was heavy with sadness. I did not want to face the reality that Auntie Dot had passed, and I certainly did not want to acknowledge the fact that another chapter of my childhood had come to a close.

After Aunty Dot's service, we gathered at the home of Emily and her family. I complimented Emily on the beautiful service she had arranged for her mother.

"Ah yes," Emily replied with a small smile, "Mum always loved a good funeral. I think we have done her proud."

I was saddened Auntie Dot had gone. I would never be able to speak with her again, never be able to share our memories—except, of course, in my memory.

Rest in peace, Auntie Dot. Rest in peace, Mickey.

Before the week had ended, I received more news I did not want to hear, Aunty Betty had passed away… and so another chapter of my life in Rabaul had closed.

CHAPTER 8

Our Favourite Places

Takis Plantation

For many years, Dad held the position as manager of the Rabaul Trading Co. Pty. Ltd. The Rabaul Trading Co. was the biggest exporter of copra and cocoa beans (copra is dried coconut that is processed to make coconut oil, and cocoa beans are used exclusively to make chocolate) in Papua New Guinea. For business purposes, Dad kept close contact with the plantations that grew the coconuts and cocoa, and as a result, many of the plantation families became our close friends.

Almost every weekend, Mum packed a picnic basket, and as many of the plantations fringed the ocean, we combined a picnic, swim, and snorkel with a social visit. Quite often at our Christmas break, we escaped town and journeyed to one or more of the outlying plantations and stayed a few days. Dad sometimes took the opportunity to talk business with plantation owners and or managers while we were there as well.

Takis was a large copra-producing plantation situated in the Baining Mountain Range. The Bainings, as we locals called the area, is located in the northeast of New Britain Island.

The Bainings, like most of New Britain, is steeped in World

War II history. In the predawn of January 23, 1942, twenty-five Japanese warships lay at anchor in a deep-water channel just off the north coast of New Britain Island. The Bainings provided a perfect geographical barrier that hid the strength of the Japanese fleet from the civilians in Rabaul.

Later that day, five thousand of Japan's elite jungle-trained South Sea Detachment brazenly marched down the old German road towards the township of Rabaul. The Japanese troops met with little resistance, and within a few short hours, Rabaul and the surrounding area lay in Japanese hands.

Takis Plantation was managed by Oscar Billings, a rather eccentric middle-aged bachelor our family was very fond of. Sadly, we did not visit Oscar or the many other plantations on the Bainings as often as we would have liked.

Dad disliked boats immensely, especially small boats, and the Bainings were only accessible from Rabaul by boat. Dad couldn't swim, and water—especially the open sea—terrified him. Apart from that, Dad was convinced that the ocean was a danger to all, full of man-eating sharks, giant octopuses, and savage rips.

It is a documented fact that during the German occupation of Rabaul, German engineers built a "good" road between Rabaul and the Bainings. However, after the Germans were ousted from New Britain in 1914, everything German—including their good roads—fell into a state of disrepair. The tropical jungle soon reclaimed a large portion of the Rabaul-Bainings road, and within a short period of time, it became impassable.

Time and time again, our Bainings planter friends issued invitations to visit. However, unbeknown to the family, whenever the question of a visit was raised, Dad declined and said we were busy.

Oscar always visited us whenever he was in town, and after dinner one evening, he asked Dad again if the family would come and stay at Takis for a few days.

Dad's face paled at Oscars' suggestion. Dad suspected that, earlier on, Mum and Oscar had discussed the possibility of a visit to Takis, and now Dad was trapped.

"Well, if Poppy agrees," Dad mumbled, "I'm sure we can work something out. Maybe we can discuss it later."

"Oh, Oscar," Mum exclaimed, "that would be wonderful, thank you." Mum looked over to me. "We'd love to visit the plantation, wouldn't we, Suellen?"

"We sure would, Mum," I said. "Please, Dad, can we?"

"Father's office is closed between Christmas and New Year, Oscar," Mum continued. "Everybody is on leave. Would it suit you if we came then?"

"Poppy, after Christmas would suit me just fine," Oscar replied.

I looked over at Dad and grinned in delight.

"Well, that's settled, then," Mum said. "How does Boxing Day sound? We can come on Boxing Day, stay a few days, and be back in town for the New Year celebrations."

"That would be wonderful," Oscar said. "Boxing Day would be perfect. I'll look forward to it."

"Oh, thank you, Oscar," Mum said with a smile.. "Oh! We are such lucky, lucky people, aren't we, Suellen?"

Dad rose from the table and made his way over to the drinks cabinet. He sighed deeply, selected a brandy balloon, pulled the stopper from a crystal brandy decanter, and poured himself a neat Napoleon.

"May I offer you a brandy, Oscar?" Dad said weakly. "Or would you prefer a Johnny Walker?"

Oscar looked at Mum and grinned. "A Johnny Walker, thanks, Cyril. On the rocks, if you don't mind."

"Righto," Dad replied, "coming up."

Mum smiled back at Oscar and picked up her cigarettes from the table.

"Let's adjourn to the front veranda, everybody, shall we?" she said. "And we can make some plans about Takis."

Mum settled herself into a cane settee and lit a cigarette. Dad handed Oscar his whiskey, reached into his top pocket, drew out his packet of pipe tobacco, and sat down next to Mum.

Oscar sipped his whiskey and lit a cigarette.

"Cyril," he said, "there is no need for you to be concerned about your boat trip to Takis. I can assure you that everybody will be quite safe on the journey over. My speedboat is very seaworthy, and I've fitted her with the best two-way radio money can buy. If, for some reason, we have a problem, I have enough life jackets on board to keep everybody afloat for a month of Sundays."

Dad took a gulp of brandy and replaced his glass on a nearby coffee table. He knocked his burnt pipe tobacco into an ashtray, refilled his pipe with new tobacco, lit the tobacco, and inhaled deeply.

"So what say," Oscar continued, "I pick you all up at Kabaira on Boxing Day morning."

Dad looked at Mum and patted her knee.

"Well, I can't disappoint Poppy and Susie, so I guess that's settled. Thank you, Oscar. What time would you like us at Kabaira?"

Dad had conceded defeat.

Boxing Day dawned bright, pink, and warm. Dad was keen to be on our way and hustled me through an early breakfast. As Mum and I made ourselves ready, Dad seemed agitated. He paced about the house and muttered under his breath about being late.

"It's a damn shame," Dad said to our dog Scamp, "that Mr. Oscar Billings has a *speed*boat and not a *flying* boat to take us all to Takis. *You'd* rather go to Takis in a flying boat, wouldn't you, old fellow?"

Dad sighed again and ruffled Scamp's ears. Scamp woofed loudly and licked Dad hand.

"Yes, I thought so," Dad muttered. "Well, old boy, we're out of luck I'm afraid. We're stuck with a speedboat. I hope it's a damn big speedboat, for Pete's sake," Dad added. "I hate small boats. I hope it's not one of those small runabout dinghies you see racing about the harbour."

In an earlier conversation, Oscar had told Mum that his speedboat was in fact quite small, and as Scamp was to accompany us as well to Takis, Oscar asked Mum to travel light. Mum agreed to pack only the bare minimum for everybody: swimming costumes, T-shirts, and shorts.

With plans all set, Mum and I eagerly awaited not only our visit to Takis but the speedboat ride as well. Not so, I'm afraid, my dad. Poor Dad; just the thought of a boat ride, any boat ride, especially if the ride entailed a journey across the open sea, left him dry-mouthed.

Every year in Rabaul, we welcomed the monsoon season. The torrential rains cooled the evenings, settled the dust, and filled our water tanks. Sometimes, however, in the late afternoon, an unpredictable cyclone-like wind blew in from the northwest and whipped the sea into mountainous waves. The wind, the waves, and the driving rains created dangerous conditions for small boats. As it was now December and well into the monsoon season, it was imperative, lest the nor'wester turned the sea savage in the afternoon, that we be on our way to Takis as early in the morning as possible.

Many of the Baining planters travelled by speedboat from their plantations to Kabaira Bay—a wide sheltered bay on the east coast of New Britain. While in town, they either moored their boats in the calm waters of the bay or beached their boats at a designated beach clearing. Rabaul was easily accessible from Kabaira, connected in part by the still usable portion of the old German road.

Over the years, a collection of tin sheds and huts had sprung up around the beach clearing, and Oscar advised Dad to park our car at the clearing next to the shed marked Takis. Oscar also informed us that, as he needed to ready things at the plantation before our visit, his assistant manager Donald, who was also well known to the family, would meet us with the speedboat instead.

We made good time to Kabaira Bay that Boxing Day morning,

and as we turned off the main road, we saw Oscar's little speedboat tethered to a coconut tree at the water's edge.

"Hello, hello everybody," Don greeted us as we alighted from our car. "How was your Christmas? Let's load up quickly and be off before the nor'wester blows in. If the weather permits, I may have a surprise for you all."

Dad eyed the speedboat with trepidation. He shook hands with Don and returned his greeting.

"That's a very small speedboat, Don," Dad commented. "Are you sure we can all fit in? We have the dog with us ... and, er, Poppy and Susie have clothes ... and, er, perhaps ..."

Mum glared at Dad. "Oh, for goodness sake, Father," she whispered, "stop being silly. Oscar wouldn't send the boat if it wasn't big enough for all of us."

Don ignored Dad's remark, grinned at Mum, and winked. "Hop in, Cyril," he said. "You sit in the middle. I can assure you that you'll all be quite safe. Besides, if need be, I can be in radio contact with Oscar at the touch of a button. I've bought this for you, by the way," Don added as he handed Dad a bulky white kapok-filled life jacket, "to put on as well."

Dad looked at the jacket with disgust and slipped it over his head. Dad then tied the straps tightly around his waist and secured the straps with a double knot.

We all scrambled aboard, threw our bags under our seats, and settled Scamp. Don pushed the boat off the sand and eased her into deeper water.

"Ready?" he asked.

We all nodded.

"Then we'll be off, shall we? Time's getting on."

Don pushed the engine throttle forward. The twin Mercury 100hp outboard motors revved to life. The boat lifted her bow and rose out of the water. Dad closed his hands around the side of his seat and his knuckles turned white as he hung on for dear life. As

169

Don edged the speedboat out of the bay and into the open waters, a low dark smudge sprang into view on the horizon. Dad kept his eyes fixed firmly on the dark smudge ahead, scared the smudge might disappear.

We sped along quite happily for an hour or so until Dad was unable to contain himself any longer.

"How long before we get to Takis, Don?" he asked.

As if on cue, the boat radio crackled loudly. "Takis to Don, Takis to Don, come in, Don ... over."

Dad looked relieved at the outside communication.

Don picked up the microphone. "Roger, Takis," he responded. "Over."

Although the radio communication was somewhat static, we heard that Oscar and Cleopatra, whoever that was, were on their way to meet us.

Don smiled as he hooked the mike back on its cradle. "That was the surprise I was telling you about earlier on," he said. "Oscar's decided to come out with Cleopatra. They've made good time, too. So keep a look out, everybody. We should be able to spot them soon."

As Don spoke, one of the outboard motors gave a low cough, Don turned the key to "off" as the motor spluttered and died. Dad drew in a sharp breath. He looked over at the motor with wide eyes.

Mum looked at Dad's fear-filled face. She dared not ask Don why the motor had stopped.

"Who is Cleopatra?" Mum asked instead. "Er ... is there a new lady at Takis?"

"Um ... sort of," Don grinned. "You'll soon meet her. Oscar asked me not to tell. I'm just going to change fuel tanks. Won't be a tick and we will be on our way again."

Dad exhaled in relief and wiped his brow with his hanky. He shaded his eyes against the glaring sun and peered longingly towards the land ahead.

With a deft hand, Donald switched fuel tanks, turned the key to "on," pumped the foot peddle a few times, and the motors roared into life again. The little speedboat lifted her bow towards Takis.

In a small speedboat such as Oscar's, the journey to Takis usually took a couple of hours. On occasion, the monsoon rains descended mid-journey, and the driving rain and the wind turned the sea into a dangerous mess of debris and choppy waves, but not so that Boxing Day. In fact, we were been lucky—twice lucky. The weather remained clear and the waters calm.

Little did the family know, however, that Oscar had also prayed for calm weather that day because it was his dearest wish that Cleopatra should finally come out, and he wanted us to be first to meet her.

"Look!" exclaimed Mum as she pointed ahead. "There is something floating in the water ahead of us. It's blue."

Mum took off her sunglasses and wiped them on her blouse.

"What on earth is it, Don? It looks like a large blue container of some sort. It's coming straight for us. Is it a foreign fishing boat? No … not a fishing boat," Mum corrected herself, "it's the wrong shape. I must say, it looks most peculiar. What is it?"

Mum replaced her sunglasses and craned her neck over the side of the speedboat.

"Is that Oscar," Mum added, 'aboard that thing? I recognize his hat. He's waving to us."

"I expect so," Don remarked as he peered into the distance. "It certainly looks like Oscar, and that blue thing, my dear friends," he added, "is *Cleopatra*."

Don looked at Mum's puzzled expression and laughed out loud.

"They've made good time," he said with a grin as he checked his watch. "Shan't be long now till we meet them."

Mum and I peered into the distance and as the blue apparition loomed closer and closer. We watched, fascinated, as *Cleopatra* gradually took shape. Finally *Cleopatra* and the little speedboat nudged each other and came to rest side by side.

Oscar stood up, smiled broadly, and fanned his face with a wide straw hat. We could see that he was clearly pleased at our surprised expressions.

"Welcome, welcome, my friends." Oscar extended his arm and bowed with mock formality. "*Cleopatra* and I welcome you and trust you have had an enjoyable journey thus far. It's such a beautiful day, so I suggested to *Cleopatra* that we motor out and meet you. Are you hungry?"

Mum, Dad, and I were stunned into silence. With mouths agape, we all looked at Oscar and nodded.

"Well then," Oscar said, "let's transfer you all across. I'm hungry too, and I have some morning tea aboard. Once we have finished eating, we can journey back to Takis in comfort."

Cleopatra's Barge was Oscar's new "lady." However, to refer to her as a barge was most unfair. *Cleopatra* was beautiful and exotic, just as her name suggested.

Cleopatra's Barge was constructed from two strong seaworthy native war canoes joined together by three-meter-wide smoothed planks of plantation wood. A tightly secured blue and white stripped surrey (complete with fringe on top) provided welcome shade over the deck.

Four blue-and-white deck chairs faced each other on the deck, and Oscar had placed two large portable iceboxes in the middle of the chairs; the cooler boxes acted as a table for food and drinks. A small transistor radio swung from a blue peg, and positioned near Oscar's chair was a hinge-lidded shiny blue painted box that held the two-way radio, ropes, and other boat paraphernalia.

To push *Cleopatra* to a safe cruising speed, twin 100hp Mercury motors mounted her stern. *Cleopatra* really was a barge fit for a queen—and for Dad, salvation.

We scrambled abroad *Cleopatra* and spread out.

"I'll tell One Fish," Donald shouted as the speedboat drew away, "to expect you sometime early afternoon."

Donald waved goodbye and, with the speedboat at full throttle, headed for Takis.

At the dinner table later that evening, Oscar told us he had built *Cleopatra* himself from *kwila,* a strong wood (native to the tropics) that was grown, felled, and seasoned on Takis.

Oscar was a generous host. The portable iceboxes overflowed with watermelon, pineapple, and fat juicy mangoes. Bottles of lime-flavored rainwater nestled along with bags of fresh bread rolls, sliced turkey breast, ham, and assorted cheeses. Pimms No. 1 and Johnny Walker Black Label scotch completed the feast.

Dad relaxed somewhat and accepted a ham roll from Mum. He patted his life jacket and asked if we would be at Takis by nightfall. We sat on the deck, dangled our feet in the water, and filled our growling tummies with food from heaven.

After we had finished our lunch, Mum and I dived overboard to cool off.

Dad jumped from his deck chair and shouted, "For Pete's sake. Get back on board, we are in the middle of the ocean, and there sharks everywhere! You might get attacked!"

Oscar looked over at Mum, smiled, and shook his head.

"Let's pack up," he said, "and head for home."

A few hours later, *Cleopatra's* bow crunched on the sand. We had arrived at Takis.

In His creation of earth, God had honed his skills by the time He fashioned New Britain and brought forth a paradise—a paradise called Takis.

I scrambled over the deck chairs and jumped overboard. The beach sand was hard and crisp and cracked underfoot as I walked up the beach. Oscar threw me a rope and asked me to tie *Cleopatra* to a nearby coconut tree. Dad stepped over the rail, gingerly placed his foot on the sand, and jumped down. He laughed and stamped his feet. Dad was overwhelmingly pleased to be on solid ground again.

A slow throb of an engine sounded in the distance, and very soon a rusty battered old tractor bounced onto the sand. The tractor pulled a small rickety flat-topped trailer.

Oscar took off his hat and wiped his brow with his sleeve. "Ah," he said, "here is my *haus boi*. He has a most unusual name. He calls himself One Fish."

One Fish jumped off the tractor. His face sported a wide grin as he trotted over to us.

"One Fish will tend to Suellen's needs while you are here," Oscar informed Mum. "He's very reliable, just like an English nanny," he added, laughing.

One Fish nodded and hung his head in shyness.

"Just let One Fish know if Suellen needs anything at all," Oscar said, "and he will attend to them."

One Fish and his helpers swung us onto the trailer and loaded our bags. We called Scamp to jump up, and then we lurched and jostled our way up the hill to the main house.

The plantation house sat high on the hill and overlooked the vast Bismarck Sea. The house was built on low sturdy stilts. The walls were constructed of panels of woven palm fronds and sheets of white fibro. Large wooden push-out shutters acted as windows that allowed the cool sea breeze to enter the dwelling. The mixture of European and native architecture blended perfectly with the plantation surroundings.

The main living area was scattered with woven native mats and furnished with cane settees, cane stools, and assorted canvas deck chairs. In one corner stood a large coffee table topped with a native-carved lamp base and cotton shade, books, and LP records. Water-filled bowls of frangipani blooms dotted the room and filled the air with a sweet pungent fragrance. The bowls and blooms created an atmosphere of femininity in an otherwise masculine environment. The house was pleasant and friendly, and the family felt very welcomed.

We'd had an exciting day. Our journey to Takis had started just after dawn, and now we were exhausted. One Fish had satisfied our hunger with a superb dinner of fresh fish and garden salad, and we all decided to retire early.

As Oscar and Don bade us goodnight, Oscar thanked us all for our company and urged us to treat Takis as home for the next few days.

One Fish called me just after dawn the next morning. He provided me with a huge breakfast of toast, fried eggs, and slices of fresh pawpaw. When I had eaten, he cleared the table and shooed me outside. He informed me that he had to prepare breakfast for the *mastas* and *misis*.

One Fish said he would *ring im belo* when it was time to come back inside, and in the meantime, he invited me to explore the surrounding area.

A collection of small buildings and sheds stood at the perimeter of the cleared land that surrounded the plantation house. The buildings housed the tractors, trailers, and various other pieces of equipment needed around the plantation.

There was one "building," however, that was perhaps the most unique of all: the *hous pek pek*, the outside toilet.

The little outhouse was partly hidden from view by a large mango tree and was only a short walk from the main house. The sturdy three-sided hut was constructed from bamboo poles and woven palm fronds. Soft white sand crunched underfoot as you stepped inside, a small wooden table stacked with the latest *Time* magazines stood in one corner, and a roll of white toilet paper hung from a wire hook just above. Just to make things nice for us, One Fish had adorned the walls with frangipani blooms, hibiscus flowers, and small seashells. One attended their daily call of nature and watched delighted as the reef changed colour below.

The little outhouse was truly a sight to behold and very comfortable indeed. Oscar did ask us, however, to take the kitchen torch if we wished to visit the *haus pek pek* at night, as he did not want us to stumble and roll down the hill.

It wasn't long before One Fish struck the large outside bell and called me to the house. Dad, Oscar, and Don had left soon after breakfast to tour the plantation, and Mum had decided that she and I would spend the morning snorkelling the coral reef that lay at the bottom of the hill.

One Fish drove the tractor to the back door and waited patiently, along with Scamp, as we changed into our swimmers and gathered our towels, goggles, and sandshoes. Once aboard, One Fish pumped the tractor peddle. The tractor roared to life, back fired loudly, and lurched forward. We were off.

"Hang on," Mum shouted above the motor noise. "The ride down the hill is bumpy."

Ten minutes later, we crunched onto the sand.

Cleopatra's Barge rocked gently in the shallow water as we drove past. She was still tethered to the coconut tree where we'd left her yesterday, and as we drove past, Mum called out to her in delight.

"Good morning, *Cleopatra*, you're a beautiful girl. I love you and wish Oscar would let me take you home with me."

It was a glorious tropical morning. One Fish parked the tractor under an old fig tree, and Mum and I jumped off.

"*Misis*," One Fish said, "I will come and get you and the *pikinini* when it is *belo.*"

The brilliant white crushed coral sand, already warmed by the sun, was hard and firm under our feet. The branches of the old fig, twisted and gnarled by decades of wind and water, hung low over us and, even though it was still early, provided shade from the tropical sun.

Beyond the sand, the crystal clear shallow water shone like white diamonds. As the water deepened, a rainbow of colours sparked in the morning sunshine: emerald green, turquoise, and deep indigo—a hue so common for an underwater channel.

Filled with eagerness to explore, Mum and I sat in the shallows, jammed our feet into our well-used sun-bleached sandshoes, and waded into the water.

The coral reef that fringed the shore at Takis was a virgin reef in the true sense of the word, the isolation from the outside world a testament to her abundance and her beauty. Nurtured by nature, the underwater Garden of Eden flourished and multiplied as God intended.

The coral heads that lay just below the surface looked strong and yet beautifully fragile. Purple-tipped staghorn coral reached for the sunshine, round balls of brain coral sat like orbs of burnished gold, and plate coral—the umbrellas of the reef—threw shade over small patches of white sand.

As we swam over the coral, the underwater world swayed and pulsated with life. Tiny electric-blue reef fish scattered as we glided past. Parrot fish, their birdlike beaks sharp and strong, nipped and chomped at fallen coral debris. Angel fish of yellow and black fled in startled fright, and here and there, a pair of black-and-white-striped butterfly fish spread their barbed fins and eyed us with suspicious indignity.

Fat, curly, brightly coloured Christmas worms retracted into their burrows at the touch of a hand, and black feathery brittle stars clung along white shafts of whip coral. A platoon of little crabs, nippers extended in defence, scampered for cover as lazy star fish, their blue arms motionless, waited in hope of an early morning breakfast.

The Takis reef was alive with a million shells: *Cypraea tigris,* one of my favourite shells, with their transparent mantles of mottled brown; cones, their deadly barbs hidden; thick rubber-lipped clams of all sizes; and murex with spider-like arms.

Like all of the tropical reefs that fringed our island home, the Takis reef housed a plethora of anemone, from small anemone that fitted into a woman's palm to big ones that covered the bonnet of a small car. The anemone is a polyp attached by a foot to a surface below. The polyp fans out and forms a disk-shaped body studded with tentacles armed with nematocysts that stun their prey.

I find the anemone (*Actiniaria*) the most intriguing of all sea creatures, for it shares a symbolic relationship with a fish. Even though not kith and kin, one could not survive without the other. As the anemone is carnivorous (especially enjoying fish, mussels, and other small crustaceans), the anemone is reliant on the clownfish to attract their food. The clownfish is protected from the nematocysts by a special mucus covering.

The fish dance around their anemone and lure unsuspecting prey into the heart of the waving mass. The prey is stunned and then consumed by the anemone. As a reward for their efforts, the clownfish are offered a safe haven from predators in the anemone's poison-filled tentacles. The clownfish possess an aggressive nature and dart about in a flurry if an anemone is approached.

On my visit to Rabaul in 2013, my dive buddies and I were granted permission from the local landowners to dive a number of small wrecks set down in the calm waters off the Kulau Lodge. The artificial reef is comprised of a number of sunken barges and plays host to some very large anemone. As I hovered above a particularly beautifully coloured anemone, a large clownfish zoomed out and nipped my finger. The nip hurt and drew blood. As I backed away, I laughed and thought, "Now, I can truthfully say I have been bitten by Nemo."

As the morning wore on, Mum and I ventured further and further from the shore. The coral carpet gave way to deep valleys and gutters of white sand peppered with whip coral and clumps of spongy soft coral. The deep gutters of a coral reef are hunting grounds for schools of larger reef fish, pelagic nomads, and reef sharks. The sharks are ever on the lookout for an unsuspecting morsel. Even though the reef shark is shy and elusive, Mum and I kept a sharp lookout for them, just in case they fancied a meal.

I have scuba dived the reefs in the South Pacific many times in recent years, and as a diver have shared my dives with many reef sharks. I become excited whenever I see a shark and am eternally grateful the sharks allow me to share their home in peace. Along with the anemone, the reef shark is one of my favourite sea creatures.

Time stood still as the morning sun rose higher and higher. Over the next few hours, Mum and I drifted through deep gutters and snorkelled over patches of staghorn coral. We chased turtles and shooed clown fish away from our fingers. We hid behind the brain coral and blew bubbles at parrot fish that spat coral rubble over our sandshoe clad feet, and as we immersed ourselves in God's underwater garden, we branded the images of the virgin reef at Takis, in our hearts and minds forever more.

Back on the beach, we sat under the spreading branches of the fig tree. The long swim had made us thirsty. One Fish had provided us with a cooler box full of freshly cut pineapple, mangoes, and *kulaus*. We devoured the fruit with relish and quenched our thirst with the sweet water from the young green coconuts.

It was close to midday, and to our delight, the sand was alive with hermit crabs. Whenever we were at the beach, we kept a sharp lookout for the crab, because unbeknown to them, the humble hermit sometimes provided us with a treasure.

The hermit crab is perhaps the envy of modern-day society, for it can change its house with the flick of a claw. This agile soft-bodied creature makes it home in dead and discarded seashells. The crab chooses a shell to accommodate its size, and as the crab grows bigger and the shell becomes too small, it finds a larger shell, discards its current home, and simply moves on in. The discarded shell then becomes vacant for the next occupant.

What a wonderful way to update your home—just grab the big one down the street, wait until the owners are away, and move in.

The hermit crab can be found on any beach in the tropics and roams at will between the high tide mark and the water's edge. Sometimes as we sat on the beach after a snorkel or swim, we found a hermit crab whose shell-home we need for our shell collection. I always sought permission from Mum (heaven help me if I didn't) before I attempted to entice the poor unfortunate crab to leave its current home. At times, I was successful and we had a new shell; at times, I was not and the crab retained its home. Many a time the hermit crab delivered a nasty nip that hurt and drew blood, so I dropped the shell and just let the crab be.

As a child, I developed a talent for removing a hermit crab without causing the crab too much discomfort. As a result of my talent, Dad named me "Chief Hermit Crab Remover."

Mum had found a large cone shell nearby and decided to add the shell to our collection. Alas, another poor unfortunate hermit crab was about to be evicted from its home.

"Here's a present for you, Suellen" Mum said as she handed the shell to me. "Can you remove the crab, please, and don't hurt it by doing so."

I took on an air of authority. I grasped the shell firmly between my fingers, puffed out my cheeks, placed the shell close to my mouth, and whistled softly—a hazardous act, for if the crab was in a bad mood, a soft pouting lip is an easy target for a clicking nipper.

I whistled soft and low. The crab, attracted by my whistle, uncoiled its body from inside the shell, and two stalk-like eyes appeared. Unafraid, the crab uncoiled further, and very soon, large nippers appeared, followed by a head and smaller legs. Mum held her breath. I whistled again. The curious crab inched further out of its shell-home. I slowly moved my hand behind the shell and gently closed my fingers over the crab body. I took a firm hold of the crab, whistled and tugged and whistled and tugged, and enticed the crab from its home. I placed the crab onto the sand. Eager to find a new home, the crab scampered away, and we had another shell for our collection.

A gong sounded in the distance, and very soon the rickety old tractor bounced onto the sand and made its way over to us. One Fish had arrived to ferry us back to the house for lunch.

One Fish was a one-in-a-million find for Oscar and Donald. Somewhere, somebody had trained him to cook European-style. He fried fish to perfection, and dished up treats of vegetables and homemade macaroni cheese. As we jumped aboard the tractor for our ride up the hill, Mum loudly gave thanks to that somebody for their patience and skill when they trained One Fish to cook like a chef rivalled by no other .

The next morning, we took to *Cleopatra's Barge* again. Oscar had decided we should spend the day on one of the small islands that dotted the coast off Takis. He told us it was turtle nesting time, and if we were lucky, we might see some turtles as they came ashore and laid their eggs.

We were really excited. We had seen lots of turtles in our waters, either on the surface or when we snorkelled. However, turtles are fast swimmers, and the turtles quickly swam away if we ventured too near.

We set off. Dad donned his life jacket and settled himself in the middle deck chair. He asked the usual question about how long the trip would take.

The early morning was still, the sea smooth and glassy. As the reef slid by under *Cleopatra's* bow, the crystal clear waters changed colour from turquoise to blue to deep sapphire blue. We motored along for an hour or so. I took turns at the wheel of *Cleopatra* until Dad, unimpressed, gave me a stern warning.

"Susie, will you drive in a straight line please. Otherwise, somebody will get seasick, and if that happens, watch out. It will home again, and … no turtles!"

Oscar cut the motors, and we glided into a small lagoon tucked inside a tiny island. It was dead low tide, and the waters of the lagoon were shallow, hot, and still.

I jumped overboard. The sand beneath my feet felt soft and

smooth like wet velvet. The lagoon was studded with tufts of short grey-green sea grass, submerged split coconut shells, and soft-bodied black sea cucumbers.

Oscar threw me a rope. "It's too shallow to go any further, Suellen," he said. "Can you pull us in a bit closer to the beach, please? We'll tie up later when the tide comes in."

The beach was wide, and the sand was pure and fine, like talcum powder—quite different from the sand on the Takis beach. Long grooved furrows snaked up the beach and disappeared under the coconut trees.

Oscar pointed to the tracks. "Look," he said, "the turtles were here last night. They'll be back later on the high tide. In the meantime, we can just relax and enjoy ourselves. You can explore the island, Suellen, if you want," he added. "It's quite safe, and there is lots to see and do."

Earlier that morning, One Fish had packed our lunch into the bright blue cooler boxes. We unloaded the boxes from *Cleopatra*, ferried them up the beach, and placed them under the shade of the coconut palms.

The high tide was still yet to come, and with it the long-awaited turtles. I wandered down to lagoon. It was too shallow to swim, but even with the absence of my beloved coral reef, the water still fascinated me. For the next few hours, I wallowed in the hot shallow water, played with the sea cucumbers, and when the sun had burnt me to a crisp, I roamed among the coconut palms and explored the island.

Later that afternoon, the tide turned. The water rushed into the lagoon and stirred the sea into life.

Just at dusk, Mum spotted our first turtle. The leatherback turtles that populated the islands of New Britain foraged far and wide. However, the turtles always returned to their island home to lay their eggs. The little island off Takis was a perfect nesting place for a large number of turtles big and small: the beach sloped gently towards the water, the smooth sand made it easy for the turtles to glide over on their bellies, and the coconut palms that grew in abundance on the island offered the nesting turtle protection as she laid her eggs.

The turtle entered the calm water of the lagoon and swam slowly towards the darkened beach. She was tired after her long sea journey, and her body—so swift and streamlined in the deep water— struggled as her flippers struck the shallows. She rested a while, the silence around her audible as she scanned the beach for danger. She heaved her cumbersome body from the water and, with slow heavy movements, lumbered towards the sanctuary of the coconut palms.

Far above the high tide mark, the turtle scraped a hole in the sand.

We crawled close to her and watched as she deposited her eggs. The fat white mucus-covered eggs glistened like South Sea island pearls as they dropped one by one into her sand-hole.

The moon rose higher and higher, and as the night worn on, we witnessed an army of turtles as they marched up the beach and laid their precious eggs in the sand under the coconut palms: grandmothers old and craggy (their shells studded with barnacles and seaweed; would this be their last visit perhaps?), their daughters (primed for breading for many years to come), and their daughters' daughters (were these turtles first-time mums?).

Close to midnight, we loaded *Cleopatra* with the empty cooler boxes. Tired and sunburned, we huddled together as *Cleopatra* nosed her way out of the lagoon. Mum pointed to the Southern Cross and told me how she had waited forty years to gaze upon the Cross from an island in the middle of the Pacific Ocean.

Many years later, I was employed as scuba diving guide on Heron Island on Australia's Great Barrier Reef. I was lucky enough to be on the island during turtle nesting time. As I walked back to my room one evening, I noticed a large turtle as she lumbered up the beach. I fell in step behind her and sat quietly as she dug her sand-hole and laid her eggs. It had been many years since I had witnessed a turtle as she nested. The sight brought tears to my eyes as I remembered the last time I had experienced this wonder of nature.

A few months later, I visited Mum in her home in Queensland. When I related the story of the nesting turtle on Heron Island, I asked Mum if she remembered our stay at Takis and our trip to the little island.

"Of course I remember," Mum said. "It was quite wonderful, and did you know that Phyllis Curtis (the Curtises' plantation was just around the bay from Takis) used to make the most wonderful sponge cakes using turtle eggs. She said the turtle eggs made the sponge light and fluffy, better than chicken eggs. I tasted a piece of her cake once, but I felt sorry for the turtles and only had a small bite, just to be polite."

One Fish had built a bonfire of driftwood on the beach at Takis, and as we turned into the open sea, the bonfire burned clear and bright and guided *Cleopatra* safely home.

We spent six wonderful days with Oscar, Donald, and One Fish. We snorkelled the reef, swam in the warm tropical waters, enjoyed superb fresh food, and rode the rickety old tractor. If I departed this Earth tomorrow, I would tell God I had experienced the very best of His creations.

The memory of my visit to Takis Plantation is forever etched in my heart, and to this day, I am reminded of a lifestyle which I still crave.

Shelly Beach

When I lived in Rabaul, my family and I experienced the very best of everything—freedom to do as we wished, endless days of warm sunshine, a bountiful supply of fresh tropical fruit to devour at whim, and good friends to share good times with. But the one thing that reigned supreme with all of us was immediate access to the glorious Pacific Ocean and all she had to offer.

Rabaul was born in the heart of an ancient volcano. The volcano, extinct for millions of years, laid the foundation for the natural horseshoe-shaped harbour, long wide beaches, and small deep inlets. As a result of past and present volcanic activity, most of the shoreline close to the township of Rabaul consisted of black volcanic sand, crushed pumice stone, and coral. As we loved the water so much, Mum and I cared little that the sand was black and volcanic, and we swam or snorkelled every day just for the sheer pleasure.

Shelly Beach is located in Rabaul Harbour. The Shell Oil Company had a conglomeration of buildings on the shoreline there, but everybody just called the area Shelly Beach.

Shelly Beach was situated close to the main wharf, although far enough away that I could play in the water safely without being run down by a large ship. Ordinarily we didn't swim in the harbour; the tranquil waters were a popular anchorage for cruising yachts, wide-decked Asian fishing boats, and foreign marine survey craft, and as such, the water traffic was at times quite busy.

In the monsoon season, vessels of all shapes and sizes sought refuge in our calm deep-watered harbour; the vessels vied for space like barnacles on a whale's back, as they clustered together around the weed-encrusted moorings.

Apart from the boat traffic, thousands of sea urchins clung to the rocks that lined the foreshore. If trodden on, the long black spines of the urchin easily penetrated a carelessly placed paw or soft-soled sandshoe.

Shelly Beach was about five minutes' drive from our home. As far as I was concerned, Shelly Beach rated a very poor second to any other beach or location we frequented. In fact, the underwater was quite uninteresting. There was really nothing to see: no coral, no shells, and no pretty little fish, just black sand underwater. However, if the weather threatened rain or we just wanted a quick swim with our dogs, Dad would drive us to Shelly Beach.

Sometimes I grumbled to Mum when I heard we were to swim

at Shelly and not Pila or Nonga, but Mum always had an alternative for me.

"You don't need to come with us to Shelly Beach, Suellen," she always said. "You can stay at home and do your homework instead if you wish. The choice is yours."

The lure of the water or the thought of homework always sent me scurrying to change into my swimmers.

As always, once in the water, I soon forgot my feelings of misfortune and swam and played with Charlie or Dizzy until the exhausted dogs made their way back to the car and threw themselves on the back seat.

I find it wonderful how sometimes the universe delivers an unexplained opportunity that can lead to a series of never-forgotten events. Not long after Charlie came to live with us, the universe offered me what I considered the opportunity of my lifetime. Shelly Beach introduced me to a horse.

One afternoon, as we pulled up at Shelly Beach for a swim, I saw two *real live* horses tethered to a coconut tree. We did not have livestock in Rabaul; no cows or sheep and certainly no horses. The sight of the horses excited me beyond belief.

After a brief glance, Mum and Dad ignored the horses. I, however, leapt from the car and ran up the beach to investigate. A local native approached me and introduced himself as Pus. He told me the horses belonged to an old *masta* who lived in town. However, the *masta* didn't like the horses very much, and therefore he never came to see them. Pus told me later that he was the old *masta's haus boi*, and in addition from his normal house duties, Pus was to "look after" the horses.

The very fact that the old *masta* never visited the horses horrified me, and after a brief discussion with Pus (and with no thought of mind or matter, even though I knew nothing of horses or how to care for them), I decided to adopt the horses as my own.

Pus said that, as far as he knew, the horses did not have names, so

I decided the call them Moneybar and Trigger—Moneybar because he was a silver-grey colour and Trigger because he looked very much like the horse ridden by the famous cowboy Roy Rogers.

Moneybar and Trigger lived in a half-fenced sandy "paddock" next to the Shell Co. buildings. As the horses were rarely tethered, they roamed the beach at will and grazed on the short tuffs of grass that grew around the base of the coconut palms. To the back of the sandy area stood a bamboo lean-to attached to a small derelict tin shed, a few abandoned forty-four gallon drums, and some sheets of rusty tin.

When I explored the tin shed, I found an old forty-four-gallon drum that contained a coil of old rope, two well-used bridles, and a few old horse brushes.

At school the next day I told my friend Pam about Moneybar and Trigger. We decided that after school, we would meet at Shelly and ride the horses. After many attempts, we managed—no doubt incorrectly—to fit the bridles to the horses; luckily, Moneybar and Trigger possessed a placid nature and stood quietly as we fiddled with the buckles and straps.

Pus was nervous when he saw the bridles on Moneybar and Trigger and told us he would have to ask the old *masta's* permission first before Pam and I rode the horses.

I informed Pus that, as the old *masta* didn't like the horses anyway, the old *masta* wouldn't mind if we "exercised" the horses for him. Pus, however, displayed some misgivings. Pam and I were unfazed by Pus's nervousness and promised him, just to make him feel better, that we would bring him some European cigarettes when we next visited. Pus's face split into a wide grin. There is no honour among thieves, and the thought of some European cigarettes to smoke was enough to convince him to keep our secret. Pam and I assured Pus that if he wasn't there when we next visited the horses, we would leave the cigarettes in the old drum in the tin shed.

Just for the record, there was an endless supply of cigarettes at home. Dad bought cigarettes by the carton, and Mum always filled the alabaster cigarette box, which sat on the coffee table in the lounge room, with the cigarettes as a gesture of hospitality for our guests whenever they visited. It was easy for me to swipe a handful of cigarettes for Pus.

With Pus sorted, I knew my ever-protective Dad would also disapprove of me riding the horses, so whenever we visited Shelly Beach, I invited Pam along. We always busied ourselves with other "horse duties" until Dad's attention was diverted.

The abandoned forty-four-gallon drums in the paddock provided a somewhat wobbly platform for us to mount Moneybar and Trigger. Once mounted, we galloped the horses up the beach as far away as possible from Dad.

Pam and I rode Moneybar and Trigger until the horses were lathered in sweat. To cool them off, we walked them into the water, jumped off their backs, and swam them into deeper water. We jumped back on, made our way into the back to the shallows, and raced each other up the beach again. It was great fun.

One afternoon, as we frolicked in the shallows with Moneybar and Trigger, Dad walked briskly towards us. I could see he was agitated.

"Where did those horses come from?" he scowled. "Whose are they, and who said you could ride them?"

"They just live over in that paddock," I informed Dad, "and Pus told us anybody can ride them, and ..."

Dad cut me short. "Who, for Pete's sake, is Pus?" Dad asked. "What would *he* know about horses anyway? I think you had better get off them and put them back in the paddock now. I'm sure Pus has it all wrong. Besides, these horses are wild, and one of you might get kicked."

Dad turned a deaf ear as I howled in protest. He stood well clear of Moneybar and Trigger as he escorted Pam and I back to the paddock. Clearly, Dad was not amused at our antics, and he lectured me on the dangers of horse riding all the way home.

My father was a great storyteller, and if he wanted me to take heed of his advice, he invented a tale to reinforce his issue. When Dad came home from the office the next afternoon, he informed me he wanted to "talk to me about something" and asked me to join him on the front veranda.

"Now Susie," Dad said. "Those two horses at Shelly Beach have both raced in the Melbourne Cup."

Dad attempted to look stern. He clasped his hands behind his back and paced up and down in front of me, and they are only there because they keep bucking their jockeys off, and the horses have to be sorted out!"

Dad had obviously put some thought into his little anecdote. However, Dad had forgotten one very important factor: I was a child who lived in New Guinea, and I knew nothing of horse racing, jockeys, or the Melbourne Cup.

Dad looked at my blank face. He knew he had missed the point.

"Now Susie, I want you to listen very carefully," Dad said. "The Melbourne Cup is a very fast horse race. Brave men called jockeys ride horses in it, and it goes on down south in Melbourne. The only horses that are allowed to run in the Melbourne Cup are thoroughbred Arab horses and Palomino horses, and they go flat out and buck their jockeys off. Those two horses at Shelly Beach are thoroughbreds. The grey one is an Arab horse, and the brown one is a Palomino horse, and that's why they run in the Melbourne Cup. I know those two horses have raced in the Melbourne Cup, because last year I listened to the Melbourne Cup race on the radio at the office, and those horses ran so fast they won!"

I loved Dad's stories, especially if they related to me and the fact that I now "owned" two very fast racehorses pleased me no end.

However, that wasn't the point of Dad's story. Dad wanted to scare me away from Moneybar and Trigger, but when Dad saw my enthralled face, he knew he had failed miserably. So Dad decided to embellish his story somewhat.

"The fellow who owns those horses," Dad told me, "knew that the horses ran very fast, so he decided to enter them in the Melbourne Cup horse race. The horses ran so fast that they left all the other horses for dead and won the race. The horses were so excited that they bucked off their jockeys, crashed through the finish tape, and trampled half the crowd! The managers of the race were so angry that they banned those two horses from ever racing down south again. Les Clarke (Dads' shipping agent in Sydney) arranged for the horses to come to Rabaul on one of the *Bank* ships to be 'sorted out.' When the ship got here, the horses kicked and bucked and everybody ran away. The horses then galloped off to Shelly Beach, and that is why they are here now. So there you have it. Those horses are wild, and your mother and I want you to stay away from them!"

I looked at Dad and grinned from to ear to ear. I loved my Dad unconditionally and believed every word he told me. I knew in my heart that Dad always tried to protect me from harm, but as far as I were concerned, the "managers" of the Melbourne Cup horse race didn't know Moneybar and Trigger as well as I did, and if the horses had behaved badly at the Melbourne Cup race, it was the managers' fault and not the horses!

Dad looked at his watch and frowned. "Your mother wants to go for a swim," he stated, "so you just think about what I have said."

Dad strode off and told Mum that he had sorted out the problem of the horses at Shelly. But his wonderful story of Moneybar and Trigger, the Melbourne Cup, and the brave jockeys had struck a chord of recognition with me. My body tingled with anticipation as my imagination went into overdrive. I couldn't wait to jump on my bike and hightail down to Shelly Beach.

A few weeks previously, the award-winning movie *Lawrence of Arabia* had come to town. The movie was spellbinding. The story of Thomas Edward Lawrence, who fought for what he believed in;

the desert tribesmen, their long headdresses billowing behind them as they charged, swords raised, towards the enemy; and of course, the magnificent horses as they flew across the sand dunes, filled me with excitement.

I was especially taken with the Arab horse ridden by Auda abu Tayi. Dad had mentioned that Moneybar was an Arab horse, and as realization dawned on me, my heart swelled with pride to think I "owned" a famous Arab horse, just like the desert horse in *Lawrence of Arabia*. Dad's warning about riding fast, falling off, and bucking horses fell on deaf ears yet again.

Pam and I always made sure we hid the bridles well in the lean-to. We didn't want anybody else to ride Moneybar and Trigger—but as in all small towns, there was talk at school, and the secret hiding place was soon discovered. The town kids descended on Shelly Beach in droves. It was the case of first in, best dressed; whoever arrived first pinched the bridles and rode off with Moneybar and Trigger.

Pam and I felt cheated and stood united in our quest to keep the intruders at bay. Alas, much to our disgust, we were rendered powerless.

One afternoon after school, a gaggle of town kids collected at Shelly Beach. A young girl called Carole tried to fit Moneybar with his bridle. Moneybar spun around and kicked Carole in the face. Moneybar's unshod hoof clocked Carole square on the nose, smashing her nose to pulpy mess and slashing her eye in the process.

The next day, Pam and I confronted Carole at school. How dare she ride Moneybar? We had little sympathy for her black weeping eye, nasty cuts, and swollen nose, and we waved away her tale of woe with "Serve yourself right for getting kicked, you can't ride properly. Anyway, he's our horse."

Word of the Moneybar's kick spread like wildfire. Moneybar was branded "unbroken" and "wild," and the town kids gave him a wide berth.

It was inevitable that Dad heard Moneybar had kicked Carole, and Dad was not amused. That afternoon, he summoned me to the front veranda and subjected me to another lecture on kicking horses. Dad finished with, "I told you so," and then instructed me, in no uncertain terms, to keep away from Moneybar and Trigger. Pam and I were devastated. Mum, however, was angry.

"For goodness sake, Father," Mum said, "you simply cannot wrap Suellen in cotton wool. If she wants to ride those horses, then let her. She will never have the opportunity again, and those horses won't be here forever."

"But that Arab horse is wild!" Dad said. "That poor girl will have to have her face fixed when she is older. That horse gave her a nasty kick."

"Well," Mum said, "I doubt that very much. Her face looks fine to me. Anyway, it was her own silly fault. Doesn't the stupid girl know you shouldn't walk behind a horse? No wonder the horse kicked her. She should have kept well away."

Dad sighed deeply. He knew the horse discussion with Mum was closed. He shook his head and muttered under his breath that "the only people who ever listened to him were office *bois*."

Pam and I were delighted that everybody was scared of "our horses." We had Moneybar and Trigger to ourselves again. We rolled our beach towels into headdresses, scoured the beach for "stick rifles," and for many months to come "chased" off the enemy as we rode "our" horses hard and fast up and down Shelly Beach.

The next year, we left Rabaul for annual leave in Sydney. Mum took me to the local horse-riding school and enrolled me in Saturday morning riding lessons. A pony called Treasure didn't like my Rabaul-style riding habits and bucked me off. I fell against a tree and broke two ribs.

I decided there and then that horse riding was not for me. When we returned to Rabaul, rather than ride Moneybar and Trigger whenever we visited Shelly Beach, I left the horses to the mercy of others. I much preferred to accompany Mum and our dogs in the water instead.

One afternoon, as our dog Charlie emerged from the water at Shelly beach, Mum noticed that his coat was smothered in engine oil.

The next morning, Mum phoned the manager of the Shell Oil Company and demanded to know why there was oil in the water. The manager told Mum the company had installed new oil storage tanks and had emptied the oil from the old tanks into the water off the beach. Mum, of course, gave the manager a blast of abuse, and we never swam at Shelly again.

A few months later, Moneybar and Trigger disappeared from Shelly Beach. Pus told us the old *masta* had loaded the horses into a truck and taken them to his plantation at Kokopo.

We never saw Moneybar and Trigger again. I often wondered if Dad "convinced" the old *masta* to relocate the two horses to a plantation; I have no doubt Dad knew who the old *masta* was. Whatever the reason, I always hoped the horses, wherever they were, enjoyed a happy, peaceful, and long life.

Now that I have lived in Australia for a number of years, I along with most of my countrymen listen to or watch the Melbourne Cup on TV. "The Race that Stops the Nation" is broadcast live, and as the horses thunder down the track, I remember Dad's story of Moneybar and Trigger.

My dad was truly the Rudyard Kipling of our family and invented a tale for nearly every circumstance that touched my life.

Nonga Beach, Tunnell Hill, and Watom Island

Nonga was a small settlement about a fifteen-minute car drive from town. The settlement consisted of a number of small native villages (complete with their gardens of Taro, Pitt-Pitt, and scraggly chickens), Chinese trade stores, and marine workshops.

The Nonga Base Hospital serviced the native and European population alike, and it was therefore the focal point for folk who were ill. However, for my family, a wide strip of black sand, situated just before the hospital turnoff, held a special interest. We simply called the area Nonga.

For most of the day, the road to Nonga was, by Rabaul standards, a busy road. Malaguna Road was the main thoroughfare from town to Kokopo and Kerevat, and the road was always thick with *boi* trucks, utilities, and cars. At the end of Malaguna Road, the road ventured left to Kokopo and right up Tunnel Hill to Kerevat.

Like many areas in Rabaul, Tunnell Hill was steeped in history. In the early 1900s, the Germans blasted a tunnel (known as Ratavul Tunnel or Ratavul Pass Road) through the ridge to access Tallili Bay. However, the tunnel collapsed after an earthquake. As the tunnel was a vital link between Rabaul and the west coast of the island, the debris was cleared and a road established instead. The road still retained the name Tunnel Hill. Prior to the Japanese occupation, a volcanology observatory was established on the hilltop to monitor the seven live volcanoes that encompassed Rabaul Harbour.

In 1941, Rabaul fell to the Japanese Imperial Army. The Japanese took advantage of the thoroughfare and established concrete underground bunkers with interlocking tunnels throughout the hill. The underground bunkers housed war equipment (including antiaircraft guns that pointed over Simpson Harbour) crucial for the defence of the Gazelle Peninsula.

After the war, the old concrete Japanese bunkers were put to good use and rather than hide Japanese antiaircraft guns, the bunkers now housed the necessary equipment to record seismic activity.

In 2000, the US Geographical Survey installed a real-time GPS monitoring upgrade for the Rabaul Volcano Observatory. The real time GPS collects data from remote receivers every ten seconds. Rabaul and the surrounding area are still considered volcanically unstable, and for the safety and well-being of the population of Rabaul, the collected data is used as an early warning sign should an evacuation of prove imminent.

On my visit to Rabaul in 2013, I visited the observatory at the top of Tunnel Hill. I had been to the observatory many times as a child, and as I stood next to the old Japanese bunkers and looked over Simpson Harbour, my heavy heart broke, as it had done *so* many times in the past few weeks. My childhood hometown lay in ruins before me, buried under tons of volcanic ash.

I looked over at Tavurvur Volcano, a volcano I had climbed as a child. A steady stream of volcanic ash spewed from her crater. The soft afternoon breeze carried the ash across the harbour and settled on my skin. Never before had I witnessed such an extreme power of nature. Most times I am in awe on nature, but that day I wondered why she was at times so very cruel. In one whimsical moment, she had shattered the lives of so many.

The road up Tunnel Hill was steep. However, the road was sealed with bitumen, which was a bonus. It was always heavily laden with vehicles going to and from the outlying villages, and we inevitably choked on exhaust fumes all the way up the hill until Dad was able to zoom past the cars, utes, and *boi* trucks on the downhill run.

Just before the hospital turnoff, a dirt road led to Nonga Beach. In the past, the area had supported some light commercial businesses (mainly marine workshops) and as a result, the area was littered with abandoned debris.

An old fig tree grew at the end of the dirt road, and the fig tree marked the spot where Dad parked our car. A crudely made wooden table and bench sat under the tree. The table made a good dumping spot for our towels and beach bags,

Nonga was not a particularly pretty spot to swim in. Although the water was clean and unpolluted, like Shelly, the underwater was totally devoid of coral, rocks, sea-grass, and fish. Nonga did, however, have two very attractive advantages: the calm water was a near-perfect environment for a seashell we converted for our collection and a floating raft anchored just off the beach.

For many years, we sought an *Oliva funebralis* (a small oval-shaped marine snail) to add our shell collection. The *Oliva funebralis*, which we just called a "black olive," was quite rare, and each time we visited Nonga, we hoped we would be lucky enough to find one.

Our quest for a black olive drew us to Nonga time and time again. However, it was many years before we finally chanced upon one.

For the most part of the day, olive shells buried themselves in the sand close to the water's edge. Just at dusk, the shells emerged from their sand holes to feed. Their sand trails, clearly visible in the warm shallow water, snaked and crisscrossed each other like underwater roadmaps.

As we had quite an extensive collection of olive shells (they were one of our favourite shells), we adhered strictly to Mum's policy of only two shells of each kind in our collection. The only olive shell we sought at Nonga was the black olive, and after a cursory glance at the other olives, if they were multicoloured and not black, we left them in peace to enjoy their dinner.

We rarely stayed long in the water at Nonga—just enough time for a quick dip to cool off. We preferred to walk in the shallows and often gathered handfuls of olive shells and sat, as the water lapped our toes, eyes peeled for the elusive one.

After a fruitless search, Mum and I often felt defeated, so we just abandoned our quest and swam out to the floating raft for a spot of fun.

The raft was made of four floating forty-four-gallon drums joined in the middle by lengths of wooden plank. The platform formed a perfect diving board for us to bomb any unsuspecting shell collectors who invaded our territory. The raft was anchored to the sea bottom with a long piece of rusty old chain attached to a concrete block. The concrete block, chain, and drums were encrusted with seaweed and barnacles that formed a mini artificial reef that attracted a large variety of little fish and sea creatures.

In later years, I learnt to waterski at Nonga. Most of our friends owned speedboats, and the family also belonged to a waterski club.

Mum always encouraged me take advantage of all water activities and it wasn't long before I were quite proficient on one ski. However, whenever I sought an alternative past-time other than exploring my beloved coral reefs, fate stepped in.

I was at Nonga one morning, skiing with a group of friends. As the boat sped towards the shore to drop me off, I miscalculated the distance to the shoreline and let go of the ski rope too late. The ride up the beach tore off my bikini (in those halcyon days, I was ignorant of the need to wear a wetsuit or life jacket) and the sand rash on my bottom, arms, and legs stung for days.

I was mortally embarrassed at my unladylike beach slide, and for a number weeks, gracefully declined any further offers to waterski. It took a while for my ego to heal, and even after it did, I was somewhat less enthusiastic to don my ski again.

When you stood on the beach at Nonga and looked out to sea, Watom Island came into view: Watom, an island of mystery and heartache.

In February 1942, Singapore fell to the Japanese Imperial Army. In October of that same year, 620 soldiers from the British Artillery Regiment were transported to Rabaul as POWs. Of the 620, some 480 were relocated to Ballalae Island, just south of Bougainville Island. The soldiers who remained were forced into work parties and along with Indian and Pakistani POWs dug many of the tunnels that surrounded Rabaul.

An unknown number of the British POWs. were also dispatched to Watom Island to clear the vegetation, build bunkers, and dig tunnels.

In 1945, Rabaul was liberated by the Allied Forces. Sadly, only eighteen British soldiers survived to tell their story.

The Japanese forces who invaded Rabaul neglected to keep accurate records of their POWs; therefore, many of the human remains found after Rabaul was liberated could not be identified. The unidentified soldiers, along with the many other soldiers who perished at that time, rest eternally at the Bitapaka War Memorial near Kokopo.

May they all rest in peace.

Pila Pila

These days when I go to the beach for a swim or even just to walk the sands with my dogs, I marvel at the assortment of water toys that accompany most families with children—surfboards, boogie boards, kneeboards, floats in the shape of whales and fish, balls, and Frisbees. Some young people, I have noticed, have cords plugged into their ears and bop their heads in time with the music played on their smartphones.

Modern technology is wonderful in every sense of the word. However, I *do* wonder if we rely on too many other "things" to keep us entertained when, in fact, nature and all she provides is the best entertainer of all.

When I lived in Rabaul as a child, Mother Nature—whatever her cloak, bountiful or barren; whatever her mood, benign or boisterous—provided me with the biggest and best water toy of all: the Pacific Ocean. The mighty Pacific, with her coral reefs and sea creatures, her seashells and driftwood, her playful hermit crabs and baby turtles, offered my family a landslide of fun. Her abundant gifts, coupled with our imaginations, was all we needed to keep us entertained hour after hour, day after day, week after week, year in and year out.

To be brutally honest, I sometimes wonder who had the better deal: the kids of today or us who had nothing except rubber-skirted face masks and cheap trade-store sandshoes?

Pila Pila—we just called the area Pila—was our water wonderland, our very own theme park where hijinks and hilarity took precedence over all else. Pila was *the* place to walk on the wild side. I didn't go there to drift over a coral reef, or to scan the shallows looking for olive shells, or to chase and whistle a hermit crab from its home, or to sit in the moonlight and watch turtles. I went to Pila for one purpose and one purpose only: to frolic and play and *really* have fun in the water with my mum.

My mother always maintained that "the best parts of Rabaul lay under the sea" and often reminded me to be grateful for the opportunities offered to me. Mum and I are strong swimmers, our skills honed by our long drifts over a coral reef and our playtimes in the deep waters of Pila or Nonga.

Dusk falls very quickly in the tropics, and on the afternoons we went to Pila, we called our dogs and left home as soon as Dad had finished his after-work cup of tea. Pila lay on the other side of Tunnell Hill, and even though it was a good fifteen-minute drive from town, the spot was a popular recreational haunt for many of the townsfolk.

When I lived in Rabaul, the tarred road finished just past the bottom of Tunnel Hill, and as we turned left onto the Pila road, we braced ourselves for the dusty ten-minute bone-rattling ride to Pila Beach.

Pila Pila settlement was held as native title, and as such, rather than being just tropical jungle, it was home to a small native village. The village had a collection of thatched huts and small fibro dwellings surrounded by neat plots of coconut palms, cocoa trees, and market gardens. The little village was clearly visible from the road and—complete with the ever-present brown speckled chickens and barking dogs—was a pleasant sight after the hustle and bustle of town.

Tall coconut palms strung with broken fence wire marked the entrance to Pila Beach, and as we turned off the road, a welcome salty breeze swept through the car. The clean smell of sea and wet sand filled our nostrils and chased away the sting of road dust. The black sand under the coconut palms was hard, compacted, and flattened by use, so it was safe for Dad to park the car. However, the coconuts at Pila Beach were rarely harvested, and the risk of a falling coconut—or indeed coconuts, especially during the monsoon season—proved hazardous for a carelessly parked car. Dad, when he remembered, always tried to park under a palm with green immature nuts rather than ripe brown ones, which fell heavily without warning.

Pila Beach was wide and sweeping and sloped down quite sharply to the water's edge. In the dry season from March to November, the water was dead calm, broken now and again by champagne-coloured ripples that ran along the beach and clawed their way silently up the slope towards dry land. The surface of the water shone clean and bright, and if you ran your fingers lightly over the top, the water felt smooth and slick like new glass. The water was deep, too, close to the shore—without any coral, rocks, or sea urchins—so we could race down the hot sand and dive straight in without fear of injury. The seabed fell away in sharp undulations, and smooth pieces of broken shell lay scattered here and there like handfuls of multicoloured gems thrown carelessly over a black velvet cape. As the sun shone through the water, the shell pieces winked and beckoned us to take a closer look. The urge to touch, stroke, and fondle them at times overwhelmed me.

November marked the start of the monsoon season in Rabaul, and overnight, it seemed, the ocean shucked her veil of tranquillity and, from then until March, relentlessly pounded our shores with wild unpredictable seas. The once-calm waters at Pila boiled with raging surf, and the sea became a giant washing machine filled with seaweed clumps, bobbing driftwood, and floating debris

It was too rough to swim at Pila during monsoon season, so I bodysurfed (as best I knew how) instead. I screamed in delight as the waves carried me up the beach and held my breath as the wild surf rolled and dumped me hard into the sand. As the receding wave dragged me back towards the breakers, I dug my hands deep in the sand and watched as the water pooled and furrowed around me. As the next big wave washed over me, I relaxed and let the powerful undertow suck me back towards the breakers again. Again and again

I bodysurfed the big waves until, spent of energy, I swam out beyond the breakers for a float on my back and rest.

In the dry season, when the waters off Pila were calm and still like an English mill pond, Mum and I swam out into deep water. We floated on our backs, treaded water, and rode each other piggyback. We duck-dived, lay on our backs, and blew underwater bubbles. Sometimes Dad became worried that we were out to far or had stayed too long. He stood on the beach and beckoned us to come in closer to shore. Mum and I just ignored him and continued playing.

My time with Mum in the waters off Pila honed my water-skills and gave me the supreme confidence I have in the ocean today.

The only "shell" we ever found at Pila was the *operculum* or "door" to the Gold-Mouth Turban *Turbo chrysostomus*. The *operculum* varied in size from a small dot to a five-cent piece and is the image of a cat's eye. The cat's eye was used extensively as decoration by the local wood carvers.

As Pila was fairly close to town, we mostly swam at Pila on the weekdays after Dad came home from the office. Even though the weather was hot, Dad rarely swam. He preferred to walk the beach instead, looking for shells or odd pieces of driftwood left by the high tide.

My favourite past-time of all is to explore a coral reef. However, the times I shared in the water with Mum and our dogs at Pila remain a highlight of my lucky, enchanted childhood.

When Mum passed away, I inherited much of our shell collection. The collection is now housed in a glass-top table situated on my back veranda. Scattered throughout the collection are many many cat's eyes Dad found at Pila.

Many years ago, Mum and Dad purchased a house in Hervey Bay, QLD. The house is within walking distance of Shelly Beach. Mum chose the location because, she said, "the calm water of the bay is just like the calm water of Pila, and when I go for a swim, it feels just like home."

Tovarua Plantation

The family had only been in Rabaul a few weeks when we received an invitation to visit Tovarua Plantation. Most Sundays, the local plantation owners and their families gathered at Tovarua for a day of rest and relaxation. Dad said it was the perfect opportunity for the family to meet some new people, and so it was decided we would visit the plantation the following Sunday.

Tovarua Plantation was about an hour's drive south of Rabaul, just past the little outpost of Kokopo. The plantation fringed the coast and stood in the very heart of the rich copra-producing belt of New Britain.

Kokopo and much of the surrounding area was synonymous with what the locals called "old German plantations." In 1884, Germany formally annexed northeast New Guinea and the islands adjacent thereto, of which New Britain was one, and in the years immediately after annexation began reorganising her new colonies.

The German administration renamed New Britain "Nue Pommern" and Kokopo "Herbertshohe." After the Germans realized the rich black volcanic soil was perfect for growing coconuts, they actively encouraged the settlement of individual German planters in the Herbertshohe area.

Queen Emma, over the years, had acquired vast land holdings in Herbertshohe area. However, at the time of annexation, the Germans wanted the area all to themselves. In 1885, the German administrators applied various strong-arm tactics in an effort to acquire Emma's land and local interests. The German administrators failed miserably; Queen Emma outfoxed them all. In a series of perfectly legal, smart business moves, Emma retained *all* her land, including her plantation Ralum and her local businesses.

In the years to come, Queen Emma decided to keep her adversaries close to hand and thus married off a number of her pretty nieces to her wealthy German neighbouring planters.

From the late 1880s until World War I, the German plantations flourished. After Germany was defeated in World War I, the German plantations were confiscated and the Germans "asked" to leave New Britain as they came: with nothing. Unfortunately, between World War I and World War II, most of the plantations were left unattended, and the plantations fell into a state of disrepair.

In 1942, the Japanese Imperial Army invaded Rabaul and very quickly established a network of underground tunnels in and around the Kokopo area. The Allies knew the tunnels were a vital part of the Japanese war machine and held a vast amount of ammunition and equipment (including Japanese mini submarines, barges, and armoured vehicles) as well sleeping quarters, kitchens, and fully operational hospitals. In order to weaken the Japanese resolve, the Allies bombed and strafed the Kokopo area on a regular basis. As a direct result of the bombing and the retaliation administered by the Japanese forces, many of the plantations in the area, including Queen Emma's Ralum were devastated or destroyed.

After peace came to New Britain in 1945, the boundaries of the plantations were re-marked and most of the plantations re-established. When my family and I lived in Rabaul, many of the old German plantations in the Kokopo area were owned by a multinational company and managed by local European families. Our family was fortunate indeed to have the opportunity to visit many of these plantations on a regular basis, and we witnessed firsthand a perfect blend of the old and the new.

For many years, Tovarua was an all-time family favourite Sunday picnic spot. Nobody really minded the long drive to the plantation. Besides, we usually stopped at Kokopo for a spell, to buy some bread and let the dogs out for a run. Kokopo had three Chinese trade stores, and *all* Chinese trade stores sold Chinese salted plums and Mum's favourite coconut candies.

The Kokopo Road was a dust-choked, unsealed narrow track that hung on, at times, almost precariously to the winding coastline. The Japanese tunnels, constructed during World War II, riddled the hillside next to the road, and their gaping mouths, black and silent, were a constant source of fascination for me. The tunnels were large enough to drive a double-decker bus though. Sometimes Dad stopped the car at the entrance of a tunnel, and he and I walked in a short way.

I remember that in one of the tunnels, there were pieces of broken electrical wire poking from the wall. Further in, we found a few Japanese sake bottles, a few one-toed thongs, broken wooden boxes, and sadly a photo of a Japanese family.

Dad always said that the war in Rabaul was a terrible time for all concerned, and we shouldn't take anything Japanese from the tunnel because it was disrespectful.

I also remember Dad adding, somewhat wistfully, "Besides, your mother would have a fit. You know what she is like, and if we pinched something and she found it, she would throw it out anyway. So we best leave everything as it is." So we left the items to rest in peace for all time.

Just for the record, Mum would refuse to accompany Dad and me into the tunnels. Mum said we were both mad for wanting to go inside, and she would sit in the car smoking nervously until we reappeared.

As we passed the tunnels and neared Kokopo, the road seemed to swell with vehicles of all shapes and sizes. Each car or truck honked its horn madly. Ignorant of safety or road rules, they passed each other willy-nilly to escape the swirling dust.

We always breathed a sigh of relief when we left Kokopo behind and turned onto the crushed coral track (left over from German times) that marked the boundary of Tovarua Plantation. Almost immediately, the surrounding area changed, and a cool feeling of serenity descended into the car.

The coconut palms that formed the plantation were a testament to the German pioneers. More than seven decades later, the palms had grown to twenty metres or more tall. Ramrod straight, majestic and strong, they lined the horizon in every direction. Set out long ago in perfectly straight lines, the mighty palms had matured to be all the same size, all the same colour, and all the same shape—a statement to the Germanic gene of uniformity.

The old German Tovarua coconut palms had, over the years, served many masters. The palms had defied tropical storms, volcanic activity, war, and neglect. Now, more than half a century later, the pungent oily smell of drying copra filled our nostrils and told us the palms still brought forth an abundant supply of the white-fleshed fruit.

The clean dust-free track led us deeper into the plantation, and eventually we came to a line of short-stumped thatched sheds set about in a large, neatly swept clearing. Orange glowing embers were visible beneath the sheds, and large piles of discarded coconut husks lay nearby. The air was thick and smelled sweet, and a fine oil-like film covered everything.

When we first visited Tovarua, Dad told me these sheds were the drying sheds, where the coconut flesh became copra. He then explained the process.

After the coconut had been harvested and husked, the hard inside nut was split open. The flesh was then removed by hand with a small sharp knife. The flesh was painstakingly placed in the sheds on wire racks. Heat from a layer of glowing embers, constantly fed with the discarded coconut husks, dried the coconut flesh. After the drying process was completed, the shrivelled and brown pieces of coconut were known as copra. The copra was then sorted to discard any inferior pieces, bagged, and subsequently trucked into town. The copra was then processed at a factory to extract coconut oil. The coconut oil was then used for cooking, cosmetics, and suchlike.

I guess these days this method of harvesting, drying, bagging, and transportation of the copra is a fairly primitive process and labour intensive as well. However, the method was tried and true and was used extensively throughout New Britain and the New Guinea mainland.

Sometimes we stopped briefly at the drying sheds just to have a look around, although as we were mostly there on a Sunday, all was usually quiet. Sometimes I would pinch a few pieces of copra to nibble on later.

I love the smell of coconut oil. It reminds me of drying copra, and even now, so many years later, that smell brings me straight back to Tovarua and floods me with an overwhelming feeling of homesickness.

The Sunday gathering at Tovarua took place at a little beach clearing in the heart of the plantation. We were told that everybody picnicked, so Mum packed a picnic lunch for us. We were informed that the coral reef that fringed the clearing was quite good, so we threw in our goggles and sandshoes as well. Mention was also made of the beach sand at Tovarua. The sand was white, not black volcanic, like it was in town.

I remember quite clearly the very first time I encountered the splendour of Tovarua. As we turned off the main road and entered the plantation, the coconut palms blotted the sun and plunged the car into dappled light. I had never seen such tall coconut palms; they seemed to touch the sky. When I asked Dad later why the palms were so tall, he told me they were very old and had been planted at the beginning of the century by the (then) German plantation owners.

It was mid-morning, and a few of the plantation families has already gathered at the beach clearing. The bush wood tables that dotted the clearing were spread with *laplap* tablecloths, foam cooler boxes, and beach towels. As we alighted from the car, I noticed the sand was white, just as we had been told. Whiter than white, in fact—a stark contrast to the black sand in town. As I walked down to the beach and looked out to sea, the sunlight danced across the coral reef and ignited the water in a blaze of opal colours. Even at such a young age, I remember being awestruck by the sheer beauty Tovarua offered.

After introductions, I was herded into a native canoe by a scowling, pimply faced boy. The canoe, we found out later, stayed permanently on the beach at Tovarua and was available to all to use at their leisure throughout the day. Earlier, that same boy had shown annoyance at his mother's suggestion that he show me around, as it was my first time there, and grumbled under his breath about babysitting as he dragged the canoe into the water.

I was quite nervous as the boy paddled the canoe furiously out to the deeper water. With a snigger, he told me to put on my goggles and sandshoes. As I bent to tie my laces, the boy prodded me furiously with the back with his paddle and, with a sneer, pushed me over the side.

I never liked the boy after that, and when I complained later to Dad of the boy's actions, my ever-protective Dad took the boy aside. After giving him a severe dressing down, Dad let the boy know that any "thuggish bullying" behaviour towards me would not be tolerated. From that day on, the scowling pimply faced youth left me alone.

Today, however, I give thanks to that boy for pushing me in, for as I looked underwater through my goggles that fateful morning, the scene took my breath away. A deep-water coral reef lay beneath me. The explosion of colour and beauty touched my very soul, and even in the naiveté of my youth left me awe-inspired.

My love affair with the coral reef and her many creatures was born that day at Tovarua, and ultimately my passion for the sea would to lead me to abandon a safe, secure, and utterly boring career in banking to pursue a dream.

The little clearing on the beach where we swam and picnicked was ringed with coconut palms and figs trees gnarled by the wind and tropical weather. The trees threw shade over a small collection of roughly made bush-wood tables and benches. The dazzling white crushed coral sand, swept clean by the tide, was rough and hard and yet cool to walk upon.

Directly in front of the clearing, starting right at the water's edge, grew a soft grey-green carpet of short sea grass. To the untrained eye, the sea grass was a mere covering, a pathway that led to the rich reef beyond, but the sea grass contained hidden gems and enthralled Mum and I just the same.

A great many cowrie shells sought haven in the sea grass. The tiger cowrie, *Cypraea tigris*—complete with a mantle even more striking in appearance than the shell it adorned—was commonplace, as was *Cypraea mappa*, so-called because the marking on the shell resembled a map. A little white cowrie, *Calpurnus verrucosus,* slashed with a purple stripe with a knoblike "tomato seed" stuck on each end, was also abundant at Tovarua. *Calpurnus verrucosus* was one of Mum's favourite shells.

The poisonous cone shell lived in the sea grass as well. The most venomous of all cones, *Conus geographus,* thrived undisturbed. A white cone with black markings much the same as newsprint, *Conus litteratus,* grew as big as a house brick.

When Mum and I first snorkelled the reef at Tovarua, our plastic bags bulged with live shells, but even in those days, Mum only allowed me to take shells we did not have in our fledgling collection. I soon learnt to leave the shells we did not need.

As the water deepened and the sea grass thinned, a thicket of staghorn coral sprang from the white sand. The seemingly impregnable thicket guarded the reef beyond just as the wall of thorns guarded Sleeping Beauty's castle. The thicket, when penetrated, held a promise of wondrous things to come.

Beyond the thicket, the reef lay in all its glory. As the coral followed the contours of the continental shelf, the water deepened considerably and dropped away to infinity. The soft corals flourished in the deeper water, and the hard corals—though abundant in many forms—paled into insignificance.

It would be remiss to give centre stage to only one type of soft coral that grew at Tovarua, for each one seemed to flaunt its beauty in radiant defiance of the hard coral. The soft corals carpeted the reef as far as the eye could see. Some lay like a yellow blanket thrown carelessly over an unmade bed, while others stood erect, their bodies tree-like, stark white, with branches sprouting red leaves. My favourite of all the soft corals we saw at Tovarua was the *Sinularia*. The *Sinularia* was drab and brown and seemingly insignificant, but sometimes, when I parted the fleshy folds ever so carefully, I found a treasure: *Ovula ovum*, commonly known as the egg cowrie.

Wherever there is healthy coral in abundance, there are healthy fish in abundance, and Tovarua was no exception. The clear unpolluted waters pulsed with reef fish of all sorts and sizes. Tiny electric-blue neon tetra fish swarmed in the branches of staghorn coral, multicoloured parrot fish nipped and pecked at brain coral, and the beautiful but deadly black-and-white-striped lion fish lurked in nooks and crannies. Anemones were also abundant at Tovarua, and I often laughed underwater as the little clown fish, turbo fins vibrating at lightning, charged me in warning to keep my distance. Sometimes, if I was extra lucky, a manta ray rose from the deep and, for a second or two, blocked the sunlight as it glided overhead.

Many years later, I was scuba diving in Palau in Micronesia. Palau is a world-renowned mustering station for manta rays. As I swam with the mantas each day, the sight filled me with nostalgia as I recalled the days of my childhood and the mantas I saw at Tovarua.

Perhaps one of the most bizarre creatures we ever saw at Tovarua were the naked gill sea slugs, known collectively as a *Nudibranchs*. These ornate little creatures do not have an outer shell as many others do and are quite alien in appearance. A striking feature with *Nudibranchs*, apart from their bright glowing colours, is a cluster of branched gill-plumes that seem to sprout from their posteriors. *Nudibranchs* tend to cling to coral and ledges and slide around, much like a garden slug, when on the hunt for food. There is one *Nudibranch*, however, who dances to attract or repel attention: the *Hexabranchus imperialis* or "Spanish dancer."

An adult Spanish dancer can grow up to ten centimetres long, as they did at Tovarua. Delicate and bewitching, the Spanish dancer populates only a few sheltered coral reefs. I saw my very first dancer at Tovarua when I was a young child, and even then I found her graceful movements spellbinding. I came upon her quite by chance, my attention drawn to a swirling mass of tiny neon tetra fish sheltering under a clump of staghorn coral. As I ran my fingers through the mass, the little fishes parted, and there she was, hovering above a patch of pure white sand, serene and poised, as if holding court in a fish's castle.

Ever so slowly, I reached out to stroke her. Startled at the intrusion, my dancer fluffed her skirts and began to dance. As she pirouetted before me, her white, orange, and yellow petticoats rose and fell in delicate overlapping waves around her, like a Spanish dancing lady with skirts undulating in full flight. With each twirl, my dancer appeared to grow larger and larger, seemingly to warn me off. Faster and faster she twirled until her skirts became a spinning kaleidoscopic mass. As I withdrew my hand and backed away, my Spanish dancer slowly settled again and dropped her skirts. Every now and again she gave a little ruffle, as if to tell me she was watching me.

After a few minutes, the little neon tetras returned to her side to fluster and wait in the wings, and my *Hexabranchus imperialis* again took centre stage, hands folded in her skirts, serene and poised in her underwater theatre carpeted in pure white sand.

In the years to come, each time I scuba-dived a coral reef, I'd search for my Spanish dancer, hoping against hope I'd lucky enough to encounter one again.

In 2012, Andrew and I were on a scuba-diving holiday in Gizo Island, Solomon Islands. We were diving on the Japanese shipwreck the *Toa Maru* when I saw a Spanish dancer flutter against the dark ship hull. It had been many years since I had seen this shy and elusive little *Nudibranch*, and as she danced before me, I was again filled with nostalgia for my childhood days and the coral reef at Tovarua.

Dad was always comfortable at Tovarua. There was shade for him and the car, there were no mosquitoes to sting him, and he could eat his lunch in a "civilized manner" with a knife and fork at the wooden tables provided. Apart from all that, Dad loved Tovarua because he could swim there in peace and quiet.

Close to the beach clearing, right on the low tide mark, grew a very large, very old fig tree. The old fig had a thick, wide second trunk that grew from its gnarled, knotted base. The second trunk, thick with branches and wide fat leaves, grew at right angles over the water below and threw shade over a small shallow coral-free alcove. The alcove was the only place I ever remember my Dad swimming.

After lunch, when the sun was at its hottest, the family, along with our dogs, gathered under the cool of the fig tree to amuse ourselves in the water. Sometimes, if it was really hot, Dad donned his waist-to-knee swimming trunks and joined Mum and me in the water. Tentatively, Dad waded in until the water lapped his chest.

At times, if I was persistent, Dad ventured a little further into the water, flapped his arms about, and frog-kicked in an uncoordinated breaststroke fashion. Dad was quite convinced he was swimming and was always pleased when I complimented him on his style.

In our early days at Tovarua, in the sheltered waters under the fig tree, Mum tried to teach Dad how to swim properly. Alas, Mum failed miserably. After many attempts, for the sake of family peace, she just gave up.

The alcove under the fig tree also pulsated with life. The shallow waters were filled with tiny sand-coloured fish, black sea cucumbers, and bright blue starfish. The grey-green seagrass hid cowrie shells, small cone shells, and banded coral snakes.

In 1989, I left my career in banking behind, gathered my limited funds, steered my daughter Leanne into safe secure employment in business and finance, and then, after many years of study, I became a professional scuba diver. My chosen career path has taken me to many parts of the world, to dive and to teach, but I can honestly say, I have *never* encountered the splendour of a deep coral reef such as the one I snorkelled over as a child at Tovarua.

After becoming a scuba-diving instructor, I was fortunate to secure a position as a dive guide on Heron Island on the Great Barrier Reef. One morning during a morning dive, I came across a lone *Sinularia*. As I parted the drab brown fleshy folds, my heart swelled at the sight of a pair of perfectly formed snow-white egg cowries. When I dived the same site a few days later, the eggs cowries had gone—souvenired by a diving tourist.

Sometimes as I struggle into my stiff wetsuit on a winter morning, my heart fills with dread at the cold water that will soon envelope me. Yet at the same time, I am uplifted, as I remember the warm waters of Tovarua ... a deep coral reef ... a *Hexabranchus imperialis*.

CHAPTER 9

The Planters Annual Dinner.

Every year, the Planters Association of Papua New Guinea, of which Dad was general secretary, held its annual conference and dinner. The conference, which lasted three or four days, covered a variety of topics, such as the world price of cocoa and copra, financial status and budget of the Planters Association, committee enquiries and news, and any future changes to the association. The committee reviewed Dad's salary package as well.

The planters came from near and far for this annual gathering. Some flew in from the New Guinea mainland, Manus Island, and Kar Kar Island, and others took the daily shuttle flight from Bougainville Island. For those planters who lived close to us on New Ireland, the journey was a quick hop, step, and jump in a DC3 aircraft—or if they preferred a more leisurely trip, an overnight boat ride. The conference and dinner was also well attended by our local New Britain planters.

Most of the plantation folk who lived in the remote areas only came to town a few times a year, so during conference week, when the men were busy discussing business, the wives shopped, visited the hairdresser for cut and set, and caught up with old friends.

At the end of the week when all the business was finished and

done with, everybody looked forward to the social event of the year:
the Planters Association Annual Dinner, or as we called it, the "the
Planters Do."

The do was by official invitation only. The invitations were
always beautifully printed in gold on white high-gloss paper, and if
my memory serves me correctly, worded something like this:

> The Planters Association of Papua New Guinea,
> together with Mr. and Mrs. C. E. Holland, request the
> pleasure of your company at the Planters Association
> annual dinner at the Guinea Club at 7.00 p.m. on
> Saturday 19 August.

Only financial members of the association and their wives were
invited, and Dad often remarked how quickly the late fees came
in once the first invitation had been mailed. Invitations were also
issued to the managers and wives of other businesses associated with
Planters, as well managers of the local banks, one or two solicitors,
and accountants.

The dress code for the dinner was formal. The ladies were required
to wear a long dress and the gentlemen long trousers, long-sleeved
shirt, and tie—although Dad sometimes chose to wear a cravat rather
than a tie. As the weather was hot, the men were not required to
wear a coat. Mum always made a new dress for herself. The dress
was, mostly a simple black Thai silk straight A-line. Sometimes
Mum wore her crystal beaded collar-necklace or her turquoise and
gold collar-necklace to accentuate her dress. The necklaces had been
bequeathed to her by her late grandmother, so they were very much
cherished.

The preparation for the do went on for weeks beforehand, and
mostly things went according to plan, as best as they possibly could
in Rabaul anyway. Food was a very important issue for the dinner,
and Mum always made sure the caterers had plenty to work with.
Orders were placed well in advance for caviar, black and red; smoked

salmon; olives; and hard cheeses. Mum also hunted down the native suppliers of mud crab and lobster. The mud crabs were flown in from New Island and the lobsters from Bougainville. Lack of refrigeration on the aircraft that delivered the seafood was of great concern, so Mum insisted the seafood be kept alive and delivered on the same day as the do and not before.

Mum was always nervous until she received news that the crab and lobster had arrived safely. Apart from that, the native suppliers of the seafood were often elusive and unreliable, so a backup menu was needed. As well as ensuring the food was top-notch, Mum liked to add a touch of elegance to the event. Well beforehand, she organized the purchase of flowers from the *bung* for the reception hall and booked the services of the local florist to make orchid corsages for the ladies who attended the dinner.

On the morning of the dinner, the pace became frantic. Even though the list of things to do had been checked and rechecked, there was still much to attend to. The reception hall had to be decorated with flowers, place cards laid, and last-minute food-preparation organized. In the midst of all the chaos and running around, the phone rang endlessly at Dad's office and at home as last minute hiccups often arose and had to be dealt with there and then. Most years, we all coped well. One particular year, however, my mother— normally cool, calm, and collected under pressure—lost her temper.

I attended boarding school in Australia and was home on holidays. I was seventeen years old, and Mum and Dad had decided I was old enough to accompany them to the Planters do that year.

Mum had sewn me a new dress to wear, my very first full-length dress. It was white and simple with blue satin piping and a narrow blue satin sash, perfect for my first official social event, Mum said. I loved my new dress, loved how it fitted snugly around my waist and hips, and especially loved how the hem brushed my ankles as I tottered around on my first pair of low heels.

That year on the morning of the dinner, Mum also surprised

me with a gift of some makeup. It was comprised of a powder compact, complete with face powder, pale blue eye shadow, pale pink lipstick, and, as I remember so well, mascara. The makeup, Mum had instructed me in no uncertain terms, was to be applied sparingly and not painted on.

Earlier in the week, I had asked Mum if I could go to the hairdresser on the Saturday morning of the do and have my long hair styled. Mum had refused my request and said, "Freshly washed, clean, and shiny brushed hair was enough for a young lady. If you wish," Mum added, "you may pick some small flowers from the garden and wear them in your hair I instead." I declined Mum's suggestion of flowers in my hair.

I was both nervous and excited at the prospect of going to the dinner. I was growing up, and I wasn't quite sure if I was ready to become an adult. I knew in my heart there was no turning back, and I sensed that my life, as I knew it, was about to change.

Even though it was the dry season, it had rained heavily the night before. The sky behind Matupit Volcano was dark and thick with rain clouds. The weather was humid, and although it was still early, the temperature nudged thirty degrees. My dress was all but finished; only the hem needed doing. As I sat on the front veranda, needle and thread in hand, the telephone shrilled loudly. I looked up as Mum answered it.

'Your father has left his reading glasses here, Suellen. Can you take them to him at the office please? Take my car. Robin (Dad's *draivaboi*) is washing the office car, ready for tonight, and Father wants him to finish that, so … and you know your father can't see without his glasses."

Dad's office was only ten minutes' drive away, and as there was still plenty of time to finish my dress. I jumped into Mum's car and zoomed off down Malaguna Road. Half an hour later, I pulled into the driveway at home. Even before I'd switched off the engine, I could hear my mother screaming the top of her lungs. Mum's tone was a mixture of barely controlled anger and hysteria.

"Get them out of my bloody kitchen. Now ... now ... I don't want them here ... get somebody up here now ... this minute!" Slam! The phone crashed onto its cradle.

I switched off the car engine and ran up front stairs. "Mum ... Mum!" I shouted, "What's the matter? Who was that on the phone?"

"Your father." Mum threw the words at me and pointed to the kitchen. A horrified looked marred her face. Mum puffed on a fresh cigarette and shuddered.

"Oh for God's sake, Suellen!" she hissed. "What do you think has happened? Those bloody idiots from the airlines have delivered those poor unfortunate crabs here instead of the New Guinea Club. The *draivaboi* who delivered them said he was told they were to come here. If I'd sent him away with the crabs, the crabs would have just sat at the airport, in the baking sun, and died. So I told him to go and leave the crabs."

"Don't they know", Mum ranted, "the stupid airlines, the crabs are for the do tonight? What am I supposed to do with them here? I don't want them here. I feel sorry for them. It makes me sick to see them all tied up like that, ready to die. I've just rung your father and told him to come and get the unfortunate things and take them to the club. Oh! The airlines are such idiots! What were they thinking— that *I* was going to cook the crabs here in *my* kitchen? Oh my God, the thought makes me sick. The stupid bloody idiots!" Mum finally drew breath and dragged deeply on her cigarette.

I giggled to myself at Mum's face and poked my head around the kitchen door. The floor was littered with large woven native baskets. I don't know what frightened Mum more: the thought of the crabs escaping and chasing her all around the house or the thought of having to cook them herself in our kitchen!

I prodded a nearby basket with a long broom handle. The basket inched across the floor and emitted a distinct clicking noise. Indeed, the airline had delivered the crabs to our house by mistake. I took a closer look, and through the open weave of the baskets, I saw several large dark shapes. The crabs, I noticed, were New Island mud crabs: big, black, and cranky!

In due course, the office ute, with ample office *bois*, arrived. With a lot of yelling and gesturing, the baskets and crabs were loaded onto the back of the ute, and with a screech of tyres, departed for the New Guinea Club. Mum flopped onto a veranda chair and calmed herself with a strong cup of black coffee and another cigarette.

By four o'clock, all was in order. A last minute check showed everything was ready for the evening do, and Mum, Dad, and I collapsed in a heap on the veranda. Mum gave thanks the Planters' do was only held once a year.

Dad was a stickler for punctuality, so he, Mum, and I left home at exactly quarter to six and arrived at the New Guinea Club promptly at six o'clock, one hour early, as Dad always said, "just in case." By seven o'clock, the New Guinea Club car park was bathed in headlights, and our guests had started to arrive.

I was very proud to stand with my parents and greet our guests as they came through the door of the reception hall. My earlier nervousness had abated somewhat, and felt I very grown up.

My Dad was in his element, as always when he was entertained, and his voice echoed his excitement as he greeted everybody. "Harry, Joan, good evening! Lovely to see you again. Gladys, Keith, welcome, welcome to the Planters Dinner. How are the children doing at boarding school?"

For those I didn't know, Dad introduced me his own special way. "This is our daughter, Suellen," he announced, gently clutching my elbow. "She's home from boarding school and has joined Poppy and me tonight. She's a big girl now, so we brought her along."

I was slightly embarrassed at Dad's introduction. I tried to appear nonchalant at the reference I was a "big girl now" and shook hands and smiled, and sighed inwardly as Dad repeated his introduction over and over again.

Everyday fashions held little importance for the average person in Rabaul. It was far too hot to bother, and mostly the womenfolk just wore a loose-fitting dress and the menfolk shorts and an open-necked shirt. However, we did dress up whenever we socialised and prided ourselves that we looked just as smart as our Australian counterparts. Sometimes, however, when the very latest look was sourced from mail order catalogues or sewn at home from locally purchased dress material, the look, just didn't quite measure up. Much to my mother's annoyance, my dad often found the lack of fashion sense among some women very amusing.

Dad was always very proud of the fact Mum dressed smartly, especially when he and Mum went out or entertained. Like all males, I guess, he harboured thoughts as to how a woman should dress for a certain occasion. Most times, Dad kept these thoughts to himself, evident only with a brief glance or grin, followed at times by a muttered comment. Sometimes, though, from sheer devilment, Dad found it hard to contain his thoughts.

As he was in high spirits that evening, for whatever reason found the fashions at this years at the Planters do worthy of more than just a grin or a brief glance. Dad's comments, muttered under his breath, were for my ears only.

"Pet, just look at the frock Mrs. So-and-So is wearing. Those stripes make her look like a fat old bumblebee. And Mrs. So-and-So—you'd think she would choose another colour. That pink reminds me of the fairy floss you eat when we go to Manly on leave. Gosh, I wonder if that's a tablecloth that Jones woman is wearing. It's like our picnic one. I'm so glad, Susie, your mother has nice frocks."

Just for the record, the only time I ever heard Dad comment on the men's fashions was when, as a teenager, I introduced my current boyfriend to him. Upon asking Dad's opinion of the young man later, Dad raised his eyebrows and stated, "Any man who wears flowers on his shirt is of questionable character!".

There was one person, however, who always drew a comment from Dad whenever they met, a person who dazzled on all occasions special or not: Mrs. Maggie Gilbert.

In her younger days, Mrs. Gilbert—we always addressed her thus—was a house model for a large Sydney department store. She was statuesque, with a very large bosom and a full and voluptuous figure. Although not quite as slim as she was in her youth, Mrs. Gilbert was nonetheless still very striking in looks and always portrayed elegance, if somewhat faded, in her manner. Mrs. Gilbert always arrived at just the precise moment, never early and never so late as to appear rude. The smell of her Chanel No. 5 perfume preceded her as she swept into a room and waited until every head turned towards her before she greeted anybody.

She oozed extravagance in every sense of the word and dripped diamonds, emeralds, and pearls. She wore long flowing bold print floral dresses, always carried an oversized handbag stuffed with cosmetics and hairspray, and tottered on impossibly high stilettos. Just like the royal family, Mrs. Gilbert never appeared in public in the daylight hours without a hat—always large brimmed—or an entourage of children and husband, who walked, as expected, three paces behind. She carried her cigarettes in a gold cigarette case complete with matching gold lighter and smoked incessantly, her scarlet talons elegantly holding a long thin black and gold cigarette holder. I loved her for everything that she was, and so did Mum.

The reception line was nearing an end. I was grateful for that. My new shoes were rubbing my little toe, and I was hungry, my senses tantalized by the smells that drifted from the New Guinea Club kitchen.

I knew Mrs. Gilbert had arrived. I'd caught sight of a large black feather in the line and knew instinctively who the feather belonged to. I wondered if Dad had seen the feather and what he would say when he did see it. I didn't have long to wait.

As Mrs. Gilbert drew level with us, her presence seemed to fill the room. Her gown and accessories, obviously chosen with great care, outshone all else. She greeted Mum with a kiss on the cheek and extended her hand to Dad. Dad clasped her hand and shook it vigorously. He touched my elbow as a comical grin spread across his face.

Mrs. Gilbert had fashioned her long blond hair into a tight French roll. The roll was pinned high on her crown and sported a very large red and gold silk flower. The flower sprouted black stamens tipped with gold. Ever resourceful, Mrs. Gilbert had securely fastened a piece of black netting to the base of the flower with a large ornate hatpin. The netting fell seductively over her eyes and finished at the tip of her nose.

Mrs. Gilbert's fascinator perfectly complemented her evening gown. The gown was a figure-hugging, fire-engine-red, shiny satin creation with a black-feather-encrusted deep V (that disappeared into oblivion) neckline. The bottom of the gown flared out like a fish tail and was adorned with large black feathers, some of which trailed behind her like a demure fluffy python.

Mrs. Gilbert completed her look with a black beaded evening purse and oversized black feather fan. Diamond drop earrings sparkled at her lobes, and a long black feather boa snaked around her neck and hung loosely over one shoulder.

Mrs. Gilbert exchanged pleasantries with Mum and Dad and turned to face me.

"Heelloo, Suellen," she exclaimed. "My, my, haven't you filled out to a nice young lady. My, you have grown up. Home from school, are you?"

My face flushed pink at Mrs. Gilbert's compliment. I was momentarily lost for words and smiled. I dared not look at Dad; I could feel he was itching to say something about her hat and dress. I mumbled a short polite greeting and hoped she would move on.

Alas, I knew my Dad would not let Mrs. Gilbert pass without a comment.

"Beautiful frock," Dad croaked, "and I must say, what a most unusual hat."

"Why, Cyril, thank you," cooed Mrs. Gilbert as she playfully tapped Dads' arm with her fan. "And aren't you quite the gentleman to notice. I actually made my gown," she paused for effect, "and my hat myself. You see, when I ..."

Dad cut Mrs. Gilbert off mid-sentence. "Poppy's an excellent seamstress," he said. "She makes all her own frocks and Susie's frocks as well. Maybe you can give her the paper pattern for your frock so she can make one for herself to wear at our next do.

Mum shot Dad and angry look and reached in her bag for a cigarette.

"Of course I will, Cyril. As I was saying, before I married, when I was a model," she batted her eyelashes, "we girls had to learn how to sew, for little alterations and such. I was considered quite talented, and ..."

"Maggie ..." My mother's voice was sugar-sweet through clenched teeth. I knew Mum was irritated at Dad and would have something to say to him later, "Do try the pink champagne. Planters had it flown in especially from South Australia for the do tonight. It's the very best there is. It's being served now in the dining room. Please have some. I wouldn't like for you to miss out."

Mrs. Gilbert shrieked in delight and hurried away to find a waiter.

Dad grinned at me as Mrs. Gilbert and her feathers disappeared into the crowd. Mum threw Dad one of her "I'll deal with you later" looks and turned to greet the next guest.

Incidentally, I entered the Miss Frangipani Pageant that year, and Mum asked Mrs. Gilbert to give me some hints on how to walk and stand on a catwalk. My girlfriend Helen won the title of Miss Frangipani, and in later years, became a successful model. For ever after, whenever Mum saw Helen's photo in a magazine, Mum pointed to the photo and said, "There's your friend Helen. Remember she beat you in Miss Frangipani?"

The Planters Association was fortunate enough to have among its members a number of planters who had lived in New Britain before the outbreak of World War II. In early 1930, the newlywed Mr. and Mrs. Frank Curtis purchased a number of acres overlooking the Bismark Sea on the east coast of New Britain. Over the next few years, they established a cocoa plantation.

In December 1941, the Allies realised the Japanese invasion of New Britain was imminent, and the Australian government ordered the immediate evacuation of all civilian personnel to Australia. Mrs. Curtis gathered her son and daughter, packed a few possessions, and along with many other woman and children, left her home to the mercy of the advancing Japanese Army. Over the next few days, all women and children were evacuated from Rabaul. However, many of the menfolk, including Mr. Curtis, decided to defy the order and stay.

In January 1941, the Japanese Imperial Army invaded Rabaul. Of the civilian men who stayed behind, many were taken prisoner and later executed. Mr. Curtis evaded capture and shortly after became a coast watcher.

The Coast Watching Organization originated during the crucial period of WWII when the Japanese advance in the Pacific threatened Allied controlled waters and/or Allied-held Islands. The organization was administered entirely by the Royal Australian Navy through the Naval Intelligence Division, Navy Office, Melbourne.

The Coast Watchers were Australian expatriate men who lived and worked in PNG. The group (mostly patrol officers, planters, and administration civilians) were recruited by the organisation because of their knowledge of the lay of the land, intimate knowledge of their local and surrounding areas, and rapport with the natives.

The select group of men were stationed behind enemy lines and provided the Allied Forces with information covertly (via radio) on enemy movements and enemy activities. It was extremely dangerous work. The coast watchers constantly moved camp to avoid detection, relied heavily on airdrops for supplies, and were always at the risk of betrayal by pro-Japanese natives. If caught, the coast watchers were tortured and executed.

The information provided by the coast watchers (who were stationed throughout New Britain, New Guinea, and the Solomon Islands) proved so valuable to the Allies, that the Allies were able to pre-empt many of the Japanese attacks and raids. As a result, time and time again, the Japanese suffered heavy losses.

The Japanese knew the information of their movements came from the coast watchers and therefore demanded the local natives provide detailed information as to the whereabouts of any coast watcher, coast watcher campsite, or radio. The Japanese instilled fear in the native population and threatened reprisals if any information was withheld. The Japanese also hunted the coast watchers relentlessly and offered substantial rewards for capture or information.

For more than two years, Mr. Curtis and his small band of trusted native *bois* roamed the Gazelle Peninsula and reported on enemy activities and enemy movements. Every few days, he and his small band moved camp to avoid detection. One morning, however, Mr. Curtis received news his camp position had been compromised. The Japanese had information as to his location and were closing in. Mr. Curtis fled his camp, and at his next radio check-in, he was ordered to destroy his equipment and abandon his post. It was time to call it quits. The Japanese wanted him dead or alive. It was too dangerous to go on. He had served his country well, and his time as a coast watcher was over. He smashed his radio and buried the pieces, bade farewell to his native *bois*, and slipped away. A few days later, he was evacuated by Allied submarine.

Mr. Curtis was reunited with his family in Townsville, QLD, a week later. It had been almost three years to the day since he had seen his wife and children. Mr. Curtis was later decorated for his service.

Mum recalled her first encounter with Mr. Curtis. We had been in Rabaul for about five years or so, and Mum was at Dad's office listening to the weekly scheduled (known as the "sked") radio session. The "sked" was used by the remote plantations to communicate with each other or Planters to order supplies.

However, this morning Mrs. Curtis asked for assistance for her very ill husband. He was to "go south," the usual terminology for a trip to Australia, for an operation. Mr. Curtis was very ill, and Mrs. Curtis was worried about him. She had to stay and run the plantation in his absence, and she asked if somebody could meet him at the Rabaul wharf and take him to his hotel. He was aboard the *MV Tololo*, a small interisland boat, due to dock in an hour. She also asked if somebody could make sure he did not miss his flight to Australia the next morning.

Mum noted the concern in Mrs. Curtis's voice and asked Dad who these people were and why, after being in Rabaul for so long, she had not heard of them or their plantation.

"The Curtises," Dad replied, "are an old couple. Their plantation is on the Bainings. They are pretty self-sufficient and keep very much to themselves. We don't hear from them very often. It sounds like the old boy is ill."

Mum told me in later years that when she met the *Tololo* that morning, she was heartsick at the state of Mr. Curtis. He was dishevelled, delirious, and disoriented. Mum said he looked like a sick old hobo who had lost his way. Mum looked after him that day and took him to the airport for his flight to Australia the next morning. Mr. and Mrs. Curtis were forever grateful for Mum's kindness in their time of need, and from that day forward remained our loyal friends.

Mr. Curtis joined us that year at the dinner, along with his wife. As our family was very fond of them and as they very seldom ventured off their plantation, we welcomed them with open arms.

In the sixties, long hair was in fashion for men, but for the Planters do that evening, it was strictly short back and sides for Mr. Curtis. Not a hair strayed from place, slicked down with goodness knows what. He had a short back and side cut parted to one side and was clean-shaven. His khaki trousers had been neatly pressed, his white shirt was starched stiff as a board, and for this special occasion, he had pinned his dark blue tie against his chest with a thick gold tiepin.

As he shook hands with Dad, I noticed he sported gold cufflinks at the wrist and had polished his black lace-up shoes until they shone like the stars at midnight. He was the smartest I had ever seen him.

"Hello, Miss," he smiled into my eyes. "Let you out, have they?"

"Good evening, Mr. Curtis, Mrs. Curtis," I replied. "Yes, I'm here with Mum and Dad tonight, just helping out."

"Well, you have a good time then, Miss, won't you?" Mr. Curtis's reply was short and to the point. "Make sure you save a dance for me later, all right?"

"I will, Mr. Curtis, I promise."

He shook Dad's hand again, kissed Mum's cheek, and he and his wife made their way inside.

Dad frowned as they disappeared in the crowd. "That old codger Curtis is a bit forward, asking Suzie for a dance like that."

Mum rolled her eyes. "Oh, for God's sake, Father," she whispered, "he is nearly seventy! Don't be so silly."

I remember Mr. and Mrs. Curtis with great fondness. Whereas Mr. Curtis did not speak of his time as a coast watcher very often, he did on occasion share his wartime stories with us. I have enormous respect for him and every other coast watcher *and* their native *bois* who put their lives on the line to ensure my freedom.

Our line of guests finally ended. Dad tapped me on my arm. "Pet," he said, "I have something in my eye. Just come with me for a minute please, before we have dinner, and see if you can see anything." He excused himself from Mum and led me behind a tall vase of flowers.

As soon as we were out of sight, Dad started to chuckle. I knew then the "eye thing" was just an excuse, and as I knew my father so well, I knew he was itching to make a comment about Mrs. Gilbert and her evening attire. Before Dad had a chance, I said, "No, Dad, please. I know what you are up to. Please," I begged, "you're not to laugh at Mrs. Gilbert. Mum will see us and get angry at us for being rude."

'Oh! For Pete's sake, pet," Dad exploded with laughter. "That frock she's wearing—she looks like that rooster we used to have in the chook pen. You know the one I mean …what was it's name? The black and red one? It used to chase everybody."

"Ruby, Dad," I reminded him. "The rooster was Ruby."

Dad was unable to maintain his composure any longer. He exploded with laughter. "That's right, Pet, Ruby, yes." His words tumbled like a waterfall. "She looks just like Ruby. Oh, for Pete's sake! She must have plucked every damn chook in Rabaul to get all those feathers to glue onto that frock. Oh for mercy sake, it looks so silly. And that thing she has around her neck—what's that for? It looks like she made it from Ruby's tail feathers or something." Dad exploded with laughter again. He plucked blindly at his top pocket, took out his hanky, and wiped his eyes. "Oh, Suzie," he said, "how am I ever going to talk to her tonight and keep a straight face?"

Mrs. Gilbert's attire drew many comments that night. However, *I* would have been disappointed if she had turned up in anything less outrageous. *Vive la difference!*

I attended many more dos and cocktail parties with my parents and learned that Dad's comments about ladies' fashions were pure devilment, uttered only to the family in the strictest of confidence, and spoken completely without malice or disrespect. It was just one of my dad's little idiosyncrasies. It was almost time for dinner, and Mum would soon wonder where we were.

"Dad," I pleaded, "you have to stop laughing at Mrs. Gilbert's dress, and we have to go and find Mum now. She'll be really angry if she finds out what we are doing. Come on, they are serving dinner now."

Dad was undeterred by the prospect of Mum's annoyance or the fact that dinner was being served. Dad caught sight of Mrs. Gilbert as she made her way to her table and started to chuckle again.

"Dad," I begged, tugging at his sleeve, "stop laughing! I'm going to find Mum now, or we'll get into trouble." I kissed Dad on his cheek and walked off.

Mum raised her eyebrows as I drew next to her. "Where is your father?" she asked. "Dinner is being served now, and everybody is hungry. What was the problem with his eye?"

I knew Mum was suspicious. Thankfully, Dad appeared, still with a smirk on his face, and said, "Gee, I'm hungry, let's go and sit down." He gently clutched my mother's elbow and steered her towards the dining room. "Darling," he asked in all innocence as he pulled out her chair at the table, "may I have the waiter bring you some more champagne?"

The memory of the live crab and lobster in our kitchen that morning impacted Mum so much that she couldn't eat her entrée. I smiled weakly at her as she pushed a small pile of crabmeat around her plate. She quickly placed a lettuce leaf over the crab and muttered "Poor thing." Mum shrugged her shoulders and whispered to me, "I have lost my appetite. I simply can't eat the crab." My mum elegantly laid her fork aside and reached for her cigarettes.

That evening, I stayed close to my parents as they circulated among their guests. Even though I was far from shy, I still lacked the confidence to socialize alone in this adult domain. I did not wish to appear a "big head" by swanning around unaccompanied, giving my opinion. Reputations were built and slashed by a single action or word in Rabaul, and I was very conscious of my parents' social standing and untarnished reputation.

I have very fond memories of the many social occasions I enjoyed with my parents. However, the Planters' annual do holds a special place in my heart.

CHAPTER 10

The Chinese Christening and the Chinese New Year Dragon

Jock Ping was one of Dad's business associates. He was a short, always smiling, thoroughly gracious, extremely affluent Chinese merchant. Typical of the wealthy Chinese, Uncle Jock was rotund and drove an always-new top-of-the-range Mercedes Benz. Jock Ping had many business interests. He was a wheeler-dealer who exported and imported goods, grew cocoa and copra, and owned trade stores.

I remember him best for his jolly disposition, his fleet of battered old blue and white trucks, and the Chinese New Year dragon. Jock Ping also had four sons, but for many years he longed for a daughter. "You lucky man," he often lamented to Dad. "You have girl. I only have four useless son. They all the time spend money on fast car and go disco dancing."

Our family loved Uncle Jock and his family, and the two families enjoyed a mutual respect and a cherished friendship that spanned many years. Dad often told the story of how he and Uncle Jock first met.

One morning not long after Dad had arrived in Rabaul, his secretary tapped on his office door.

"Mr. Holland, there is a Chinese gentleman outside to see you.

He said if you were busy he'd wait until you are free. Shall I tell him you are busy, or …?"

"No, that's all right, Mrs. Walker," replied Dad. "Ask him to come into my office, please. I have a few minutes to spare, and would you mind organizing a cup of tea for us? Thank you."

Mrs. Walker nodded and disappeared. Dad heard her tell Uncle Jock that Mr. Holland was free and would see him now.

Dad rose from his chair and extended his hand as his visitor stepped through his office door.

"Mr. Holland, my name Ah Ping, all European call me Jock, so you call me Jock, okay?" Uncle Jock introduced himself all in one breath while pumping Dad's hand furiously.

Dad smiled and pointed to a chair. "I am very pleased to meet you, Jock. What can I do for you?"

Dad had a preconceived notion that Uncle Jock wanted a job in the office.

"Mr. Holland, I have one wife and three son and one little baby son. I also have three very good truck. My truck can take your cocoa from warehouse to shipping wharf. I give you very good special price, if only use my truck. If you use my truck, you have no worries, Mr. Holland, no trouble. You ring; I send my truck, quick time, and pick up your cocoa. Okay? What you say, Mr. Holland, we have deal?"

Dad said he was very impressed with Uncle Jock's forthright approach, and so a deal was made on a gentlemen's handshake. Rabaul Trading Company would use Uncle Jock's "three very good truck" to convey the cocoa and copra bags to the wharf to be shipped overseas.

One day while out shopping, Mum and I saw Jock's wife Edith in a loose-fitting dress. "Jocks' wife is having an infant," Dad informed Mum and me later. Dad never said so-and-so was pregnant or having a baby; he always referred to pregnancy as "having an infant." He added, "I hope the infant is a girl. That would make Jock so happy."

The family agreed, and when we heard Mrs. Ping had been admitted to hospital, we, along with the whole town, waited for the outcome. The old Chinese people lit their joss sticks and prayed even harder to Buddha. The old people knew that if Mrs. Ping was safely delivered of a daughter, their community would benefit greatly—financially, of course.

That evening, as we washed and readied ourselves for dinner, fireworks erupted over Chinatown. Just as we sat down at the table, the phone rang. Dad rose to answer it. "Jock's wife has had her infant, a girl," Dad called out, "and Jock is pleased as punch. He wants us to go over to their place tonight for a bit of a celebration. Shall I say yes to the invitation?"

"Of course," said Mum, "how lovely for them. Let's go and offer our congratulations."

The Ping family lived in Chinatown, and I loved going to Chinatown, especially to Uncle Jock's. He always made a big fuss me. He ruffled my hair and asked about school and always told Dad, much to my delight, how lucky he was to have a girl. As a family, we were very happy he now had "a girl" of his own.

We rushed through dinner and set off. As we neared Chinatown, the traffic thickened, and as we approached Uncle Jock's street, the area became even more congested with cars, bicycles, and people. Dad slowed the car to a crawl and asked Mum and I to look out for a parking space.

"My goodness," said Mum, as we circled the block for the second time. "Just look at all these people! This is bigger than Queen Elizabeth's coronation!"

"It sure is," replied Dad, "and I bet you, as sure as eggs, they're all here tonight for the same reason as we."

The Ping family lived in a large apartment above a collection of Chinese trade stores. We pushed our way up the narrow stairs and stepped inside. The apartment was full of revellers; it was impossible to see Uncle Jock or any of his sons amid the crush. Everybody back-slapped each other, raised glasses, and yelled across the room to friends. The Chinese people of Rabaul were very happy that good fortune had befallen Uncle Jock and his family that day.

We hovered by the door, and somebody called out, "Jock, Mr. Holland is here."

Suddenly, the crowd parted. Uncle Jock strode over to us. Dad pumped his hand and thumped him on the back. "Congratulations, Jock!" Dad said. "Well done, well done. After all this time, you now have your daughter."

'Yes, yes, thank you, Cyril! Yes, I now have baby daughter. Just like your daughter. Oh, I lucky, lucky man now!"

"You are indeed a lucky man, Jock, and now that you have a daughter," Dad laughed, "you have to start saving for her wedding, just like I have to."

Jock laughed. "This is true, Cyril, now I have to work hard and save for her school and wedding, very expensive …girls' wedding. Now, Poppy, you eat, Cyril, you eat, plenty food, plenty drink, you help yourself, okay? We talk later." With a chuckle, Uncle Jock disappeared into the crowd.

"Phew," said Dad, "what a turnout. It's going to be one hell of a christening party."

A few weeks later, Stewie, Uncle Jock's eldest son, popped into Dad's office and handed Dad a red envelope. The envelope contained an invitation, also printed on red paper (the Chinese believe red is the colour of good luck and good fortune), for the whole family to attend baby Veronica Ping's christening, one month from Saturday. Dad read the invitation, thanked Stewie, and accepted the invitation there and then.

The Chinese community kept very much to themselves in Rabaul, therefore an invitation to Veronica's christening was an honour indeed. Mum and Dad were very pleased to receive the invitation. Besides, we genuinely liked the Ping family, and we were happy to celebrate Veronica's christening with them. Apart from that, our attendance fostered a healthy business relationship between Rabaul Trading Co. and Ah Ping and Sons.

However, we did have a small problem. As Jock was, by now, extremely wealthy, Mum and Dad mulled over the question of an appropriate gift.

"What do you buy a Chinese baby?" wondered Mum, as the family discussed the christening at dinner one evening. "I have no idea whatsoever what to buy her, and I don't want to offend them."

Dad scratched his head. "Well, I don't know. I'm sure there must be something that she'll need. We'll just have to have a good look in all the shops."

As the date for baby Veronica's christening grew nearer and nearer, the family deliberated over the problem of an appropriate gift. We didn't have gift shops in Rabaul, only one or two or Chinese emporiums, and Uncle Jock owned one of them.

"We could give her a cheque," suggested Dad, "to start a bank account, or some cash even."

"I don't think so," Mum said. "By the time she is twenty-one, she will own half of New Guinea and a good-sized chunk of Australia as well, for that matter. I doubt is she'll need any money ever."

Dad sighed. "Yes, that's true, but what can we do? We'll have to get something suitable."

On the Saturday morning before Veronica's christening, Dad and I set off to find an appropriate gift. Dad normally went to the office on Saturday morning, but we needed to buy a gift for baby Veronica, and that was more important than Dad going to the office. So Dad rang Mrs. Walker and said he had a very important errand to attend to and would not be in the office that morning.

"Come on, pet," he said to me after breakfast. "We can look slowly through all the shops. We don't have to rush; we have all morning. I'm sure we will find something suitable for Jock's new infant."

Mum waved us goodbye and wished us luck.

Just after 12 noon, Dad and I pulled into our driveway. Mum stepped onto the veranda.

"Hello, you are back," said Mum. "Did you find anything?"

Dad kissed Mum's cheek. "We were so lucky this morning. We've found just the thing for Jock's daughter. The lady in the shop said it's the only one of its kind in the whole of Rabaul."

"Well, thank goodness for that," sighed Mum. "What did you find?"

"Just wait till you see it, Mum, it's really beautiful," I said. "I'm sure they will really like it. The lady in the shop said they would.

Dad drew a small brown paper bag from his pocket and handed the bag to Mum. "You open it," he said, "and tell me what you think."

Mum opened the bag and drew out a small blue velvet box. She carefully opened the lid. "Oh! What a wonderful idea," she gasped. Inside the box, nestled on a cushion of cream satin, lay a very large Japanese cultured pearl.

"Oh! what a beautiful pearl," Mum said. "Where did you get it?"

"At Seetos," Dad said, "that big Chinese shop just off the main street. I thought I would suggest to Jock that he buy one for the little girl each year on the anniversary of her christening, and when she is twenty one, she will have enough for a necklace."

Mum nodded. "Very, very clever, Father," she said, "very clever."

The Chinese-owned Kuomintang Hall was situated in the heart of Chinatown. The KMT, as the hall was known, seated about two to three hundred people, and as expected, was the chosen venue for Veronica's Christening party. Even though the hall was large, the parking was limited, and that posed a problem for the hundreds of party guests. As a result, by the time Mum, Dad, and I arrived at the hall, the roads and lanes around the KMT were jam-packed with vehicles of all descriptions. Suffice to say, the revellers, in their excitement *and* with little thought of parking etiquette, had crammed their cars, trucks, and bicycles into every spot imaginable.

Dad finally found a parking spot on a strip of dirt at the back of the hall near the kitchen. We alighted from the car and made our way around to the front entrance.

The front of the KMT had been decorated for good luck and good fortune. Two large red banners hung from the rafters above the double doors. The banners, proud and straight in the warm night air, were flanked each side by large translucent rice-paper lanterns; the lanterns trailed long red tassels that almost brushed the floor. The Chinese people believed the Good Luck Dragon would visit later in the evening and had tied large leafy branches to the pillars at the entrance of the steps that led into the hall. Hidden in the branches were several red paper bags. The bags, I knew, contained banknotes tied with red string.

Dad hustled us through the crowd, and we stepped inside. Jock's eldest son, Stewie, broke away from a circle of friends and ran over to meet us.

"Ah, Mr. Holland," he said as he pumped Dad's hand. "You and your family are here. Good."

He beckoned to an usher and said, "We have a special place for you to sit tonight. Please, Mr. Holland, follow the usher, and he will show you to your table. My father asked me to tell him as soon as you had arrived. I will go and find him now tell him you are here."

"Thank you, Stewie," replied Dad. "We will see you during the evening." Dad put his hand in his pocket and drew out Veronica's gift. "We have brought a small gift for your new baby sister," he said tentatively. "Where shall ...?"

"I will take it, Mr. Holland, thank you," said Stewie as he took the little box, "and put it with the others. But wait just a minute. I have to give you a number." Stewie ran off and returned a second later with a red card bearing the number 158 and handed the card to Dad. Dad looked at the card, frowned, and put it into his top pocket.

"Mr. Holland," Stewie said, "you and your family please go and sit down. I will tell my father you are here."

The hall was filled with tables of all sizes. Each table had been set with Chinese bowls, chopsticks, spoons, and glasses. The usher led us through the maze to a small table at the foot of the stage. In the middle of the table sat a red place card that read "Mr. C. E. Holland and Family." On the stage, not two meters away, stood the Ping family table—the official christening table. Dad was quite surprised that we had been seated so close to the guests of honour. It was an indication of the respect shared between my father and Uncle Jock.

The Ping family table sparkled with crystal glasses and gold cutlery. Bottles of champagne, Chinese rice wine, jugs of fruit juice, bowls, plates, platters, and serving dishes vied for space with tall vases of hibiscus and orchids. Red lacquered chopsticks had been placed neatly across each bowl, and red linen serviettes fashioned in the shape of flowers and birds gave the table a feeling of innocence. In front of the table, in full view of the adoring public, under the glaring stage lights, sat a white wicker crib. The crib—draped in white satin, adorned with bows and long trailing ribbons—was empty.

Uncle Jock trotted over as we sat down. He pumped Dad's extended hand and smiled. "Hello, hello," he greeted us, "good that you come. Stewie tell me you here and I come straight away." He broke into a belly-slapping laugh. "You like this table, Cyril? I put your family here so we can talk, but not business, this party tonight, not business," he laughed again.

"Yes indeed, Jock," replied Dad, "thank you. The table is very nice."

"Jock," Mum inquired, "where is the baby? I don't see her in the crib. And where is Edith? I wish to offer my congratulations."

"Ah …" Jock sighed. "New baby daughter at home sleeping with my wife; too noisy here, you see, Poppy. Edith say, too many people here tonight, too much for little girl to sleep. Maybe they be back later, but never mind, plenty time for little girl to party later—when she teenager,' he laughed again.

"Quite right," agreed Dad.

A master of ceremonies introduced Jock's family one by one. Uncle Jock thanked everybody and informed us all that, "My wife and new baby girl home sleeping, maybe come back later." Nobody seemed to mind, or indeed to be disappointed that the star attraction and her mother were "home sleeping," for the atmosphere that night was "party" whether they were there or not.

As soon as the speeches were over, an army of waiters appeared with platters piled with food. Over the next few hours, we waded through dim sims and dim sums, pork steam buns and platters of odd-shaped little fried delicacies, along with Peking duck, sweet and sour fish, lobster, king prawns that dripped honey, chili crab, and spicy Chinese beef. Mum said it was like "the feeding of the five thousand." Dad agreed and said that "if Buddha ate like this every day, no wonder he was fat!"

Finally, the fried rice arrived. Traditionally, to the Chinese, a serving of rice signalled the end of a meal.

"Oh, thank goodness," groaned Mum as the waiter placed the platter on the table, "the rice is here. I simply cannot eat another thing."

After the table had been cleared of dirty dishes and empty glasses, a hush fell over the audience.

Six agile Chinese youths appeared carrying a large table. They carefully placed the table right in the middle of the dance floor, disappeared, and returned a few minutes later with another table. After a few minutes, the eight tables formed a line just like a model's catwalk.

"I wonder what's happening here?" Dad said. "Maybe it's some sort of entertainment or something."

"Goodness knows," replied Mum.

A few seconds later, an army of Chinese ladies appeared carrying a bolt of red linen cloth. The ladies rolled the cloth along the table, pinned it at intervals along the edge, and decorated the now red table with red crepe-paper streamers. As if on cue, a line of Chinese aunties marched in, arms laden with gifts. They placed the gifts gently on the end table. We watched fascinated as the tables filled with boxes and parcels and packages, each bearing a card and a number.

"Oh," said Mum, "now I understand, the present. All the presents have numbers; remember, Stewie gave Father a card …158."

Dad looked disappointed. "Oh," he said and took the card out of his top pocket. "I thought the card was for a raffle or something."

"The card is for identification purposes, I think," said Mum, "so they know who gave what present."

"Oh, for Pete's sake," moaned Dad, "do you think so? In that case, I'm glad ours gift is decent one."

"Oh, I don't think it's that, Father," replied Mum. "You know how polite Jock and Edith are. I'm sure it's so they can say thank you for the right gift. Imagine how embarrassed they would be if they sent a note to say thank you for the booties if you had given a pearl."

Dad nodded. A look of relief passed over his face.

The gifts were unwrapped by the same Chinese aunties and arranged in numerical order on the tables. We watched as the line of presents filled the tables from corner to corner. It was like looking into Aladdin's cave.

"My, my," I sighed, "the baby got a lot of things. Did I get lots of presents when I was christened?"

"Ah yes," replied Mum, "you did, but not as many as Veronica. Your father had a lot of business people who gave you quite a few gifts. Although your christening was just a family affair. You were christened in the Anglican church in Madras, and after the service, we just had an afternoon tea party at home. But honestly, I have never seen so many gifts," Mum added, "not even at the big Moslem weddings Father and I used to go to in India."

Veronica's gifts were many and varied, including jade figurines, silver spoons, golden cups, exquisite little Chinese porcelain dolls, layer upon layer of silken baby pyjamas and shawls, photo frames, teething rings, and silver rattles. There were also envelopes filled with money and personal bank cheques.

Dad suddenly looked worried. "I haven't seen our pearl yet," he whispered to Mum, his voice quivering with concern. "I hope some blighter hasn't knocked it off in all this hoo-ha.

Mum raised her eyebrows. "I'm sure it's there, Father," she whispered back. "Stewie gave us a number. Remember? 158. Besides, nobody would dare pinch anything tonight, not here. Just be patient. It will turn up soon enough."

Dad tapped his pocket again. He drew out the ticket and checked the number.

The master of ceremonies announced that the guests were invited to view the gifts. A stampede erupted around us as the masses converged upon the tables. The Chinese aunties sprang into action, smacked hands, and snatched back the gifts if the gifts were handled for too long. The guests oohed and aahed, caressed and fondled, and moved on reluctantly when chastised. It was all too much for Dad.

Alarmed, he turned to Mum and said, "I'm going to look for our pearl. I can't stand it." Then, in a complete about face, he grinned and whispered behind his hand, "Maybe we can knock off some of the stuff. It will save us buying Christmas presents for Susie this year."

I was horrified. "I don't want any of that stuff, Dad," I scoffed. "It's all baby stuff. I'm too old for any of those things."

Dad patted my hand. "I was only joking, pet," he grinned, "and I know you are a big girl now."

Dad rose from the table and patted his pocket again. "Come on," he said, "let's go and have a look."

When one is on a mission, manners are forgotten, and Dad was on a mission to find "our pearl." He squeezed himself between two ladies and made room for me. "Right," he said as he cast his eyes over the table, "we have to attack this like a military operation. We will split up. I will start at one end of the table, and you start at the other. Shout as soon as you have seen our pearl."

I looked over Veronica's gifts and finally came across the pearl. The little blue velvet box was completely overshadowed by a carving of a jade bonsai tree. Dad was happy when I called out to him that I had found our pearl. That is all he wanted to see—and to make sure "'gift number 158" hadn't been knocked off.

On the next anniversary of Veronica's christening, Uncle Jock presented himself at Dad's office. He laid a little blue velvet box on Dad's office table. "Cyril, I come here to show you pearl, very expensive pearl, I buy my daughter—but I have to buy, because you buy first one." The conversation ended with a belly-slapping laugh.

The friendship between the Holland and Ping families spanned more than three decades. Week in and week out, on the strength of a gentleman's handshake and for a "very special good price," Uncle Jock's trucks diligently conveyed Rabaul Trading Company cocoa and copra to the wharf to be shipped overseas.

In gratitude for Dad's ongoing commitment, Uncle Jock always remembered my family at Christmas time. Every Christmas Eve, he presented himself at Dad's office with a basket that contained a very large Christmas ham, a gift for Mum, and a gift for me.

Over the years, Mum, Dad, and I attended many Ping family celebrations, including birthdays, engagements, and the weddings of Uncle Jock's four sons. Best of all, every year, Uncle Jock invited us to his home in Chinatown for the biggest bash of all: a humdinger an event to see in the New Year and witness the arrival of the Chinese dragon.

The Chinese New Year dragon was a scary monster, and I loved it. I still do. The elongated head sprouted bug eyes on stalks and a long red tongue framed by a white tasselled beard. The silk-embroidered body was adorned with red, gold, and green ribbons that swayed and dipped as the tassels swept the ground. The dragon was mean-spirited and short-tempered. It chased everything that moved and grabbed at anyone who ventured too close.

At each house or trade store, the dragon stopped and in explosion of red firecrackers, snatched a bagful of money from a tree branch or house post.

To add to the noise and confusion, an entourage of young Chinese youths in oversized laughing masks trailed the dragon and banged away at drums to chase away the evil spirits.

The dragon usually arrived at Uncle Jock's around mid-morning of New Year's Day. The dragon danced and roared and carried on until Uncle Jock threw him a sack full of money. Satisfied, the dragon then bestowed good luck and good fortune on Uncle Jock and his family and friends, bowed, and retreated to find its next "victim."

I still love the New Year Chinese dragon, and whenever I can, I hightail it into Chinatown on Chinese New Year's day to jostle with the crowd, throw money in the dragon's path, and wait for the Good Luck Dragon to bestow good luck and good fortune on me and my family for another year.

Many years ago, Uncle Jock gave Mum a beautifully carved jewellery box. The box sits on a glass table in my spare room. Whenever I walk into my spare room and see the box, I remember— with fondness in my heart—Uncle Jock Ping and his family, his battered old blue and white trucks, and his joyful belly slapping laugh.

On my last visit home to Rabaul, Andrew and I caught up with Stewie and his family. We enjoyed a wonderful evening of fine food and best of all, memories that lasted well into the wee small hours.

CHAPTER 11

Ruby the Rooster

We had been living in Rabaul for a couple years when, almost overnight, our animal population increased from three cats and two dogs to three cats, two dogs, and *two chickens*. Around the same time, Mum's dream came true: we were moving to a new house. The new house was at the other end of town and, according to Mum, better suited for our family.

Our new house was large and roomy. The house had four large bedrooms, two lounge rooms, two bathrooms, two dining rooms, a very large kitchen, and wide sweeping verandas. Much to Mum's delight, the house sat on an acre of ground (plenty of room for Mum to indulge in her passion for gardening) and was surrounded by a thick hedge of Hibiscus. The new house, we all agreed, was perfect for us—and, we soon realized, perfect for Ruby.

One evening, just before we moved, a young man from Dad's office called in at home with a "gift." The gift was a tiny half-dead baby chicken. The young man had rescued the chicken from a batch of hatchlings that had arrived from Australia that day. The chickens were destined for a plantation in New Ireland, and, as he was unable to look after the sick chicken, he offered the chicken to us.

The chicken was very weak, featherless except for a few tufts of amber down, and only a few days old. Mum felt sorry for the chicken and, with trepidation, accepted the gift.

Mum doubted the chicken would survive the night and told me to put the poor little thing in a small box with some water and a few flakes of Quaker Oats. I found an old cardboard box in the kitchen and placed the chicken inside. When I looked into the box the next morning, the chicken stood up and chirped loudly. We had no option other than to keep the chicken, and Dad decided to call the chicken Ruby.

Mum said that Ruby needed a friend and asked Dad to see if any of his native office staff had a spare chicken we could buy. Dads' *draivaboi* Robin told Dad he had lots of chickens at Rapindik, his home village at the base of Matupit Volcano, and that he would be quite happy for us to have one. Dad, very grateful for Robin's offer, thanked him profusely and arranged to visit Rapindik the very next Saturday afternoon.

After lunch the next Saturday, Dad and I drove to Rapindik. Robin greeted Dad and me with a huge grin and introduced us to his family and friends. He pointed to his flock of chickens and said that we could have any chicken that took our fancy.

Robin's chickens were typical of the many village chickens. They roamed free and were quite friendly, although as far as chickens go, they were quite ugly. We chose a white half-grown skinny-looking hen–chicken with short yellow legs.

The chicken did have one redeeming feature, however: she didn't struggle too much when I picked her up. Dad noticed our new chicken had a few red feathers on her back and promptly named her *Buai*.

As we were to move very shortly to our new home, Mum insisted a chicken coop be built for our two chickens. After our move, Dad bought a few more chickens from Robin. The chickens settled very comfortably into their new home and, much to everybody's delight, soon started rewarding us with fresh eggs every day.

Ruby thrived in his new surroundings. He matured quickly, and soon his short amber tufts grew into long shiny blood-red feathers that covered him from head to knee. He developed a fine proud tail and a smart yellow comb. His legs thickened and grew spurs; his beak became a formidable weapon; and his eyes, black and beady, held your gaze in insolence. Ruby the rooster certainly was cock of the walk, and he knew it.

Alas, as with some humans, Ruby became arrogant with maturity. He developed antisocial habits. He beat up his wives in public, jumped on their backs whenever the fancy took him, and if his wives so much as uttered a squawk in argument, Ruby pecked them on the back of their heads.

Every afternoon after school, I opened the chicken coop for the chickens to roam free in the garden. Ruby, much to Mum's disgust, often snuck up the back steps and trotted into the kitchen, no doubt on the lookout for titbits. When Mum screamed at him to get out and chased him off with the broom, Ruby deposited runny splats of poo on the kitchen floor.

Ruby also stalked our friends when they visited, and when they weren't looking, ran up behind them and pecked their ankles. Perhaps Ruby's most annoying habit was his loud persistent crowing at dawn. The crowing went on and on, until in desperation somebody went to the coop and pelted him with a few food scraps. All in all, in a very short period time, Ruby developed a bad reputation among our neighbours.

One Sunday morning, Dad—sick and tired of Ruby's unrelenting crowing—decided Ruby needed some more wives to keep him company. The next day, when Dad had finished at the office, he and Robin drove to Rapindik, and Dad purchased four more hens. The native hens were black-speckled insignificant-looking creatures; however, of the four new hens, two became my pets. Goodness knows why, but I called my new pets Cockle and Petrol.

Ruby loved his new wives, and for a while he was content. Our

245

new hens thrived and very soon developed into respectable-looking chickens. They also rewarded us with fat brown double-yolk eggs.

Now that Ruby had a big family to care for, he took on some airs and graces. Reinforced by the devotion of his wives, his head swelled with each passing day. He became an arrogant jealous rooster with a mean disposition who harassed everybody at every opportunity.

For some reason, Ruby disliked me intently. He stalked me whenever he was out of the coop, ambushed me, chased me, and pecked me viciously without any apparent reason. Dad said Ruby was exercising his muscle, and I was to just ignore him.

One afternoon, Ruby chased me up the guava tree. The guava tree was home to a large nest of orange tree ants. As I climbed up the tree, my leg brushed against the ant nest. The ants, angry at being disturbed, swarmed all over my legs. As I leant over to brush the ants off, I fell out the tree and landed heavily on the ground. Dad heard me scream as I crashed through the branches and ran onto the veranda

"What happened, Pet?" he said. "Did you fall?"

"Ruby chased me up the tree," I said, "and then the ants bit me."

"Oh, for Pete's sake," Dad said, "that damn rooster better watch out or he will end up as chicken curry if he's not careful. Pet," Dad added, "you just have to be strong and show Ruby who's boss. After all, he is just a rooster."

Mum would never agree to "curry" Ruby. Nothing was ever killed on our home, so we all knew Dad's threat was just an idle threat to make me feel better.

After the guava-tree episode, I decided to take matters into my own hands. I decided enough was enough, and attack was the best form of defence. I had no wish to harm Ruby' in fact, I was quite fond of him. However, I was tired of being attacked in my own yard. From then on, whenever Ruby was out of the coop, I armed myself with a native broom, yelled at him, and chased him away if he came near me. My method of rooster control worked for a while, at least.

One afternoon, after I had yelled at him and chased him away, Ruby decided that once and for all, he was going to re-establish his pecking order with me. He was fast losing his reputation as cock of the walk, and now even the dogs stood their ground and barked at him whenever their paths crossed.

Ruby's opportunity came that afternoon when Mum asked me to let the chooks out of the pen and collect the eggs. As soon I opened the pen door, Ruby ran straight for the chilli bush near the side of the house and hid under the bush. He knew I had to walk past him with an armful of eggs and the chilli bush screened him perfectly. Ruby watched as I walked up and down the nesting boxes and collected the eggs. He watched as I rolled the bottom of my T-shirt up to form a bag. When I had had finished, Ruby that saw my "bag" was bulging with fresh brown eggs.

Before I left the safety of the chook pen, I looked around for Ruby. The coast appeared to be clear. The rooster was nowhere in sight. I was safe.

As I ambled up the side path that led to the back veranda steps, Ruby watched me intently. He backed himself further under the chilli bush. Silent and seething, he allowed me to pass. As I drew level with the frangipani tree, Ruby, head down and neck stretched, charged me. Not a squawk or a crow left his beak; not a sound came from his strong spur-encrusted legs as he pounded up the dirt path behind me.

Just as I mounted the back steps, Ruby drew his head back and, with the pent-up revenge of a lover scorned, flew at my bare ankles. His machine-gun head hammered as he pecked hard, fast, and deep. I screamed at the first hit and spun around to face Ruby. With a shudder, I realized the rooster had the upper hand. I knew that, with a T-shirt full of eggs, I was powerless to protect myself. I was at his mercy.

I reached inside my T-shirt, grabbed an egg, and hurled the egg at Ruby. Ruby did not flinch as the egg sailed past him. I reach for another egg and hurled that one too, and then another. Ruby sensed the change in my attitude and decided to finish me off for good, and fast. He backed away to gather momentum, spread his wings for balance, and rose up on his toes. He was ready for the kill.

With spurs extended, Ruby launched his body at my chest. I recoiled as I saw the red missile and braced myself for the impact. The irate rooster hit my chest with the force of a tornado. The impact smashed the eggs and drove me onto my back. I screamed and let go of my T-shirt. Ruby crowed in victory and thundered towards me again. I leapt to my feet. Like two boxers, Ruby and I circled each other. We were ready for each other. Ruby wanted to fight, and *I* wanted revenge for my bleeding ankles and smashed eggs. I wasn't about to give in, and neither was Ruby.

"Rack off, Ruby," I screamed as I looked down at my slimy yoke-encrusted T-shirt, "you stupid damn chook. Look what you have done to me. You're going to get it now. You've broken all the eggs. Dad said next time you pecked me, it's the curry pot for you. You've had it now. Now … rack off!"

Ruby cocked his head at my threat of the curry pot and fixed me with steady eyes. He took a few steps backwards, lowered his head again, and stretched out his neck.

Mum heard me scream, grabbed the kitchen broom, and raced onto the back veranda. "Ruby!" she shouted. "Shoo, shoo … off you go now … shoo. Go on now." Mum brandished the broom at Ruby and started down the steps.

Ruby looked up at Mum and the broom and knew he was outnumbered. He stood high on his toes, arched his neck, and crowed in delight at the success of his mission. He turned his back on me, gave one last squawk, and tottered off to tell his wives his side of the story.

I burst into tears. "I hate that rooster, Mum. I really hate him." Tears streamed down my face as I wiped the blood from my ankles.

"He is always getting me. He was waiting for me at the back and he … he pecked my ankles and made me break all the eggs."

"Never mind the eggs," said Mum. "You forgot to take the broom with you, and you know what Ruby is like. Now go inside and wash your legs and change your T-shirt. Don't forget to put some antibiotic cream on those pecks, or they will become infected.'

Ruby fathered many children, and soon we had about twenty chooks. He became more aggressive as his family grew, and he still chased everybody who happened to cross his path. As expected, his reputation as a mean old rooster spread like wildfire. However, unbeknown to us, somebody had decided to get rid of Ruby once and for all.

One afternoon, Ruby, as usual, took off when I opened the chook pen and disappeared around the side of the house. Later, when we had returned from our swim, Mum asked me to close the chook pen door. When I checked inside, the hens had settled into their nesting boxes, but Ruby was missing.

I walked inside to the kitchen and said, "Mum, Ruby's missing. He's not in the chook pen."

"He is most likely in the garden," Mum replied. "He will come in by nightfall, I am sure."

As dusk fell, there was still no sign of Ruby. We were all worried. It was not like Ruby to stay out of the pen at night.

Dad, ever the storyteller, said to me, "Don't worry, my pet. I'm sure Ruby is all right. He is just out on the town tonight, looking for some more wives. He'll be back in the morning, you'll see."

Alas, that was not to be. Ruby never returned home. We heard the next day that the *haus boi* next door had waited until we had left for our swim, kidnapped Ruby, and cooked him for dinner.

When Dad found out, he was really angry. He told Mum he hoped Ruby was tough and that the *haus boi* had choked on his dinner.

Dad decided, out of respect for Ruby, to hold a memorial service for him. I found two red tail feathers near the tennis court at the back of the house. When Dad came home from the office, we buried the feathers behind the chicken coop near the pawpaw tree.

Ashes to ashes, dust to dust. We all shed a tear for an arrogant big-headed rooster called Ruby.

After a respectful period of mourning, Dad visited Rapindik and purchased another rooster from Robin. The rooster was a dull black common garden-variety rooster that, sadly, lacked attitude or arrogance. The family agreed that the new rooster was totally devoid of character and wasn't a patch on Ruby.

CHAPTER 12

Joseph and the Technicolour Sprinkles

Over the many years we lived in Rabaul, a number of *haus bois* passed through our door. Some stayed a few months, some stayed a few weeks, and some stayed as little as one or two days. Every now and again, we found a *haus boi* who fitted in with the family and happily stayed with us for a few years.

Joseph came to our door not long after we moved into the Balataman Street house and asked Mum if she wanted a *haus boi*. At first glance, Joseph seemed to fit the criteria Mum looked for in a *haus boi*. He was married, clean, and looked presentable, and he told Mum he knew how to wash, iron, and clean "good." Mum didn't ask much of our household staff, only that they be kind to our dogs and cats, apply liberal amounts of deodorant daily, and not chew *Buai* in her presence. Joseph agreed happily to abide by Mum's rules, and without further ado, Mum hired him on the spot.

Joseph soon learned to do things Mum's way, and surprisingly enough, he proved to be quite handy in the kitchen. He told Mum that the big *misis* he worked for before like to "cook plenty meat and plenty cakes," and she taught him how to do things in the kitchen.

Our home sat on an acre, and when we first moved in, most of the land that surrounded the house was just plain grass. Mum was an avid gardener and often said that a house without a garden was a house without a soul. She decided to plant the area around the house with trees and shrubs. Mum loved all tropical plants, and in time, our garden rivalled a botanical garden. However, when Mum told Dad she wanted to create a garden, Dad was not amused.

"Pet," he said to me, "your mother wants a garden. We have only been here for five minutes, for Pete's sake, and your Mother wants to change things. She saw some plants in a catalogue, and now she wants to order some."

The plants Mum saw in the catalogue were hibiscus, and the hibiscus had to be imported from Hawaii.

Later that evening, Mum told me that in her opinion, that plain grass was boring. "Besides," she added, "I'm forever ringing Father at the office to remind him to send over the office *boi* to mow the grass. I'm sick of it!"

Mum was never one to wait for something to happen, so the next day she ordered a number of orchids and ginger plants from the Department of Agriculture on the New Guinea mainland. Mum also placed an order for a variety of the Hawaiian hibiscus as well.

Each time a batch of plants arrived, Mum donned her large white garden hat, and with her ever-present cigarettes and cup of coffee, walked around the garden and instructed the two newly employed *gaten bois* to plant this, dig that, and remove something else. In a very short period of time, our manicured lawn became garden beds of all shapes and sizes.

The Hawaiian hibiscus thrived in our rich black volcanic soil and almost overnight produced dinner-plate-sized flowers in every colour imaginable. Mum entered a few of the hibiscus in the annual Kokopo Show, and even though her flowers came in second to Mrs. Maggie Gilberts' orchids, her Hawaiian imports set a few tongues wagging.

Mum's Hawaiian hibiscus created a wide interest among many of the ladies in town, and Mum was contacted by a committee member of the Rabaul Garden Club. Mum was *not* a member of the garden club. She loathed all committees and clubs, and refused to join clubs or attend any club meetings. However, the Rabaul Garden Club members wanted to see Mum's Hawaiian hibiscus, and after a great deal of persuasion, Mum agreed to the request. A date was set for the following Tuesday afternoon at two o'clock. Mum decided to host a small tea party of the garden club ladies as well.

Many years later, I asked Mum why she had decided to host an afternoon tea party with the ladies from the garden club. I knew Mum didn't like some of the ladies and wondered why she would extend such an invitation. Mum's answer surprised me. "Well," she said, "Had I not asked them over, they would have badgered me forevermore, so I asked them over purely to shut them up."

The ladies of the Rabaul Garden Club arrived at our place promptly at two o'clock the following Tuesday. After a tour of the garden, the ladies settled themselves in the front lounge room for afternoon tea. Mum excused herself from the group to organise things in the kitchen. The ladies expected a good afternoon tea, and Mum obliged.

Earlier that morning, Mum had baked a rich dark chocolate cake and filled the middle with whipped cream. Mum had also made some white bread cucumber sandwiches and, to cater to all tastes, decided to offer chicken liver pâté, cracker biscuits, and cheese as well.

That morning, Joseph had ironed the white monogrammed serviettes, polished the silver trays, and set out our best teacups, teapot, cake forks, and small cake plates. He hovered in the kitchen as Mum assembled the cheese platter.

"*Misis*," he said, "I can put these biscuits on the tray for you. You go and sit down with the other *misises*, and I will bring everything out for you."

"Oh, all right, Joseph," Mum said. "Thank you. Just put everything on the big silver trays. Put the cheese and pâté on the

253

same tray with some butter and biscuits, and bring it all out together on the tea trolley. Understand?"

"Yes, *Misis*," Joseph nodded. "I know exactly what to do."

Mum handed Joseph the crackers, washed her hands, and left him to assemble the food as per her instructions.

When I arrived home from school at three o'clock, Mum introduced me to the club ladies and, in the same breath, politely told me to disappear and not go near the kitchen. She told me that I could have some afternoon tea later, and I was to amuse myself quietly until then. Only the brave disobeyed Mum, so I gave the kitchen a wide berth. After I'd changed into my play clothes, I vanished outside to play. However, had I disregarded Mum's instructions not to go into the kitchen, I would have saved Mum from acute embarrassment.

As soon as Mum left the kitchen, Joseph set to work. He knew exactly what he had to do: Mums instructions were clear and concise. He placed the cheese, biscuits, and pâté on the silver tray. Suddenly Joseph had an idea. He grinned to himself and ran to Mum's bathroom.

Joseph placed the sandwiches and chocolate cake on the bottom tray of the tea trolley. He ever so gently picked up the silver platter of crackers, cheese, and pâté. With a steady hand, he placed the platter on the top tray of the tea trolley. He was well pleased with his display and hoped the *misis* would be pleased too. With a spring in his step, he swung open the kitchen door and pushed the trolley through.

Fifteen minutes had passed since Mum had rejoined her guests … a long fifteen minutes, and there was still no sign of Joseph or the afternoon tea. Mum realised the club ladies were restless, and their restlessness made Mum her feel uncomfortable. The ladies wanted their tea and cake, and time was getting on. "Apart from that," Mum said later, quite frankly, I was running out of small talk."

As if on cue, Joseph appeared with the tea trolley. He walked very slowly, as if he was pushing a sleeping babe in a pram. All eyes turned to him as he stopped in front of Mum, paused, and stood back.

The tea trolley was fully laden. The cucumber sandwiches and chocolate cake were there, along with the cups, saucers, and teapot. However, Joseph had added something extra special for the ladies. He had lathered each cracker biscuit with a thick layer of butter and topped the biscuit with a pill from Mum's medicine cabinet. Joseph had a fine eye for detail. He had selected the prettiest of pills to decorate the crackers.

The conversation ground to a halt as everybody eyed the biscuits. The first row of crackers held a white pill, the second a red, and the third a yellow pill.

Mum looked at Joseph and smiled weakly, "Thank you, Joseph," she said, "that is very nice, very nice indeed. I'll call you when we have finished so you can clear away the plates and cups."

Joseph's grin widened. "Thank you, *Misis*," he said and shuffled off.

As Joseph walked away, Mum said, "Ladies, please help yourselves to the tea and cake. I do apologise for the delay. I suggest you leave the crackers—unless of course, you have a headache."

The ladies from the garden club enjoyed Mum's cake and sandwiches. After they had said their goodbyes, Mum called Joseph to clear the dirty cups and plates. I heard the cars pull out of the driveway and raced into the kitchen for my promised afternoon tea. I exploded with laughter when Mum told me about the biscuits. In between mouthfuls of chocolate cake, I helped Mum pick the pills off the now-soggy biscuits. We flushed all the pills down the toilet and threw the biscuits into the scrap bucket for the chickens to have later.

Later, Mum asked Joseph why he decorated the biscuits with the pills from the medicine cabinet. Joseph replied with dignity that the last *misis* he worked for always put things on biscuits to make them taste better. Was he thinking of red and green pickled onions, perhaps?

Dad found the pill and biscuit story hilarious. Later that evening, Dad called Joseph into the lounge room. Dad was lousy at speaking pidgin and tried to explain to Joseph that you only took the pills when you were sick. Joseph looked at Dad and scratched his head in confusion. "Yes, *Masta*," he said. Dad rolled his eyes and muttered under his breath. The next day, for Dad's peace of mind, he fitted a lock to the medicine cabinet.

One year, I decided to send Mum flowers for her birthday. As I now live in Australia, I arranged for the flowers to be sent via an international florist. When Mum received the flowers, she phoned me, said the flowers were beautiful, and thanked me.

"There as a slight problem," Mum said. "The woman from the florist shop raided my garden, and when your flowers arrived, I recognised my own orchids and ginger. That woman," Mum added, "delivered my own flowers back to me, and *you* paid for them. What a hide. I marched back to the florist and demanded your money back. So I got your money back for you. Stupid woman. Did she not think that I would recognise my own orchids!"

"Oh Mum," I said, "I am so sorry. I just didn't think. Keep the money and buy something else." Which Mum did.

Year after year, Mum's garden produced a wealth of beautiful flowers. Many a bride carried a posy filled with Mum's orchids and ginger, as I did many years later. I was married in Australia, and a few days before I was married, Dad picked my orchids from Mum's garden. He boxed the orchids with a drop of water and guarded them on the fourteen-hour plane journey to Australia. After I was married, I pressed an orchid between the pages of my family Bible. The orchid is still there today along with a flower from Dad's funeral service and a flower from Mum's wreath.

Joseph was about middle-aged when he joined our household. His wife, Wadia, however, appeared to be much older. Wadia was a pleasant woman who kept very much to herself and was employed to wash our clothes, which she did very well. Every year, Joseph and Wadia returned to his home village for his annual holidays.

One year, however, Joseph arrived back home with a new wife.

When Mum enquired as to where Wadia was, Joseph told Mum that he had divorced Wadia and married again, all the space of a month. Joseph's new wife was very young and pretty, and in time she bore him two children.

One day, a few years later, Joseph told Mum that he was now too old to work, and he wanted to go back to his home village. We were sorry to see Joseph, Lydia, and their *pikininis* go. We had grown very fond of them. However, we wished them well. Mum bought new cloths for them all and paid Joseph well for his many years of loyal service.

CHAPTER 13

The Empty Glass Bottles

Mum told me that she and Dad brought very few possessions with them when we emigrated from India to Australia in 1956—just a few clothes, some treasured bits and pieces, the family crystal and glassware, and (much to Mum's disgust) Dad's very large tiger skin and stuffed elephant foot. Dad had shot the tiger, a man-eater, and the elephant, which was a rogue, many years before he met Mum. As he loved the skins, he refused to leave them behind in India.

The tiger skin and elephant foot had to clear Australian customs in Sydney, and customs requested Mum and Dad be present when our crates were unloaded. When Mum and Dad arrived at the wharf a few days later, all but one of our crates was sitting on the dock. As the crane swung our last crate over the dock, a cable broke, and Mum watched in horror as the barrel-shaped crate broke free and crashed onto the wharf. The barrel bounced twice, rolled down the wharf, and slammed into a low concrete barrier. The barrel was marked with yellow stickers that said "Fragile: Handle with Care." Mum realised the barrel contained the entire collection of Dad's crystal glasses and bowls.

Mum and Dad were horrified. "There goes the crystal," Dad

said. "I bought that crystal in London years ago. We will never be able to replace it now."

The barrel was stored in the back of our garage in Sydney and remained unopened for four more years. When Mum and I left Sydney, the barrel was loaded along with all our other possessions aboard the *MV Soochow* and conveyed to Rabaul. Our dog, Scamp, also travelled to Rabaul aboard the *Soochow*.

I remember quite clearly the day our possessions arrived in Rabaul. As Mum and Dad unpacked crate after crate, our driveway filled with straw and paper. I was charged with sorting our possessions, and I made many trips back and forth between the house and driveway. I recall a barrel marked with tape that said, "Fragile: Handle with Care." I knew that barrel contained Dad's crystal, and as the barrel had never been opened, I'd always wondered what Dad's crystal looked like.

There was much discussion between Mum and Dad as to whether the "crystal barrel" was worth unpacking. Mum said later that Dad became very angry every time he saw the barrel, and for the sake of family peace, she decided to open the barrel anyway.

"You never know," Mum said to Dad. "By chance, there may be some glasses that were not broken in the fall. And if we ever go to back to England, perhaps we can take a glass with us and match them."

Mum prised the lid of the barrel open and carefully parted the straw. The straw was littered with broken glass.

"I'm afraid that's it," said Mum. "The whole lot is broken. I'll just empty it so we can use the barrel again."

However, as Mum pulled away more straw, she saw that the next row of glasses were unbroken. Dad was delighted, and as Mum and Dad pulled out more straw, they found more and more unbroken glasses. When Dad tallied up the score, he was astounded. He silently thanked the Indian packers, for they had done a remarkable job.

The crystal barrel held a complete set of crystal, about fifty pieces in all. The pieces included glasses of all sizes, fingers bowls, jugs, decanters, and large salad bowls. Of all the pieces, only the top three wine glasses had broken. The rest of the crystal had survived two long sea journeys *and* a crash on the wharf!

The crystal was referred to as "Dad's crystal" or "Father's crystal." Mum wasn't particularly fond of the crystal, as it was cut-glass, heavy-based, and ornate. Mum preferred a more modern clean-cut design, but Dad loved every single piece of his crystal, and from an early age I knew the crystal was special to him. The most special piece of all was the large square whiskey decanter.

In Rabaul in the early sixties, containers for storing food were very hard to come by. Consequently, Mum usually kept all glass jars and bottles, large or small, for fridge and or pantry storage. One morning after a dinner party, Mum decided there were far too many empty jars and bottles in the pantry, so she sorted through what we had, discarded a few, and told our *haus boi* Joseph to throw out any new bottles or jars.

Later that day, Joseph showed Mum an empty caviar jar. "*Misis*," he said, "I found this in the fridge. Do you want me to wash it and put it with the others?"

"No, Joseph, it can go in the bin, thank you," replied Mum. "Remember this morning, I told you to throw out any empty glass bottles you find from now on."

"Oh yes, *Misis*, I forgot." Joseph scratched his head and grinned. "If I find anymore, I will throw them out."

"Yes, that's right, Joseph," replied Mum. "We have enough containers for the moment."

For the purpose of hygiene, all garbage and rubbish—household or otherwise—was collected every day in Rabaul. In the early hours of the morning, the bin and any rubbish left next to the bin was whisked away by silent unseen hands, the bin emptied and then returned to its spot. Therefore if something was accidentally thrown out during the day, it was lost forever.

Our house sat on low stilts and was surrounded by a wide veranda. The garbage bin lived adjacent to the kitchen at the bottom of the back veranda steps. Whenever there was rubbish to go out, Joseph stood at the kitchen door and expertly hurled the newspaper-wrapped parcel overarm across the veranda and into the bin six feet below. Dad often said Joseph was such an expert shot, he should forget about being a *haus boi* and play international cricket instead!

One evening, as Mum cooked dinner, she decided to add some pineapple to a fruit salad she was preparing for desert. The pineapple need to be skinned, and Joseph usually did that. However, Joseph was busy setting the table, so Mum decided to save time and skin the pineapple herself. After she had finished, she wrapped the pineapple skins in newspaper and walked outside to put the parcel in the bin.

When Mum lifted the lid of the garbage bin, a piece of glass buried deep in the rubbish caught her eye. Mum hesitated a moment as a ripple of anxiety passed through her body; the pattern on the glass looked vaguely familiar. However, as she said later, the thought of digging in the garbage bin repulsed her, so she pushed her feeling of uneasiness aside, threw the newspaper parcel in, and replaced the bin lid.

As Mum put the finishing touches to dinner, her thoughts turned again and again to the piece of glass buried in the rubbish. Finally, unable to drive the image from her mind, Mum decided to go back to the bin and investigate. As she lifted the lid and pushed aside the rubbish, a ball of fear formed in the pit of her stomach. Dad's most prized possession, the cut-glass whiskey decanter, lay upside down on a bed of wet sloppy tea leaves. Mum stared at the decanter and drew in a sharp breath. She sunk down on the bottom step, buried her head in her hands, and inhaled deeply. She knew exactly who had thrown the decanter away.

Mum said when she saw Dad's crystal decanter lying among the rubbish, her heart started to pound so fast, she felt she would be violently ill there and then. "In my mind's eye," she told me later, "I saw quite clearly, as if in slow motion, the sequence of events about to take place. I knew without a shadow of doubt that when Father found out Joseph had broken his decanter, Father would kill him. Quite literally murder him in cold blood. He would put his hands around Joseph's throat and choke him to death or stab him with a kitchen knife or something like that."

"I had visions", Mum continued of Father being charged, branded a murderer, and being led away handcuffed to rot in some New Guinea jail. I saw myself in the years to come struggling to educate, feed, and clothe you on my own. At the same time," she added, "I was wondering, seeing the bloody thing came from England, how on earth I was going to replace the decanter without Father knowing. Apart from that, if by some remote chance I could track one down and match it exactly, I had no idea as to what excuse I would give Father when I asked for money to buy an airline ticket to go to England. I just didn't know what I was going to do, so I thought I had better just get the bloody stupid thing out of the bin and bury it or something."

Mum prised open the lid of bin, gingerly picked up the decanter, and laid it in her lap. Surprisingly, the decanter appeared to be unbroken. Mum lifted the glass stopper and peered inside. Everything looked OK. There were no visible cracks or chips, and apart from being covered in tea leaves, Dad's very special piece of crystal looked good as new.

Mum said a silent prayer of thanks and called out to Joseph. He came galloping down the stairs and stood beside her near the bin.

"Joseph," she asked, pointing to the decanter. "Did you throw out this bottle?"

"Yes, *Misis*," Joseph replied, "it's empty. You told me to throw out all the empty glass bottles."

"But Joseph, this is *Masta's* best bottle. It came from a long way away."

"Yes, *Misis*," Joseph said, scratching his head again, "and *Masta's* best bottle is empty, so I threw it out like you said."

Mum shook her head and sighed again. "Well, I am back to square one," Mum muttered under her breath. "I just plain give up. It's useless. Joseph," Mum declared, "from now on, you keep all the empty bottles. You hear? Every last one of them."

Joseph scratched his head again. "Yes, *Misis*," he said.

If Mum was busy, she sometimes asked our house staff to help in the kitchen at mealtime. They peeled potatoes, cut onions, or washed rice.

Joseph really enjoyed working in the kitchen, as he had a great love for anything electrical, and Mum had an array of electrical appliances. Among Joseph's favourite appliances were the electric eggbeater and the electric can opener.

One morning, Dad and Joseph were in the kitchen preparing breakfast. Mum and Dad had hosted a dinner party the night before, and Dad was tired. Our dogs were barking loudly in the background, and Dad decided to find out what the dogs were barking at. He told Joseph to find a bowl, get out the eggbeater, and beat some eggs for an omelette.

Joseph was delighted. As soon as Dad walked out of the kitchen, he moved with lightning speed. He opened the kitchen cupboard and grabbed the eggbeater, flung open the fridge, selected six eggs, and slammed the fridge door shut. Joseph cracked the eggs into a nearby bowl, picked up the beater, flicked the lever onto high, and plunged the beater into the glass bowl.

Dad walked outside and noticed a native *boi* as he walked past our back hedge. "Oh, for Pete's sake, shut up, you two. Dad shouted at the dogs. "I just want to have my breakfast in peace and quiet. Stop barking, or I'll brain the pair of you with the fry pan."

Dad walked back into the kitchen.

As I have stated in the past, Dad very seldom raised his voice, so when I heard him yelling at Joseph, I bolted from my bedroom. As I burst through the kitchen door, Dad stood rooted to the floor.

"No," Dad bellowed like a wounded bison, "for mercy sake, stop, Joseph. Stop. No, no."

Joseph held the eggbeater in a vice grip and worked it round and round the bowl. Dad had told him in the past that the eggs had to be "nice and fluffy" for a good omelette, so Joseph had pushed the lever to the maximum setting. The force of the eggbeater made the glass bowl bounce along the kitchen bench, and as Joseph fought to keep the bowl still, the whirring spinning stainless-steal blades bounced off the sides of Dad's cut-glass crystal salad bowl.

"No!" screamed Dad again. He lunged for wall power switch, and the machine and noise came to an abrupt halt. The crystal bowl gave one last jerk and settled onto the kitchen bench. Dad stared at the bowl and closed his eyes. Large beads of sweat formed on his temple and slid unchecked down his cheek.

Dad groped for a kitchen chair, lowered himself into it, covered his face with his hands, and groaned deeply. Joseph looked at Dad with wide eyes. He fled the kitchen and banged on Mum's bedroom door.

"*Misis, Misis,*" he screamed, "you come quick! *Masta* is sick, he is in pain. Come quick." Mum pushed Joseph aside and ran to the kitchen.

Dad was slumped over the kitchen bench. He was drenched in perspiration.

"For God's sake," Mum said, "what on earth is the matter? Joseph said you were having a heart attack or something."

Dad pointed at his crystal bowl and groaned again. "Joseph was beating the eggs in my crystal bowl."

Mum looked at the eggs in the bowl and said, "Well, Father, you should *not* have left the bowl on the bench last night after our guests had left. You should have washed it and put it away."

"I was tired, for Pete's sake," Dad replied, "so I left it with the glasses."

Dad finally recovered from his ordeal, and the cut-glass salad bowl survived Joseph's enthusiastic treatment. However, Dad had made a decision. "I'm going to buy a lock and key," he said, "a very strong lock and a very big key. And I am going to lock up my crystal and put the key on my car key ring."

Which he did, but remember, Dad was a useless handyman, so when he fitted the lock, he fitted it upside down. Nevertheless, upside down or not, the lock worked, and the crystal was safe. And that was all my Dad was concerned about.

Unfortunately, Dad's crystal bowl was marred by deep scratches from the eggbeater blades. Every time Dad saw the bowl, he became very upset. For the sake of family peace, every time we used the bowl, Mum covered the bottom of the bowl with lettuce leaves. The lettuce leaves hid the scratches somewhat. However, whenever Dad washed his crystal bowl after a dinner party, he always retired to the front veranda with a stiff brandy, and his pipe just to calm is nerves.

CHAPTER 14

The Curry and the Moth

Rabaul had a wonderful open-air market that offered an abundant array of fresh tropical fruit and vegetables. However, most of our other foods, meat, cheese, and dry goods came from Australia or New Zealand by ship. The ship normally took about six weeks or more to dock in Rabaul, and by the time the goods cleared customs and made their way to the store shelves, the potatoes had shrivelled and grown eyes, and the meat was a tough frostbitten lump.

The fact that the meat was tough didn't really bother us. We were practically vegetarians anyway, and on the very rare occasions we did eat meat, the meat was usually curried.

It was Saturday, and that evening Mum and Dad were having a dinner party. The dinner was just a friendly social gathering—a few friends over for a curry and chat. Mum's curries had a reputation for mouth-watering excellence, so an invitation to share a curry with us was hardly ever refused.

All afternoon, the smell of spices and curry wafted around the neighbourhood. By five that evening, a chicken curry was simmering in the big blue curry pot. By six o'clock, our *haus boi* had set the table with our best crockery and cutlery (Dad always placed the crystal

266

glasses later), and the family looked forward to a relaxed evening with friends.

At seven o'clock, our guests arrived and settled themselves on the cane chairs on the front veranda. Mum placed a small platter of crackers, cheese, and smoked oysters on the coffee table and asked Dad to bring out his punch. As Mum was famous for her curries, Dad was famous for his special planter's punch. The punch was made with rum, freshly squeezed lime juice, mint, and crushed ice. Our guests were also offered scotch whiskey, gin, brandy, or just plain fruit juice if they wished.

The evening so far had been relaxed and peaceful. Just before we sat down for dinner, Dad decided to refill the ice bucket. He excused himself and trotted off to the kitchen. He returned a few seconds later, minus the ice bucket, and tapped me on the shoulder. He asked if I would come to the kitchen and "help him with the ice." As we stepped into the kitchen, Dad's face split into a silly half-grin. He covered his mouth with his hand and tried hard not to laugh.

"What's up, Dad?" I asked. "Why are you laughing? What's so funny?"

"Oh, dear pet," he said as he suppressed a chuckle, "luckily I came to the kitchen for some ice, because look what I found in the curry."

I peered over Dad's shoulder into the curry pot. What I saw made me ill. A very large moth had landed in the curry. The moth had a thick maggot-like body and large paper-thin wings. The poor moth had died and now floated among the pieces of curried chicken and potato.

"Yuck, Dad," I shuddered, "that's gross. How did that get in there?"

"I don't know, pet. It must have been attracted by the smell of the curry and fell in or something."

"Well, you'd better get it out quick before Mum sees it," I said, "or she'll be sick."

Dad's face crumbled. He groaned and said, "Oh, for Pete's sake, we can't have that. We have guests, and there'll be hell to play."

"Well, you know how Mum is," I said. "If she sees the moth in there, she'll insist the curry be thrown out."

Dad's face fell. "All right, all right," he said, "now don't get excited, we don't want a riot on our hands." Dad always used that expression if he thought things were getting out of hand and if Mum saw the moth and threw up or exploded with anger… well, that was out of hand. Dad stroked his beard and said in a quiet voice, "Well, we will just keep it to ourselves, shall we? Now just stay calm and I'll think of something."

My dad always had the ability to think on his feet, especially if he was in a tight corner, so Dad put on his sugar-sweet voice and called out loudly, "Darling, Susie and I will serve dinner. You just stay where you are and relax; after all, you have been cooking all afternoon. Now, I don't want you to come anywhere near the kitchen. We will call you when everything is on the table."

Dad's ploy worked.

"Thank you, Father," Mum called back, and the sound of conversation on the veranda resumed.

"Righto," Dad whispered, "we had better work quickly. Now Susie, bang some plates together or something. Make like we are getting things ready, and I'll try and fish this thing out of the curry. We only have a few minutes. Now, what can I use to get the damn thing out?"

I pointed to the ice bucket and shrugged my shoulders. "Try the tongs, Dad," I suggested.

Dad nodded. He picked up the ice tongs and held them like a surgical instrument. He grabbed moth's wing and squeezed the tongs together. As soon as Dad gave the wing a tug, the wing broke away from the moth's body, and the lopsided moth sank into the curry gravy and disappeared from view."

"Oh dear," mumbled Dad. People often laugh in a stressful

situation, and our situation was certainly stressful. Dad suddenly saw the funny side of whole operation and choked back another laugh. He leaned against the fridge and, barely able to contain his mirth, threw the tongs into the sink. 'Well, that's torn it. The damn thing's disappeared," he grinned. "Now what will we do? We're really in hot water. How am I going to find it in all that curry?"

"Gosh, Dad," I said, "you had better get that thing out of the curry. Mum will get really cross if she finds out. You know what she's like. If she finds out, we are all going to get it.'

Dad's shoulders stiffened. The grin left his face, and he became all hot and bothered. "All right, all right," he said, "now we don't want that, now do we? So we have to find it and get it out, or there'll be hell to play."

I pointed to a wooden spoon on the sink and said, "Well, why don't you use that spoon, Dad, and just stir the curry? Maybe the moth will float to the top, and then you can get it out and Mum will never know."

"Well, it's worth a try," said Dad. He snatched up the spoon, plunged the spoon into the pot, and stirred madly. Dad stirred and stirred, and stirred and stirred, but alas, the cooked moth failed to appear.

"Oh yuck," I said, "that's gross. I'm not having any curry, it's disgusting. I bet it's all mashed up now. I'm not eating any curry with that moth in there."

"And I won't be able to eat it either," sighed Dad, "and if your mother finds out, she'll have a fit. So for Pete's sake, don't tell her. We'll just have to leave it and hope for the best."

Dad and I assembled the food on the table. Mum had really cooked a feast. Apart from the curry, we also had pilau rice and poppadoms, and some homemade sambal as well.

Dad called everybody to the table, and we all sat down. Large drops of perspiration formed on Dad's brow. I knew he was nervous. I was too.

"Phew," he said as he wiped his face with his serviette, "it's hot. I'll just get the fan."

Dad jumped up and disappeared to find a fan. Mum looked around in puzzlement and asked if anybody else was hot. Everybody shook their heads.

Dad returned with a pedestal fan, plugged the fan into the wall socket, spun the dial to "high," and flicked the switch. A tornado of cool air blasted over the table. "There, that's better," he said as he pulled out his chair and sat down.

Somewhat annoyed, Mum said, "Now that Father has returned, we can have some dinner. Please help yourselves, everybody. Mum handed around the serving spoons and took a sip of water from her glass.

Vivian Bruce smacked her lips and held out her hand for a serving spoon. "Poppy," she said, "I just love your curries. Thank you so much for inviting George and me." She dipped the spoon deep into the pot and helped herself to a generous proportion of curry.

I was so afraid the cooked moth would appear on Mrs. Bruce's plate. I knew if Mum saw the curried moth, she would heave violently. I felt as if I was riding a roller coaster. My heart leapt each time Mrs. Bruce dipped the spoon into the curry pot and beat against my chest each time she ladled the curry over her rice. I dared not look at Dad in case Mum guessed something was amiss and questioned me later. Finally, Mrs. Bruce passed the spoon to the next person and reached for sambal. Goodness knows where the moth was. My fear abated somewhat; one plate down and seven to go.

As the curry spoon passed from guest to guest, there was still no sign of the moth. Dad perspired profusely and, time and time again, wiped his face with his serviette. When at last Mr. Bruce offered Dad the spoon, Dad shook his head vigorously. "Er … no thank you, George, I'll just have rice tonight, I think," he croaked. "I've had a bit of an upset tummy of late and, you know …' His voice trailed off.

"I'll just have rice too," I piped up. "I don't want any curry either."

My mother was a very astute woman, and she became suspicious. She shot Dad a sour *what's wrong with my curry* look and asked in a sweet voice, "Are you sure you're not having curry, Father? You didn't tell me you had an upset tummy."

"Oh, it's just a touch of the collywobbles, and I didn't want to worry you." Dad averted his eyes. "I'll be as right as rain after I've had some rice."

Mum looked at me. "Curry, Suellen?" she asked, "or do you also have the collywobbles?"

"Em ... no, thanks, Mum, I ate too many smoked oysters in the kitchen, and I'm not hungry."

Everybody relished Mum's cooking, especially her curries. The table fell silent as our guests tucked in. I gave a silent prayer, as the moth was nowhere to be seen.

However, Dad was uncomfortable. He knew Mum knew he'd lied about his collywobbles, and he knew that when our guests had left, Mum would question him. In order to hide his discomfort, Dad babbled Mum's praises.

"You know," Dad said as he helped himself to more rice, "Poppy's a marvellous cook. Even our cook in India couldn't cook a curry as good as this. You won't taste curry like this anywhere in the world, not even in the whole of India. Poppy knows just what spices to use in order to get the right taste, and ..."

Mum silenced him with a glare and a sharp kick under the table.

Finally, the curry pot was empty, the rice was finished, and dinner was over. I guessed the moth had been eaten by some poor unsuspecting soul—hopefully not my mother.

Our *haus boi* appeared to clear the table, and we all adjourned to the veranda for coffee and liqueur.

Finally, close to midnight, our guests thanked Mum and Dad for a wonderful evening and dinner, said their goodbyes, and left.

The house fell into darkness. I said goodnight to Mum and Dad and slunk off to bed. Mum cornered Dad in their bedroom. All evening, she had mulled over the strange behaviour of Dad and me. Mum was suspicious, and she was convinced Dad was up to something. Unable to contain her anger, Mum wanted some answers.

"Why didn't you and Suellen eat any curry tonight?" she asked. "What's this about an upset stomach? It certainly didn't stop you stuffing your face with everything else. Is there something I should know about?"

Dad was sheepish. "Not at all, darling. Susie and I ate too many crackers in the kitchen, that's all. Er ... do you require the bathroom? If not, I'll just quickly have my shower."

"There were no crackers in the kitchen," Mum stated. "I know because I emptied the lot onto the cheese platter. You and Suellen have been up to something."

"Nonsense, darling, the dinner was lovely."

I heard the bathroom door shut, very firmly.

The moth story remained a well-kept secret between my dad and me. We often giggled about it in the years to come. I have always hoped, however, that somebody else ate the moth and not Mum.

Many years later, Mum offered the big blue curry pot to me.

"The pot is too heavy for me to lift off the stove," Mum explained. "Your father bought it for me many years ago. I had seen the pot in a catalogue, but the pot was only available in Port Moresby. So when Father had to go to Moresby on business, I asked him to buy one. There was a choice of a yellow pot or a blue pot, and when your Father came home with a blue pot, I thought it was silly, seeing I wanted the pot for curry, so yellow would have been better, as curry stains everything yellow. But," added Mum, "blue, as you know was Father's favourite colour, so that's why I have a blue curry pot and not a yellow one."

Mum's big blue curry pot is made of cast iron, enamelled in blue on the outside and white on the inside. The pot is at least fifty years old, and although the white enamel inside is now tinged with yellow, the pot has stood the test of time.

I love Mum's curry pot and use the pot whenever I host a curry party. Not so long ago, I decided to retire Mum's pot and buy a new stainless steel pot to cook curry in. I regretted my decision, for even though I followed the recipe, my curry just didn't have the taste a good curry should. I donated my new stainless steel pot to a charity shop and now only use Mum's pot whenever I cook a curry.

CHAPTER 15

Fletcher Jones and the Japanese

Dad came home from the office one day and told Mum and me that he had to go to Japan on a business trip. When I heard Dad's news, I felt a tremor of unease. I had never met a Japanese person before, and I harboured a fear born from the stories I'd heard of the atrocities committed by the Japanese during World War II.

I knew the Japanese had invaded Rabaul, knew of the civilian executions and the treatment endured by the prisoners of war. I also knew that during the Japanese occupation, people just disappeared, never to been seen again. I wondered if Dad would be safe when he visited Japan. I was afraid Dad would disappear and never come home, or be taken prisoner for some reason.

However, I was most afraid that Dad would be executed just because he was a civilian. We had arrived in Rabaul fifteen years after the end of World War II, not a long time in the scheme of things, and the remembrance of war was still very evident in Rabaul. The gallows once used to hang the Japanese war criminals still stood near the airport and were only removed sometime after we had arrived.

Many of our friends had lost loved ones in the war, and others had been so severely impacted, they still bore feelings of ill will towards the Japanese people. Many voiced their opinions whenever the opportunity arose and refused to buy anything that was made in Japan. As a young child, rightly or wrongly, I was very influenced by what I had heard.

When I spoke to Dad of my fears, he put his arm around me and patted my shoulder. "Pet," he said, "thank you for worrying about me, but there is no need to worry now. The war is over, and the Japanese are our friends now. The reason I'm going to Japan," he added, "is because Japan is now a world leader in technology, and I'm going there to see what's cooking!"

I still had no idea why Dad was going to Japan (I learned later that he wanted to establish a business agent in Japan) and was still not convinced he would be safe. Dad's words of comfort did nothing to allay my fears, and in my heart, I did not want him to go.

Mum subscribed to *National Geographic* magazine, and I had seen some photographs of Japan and her people in a recent edition. After school the next day, I looked through the magazines until I found the photographs. When I flicked through the pages, I noted the Japanese people looked nothing like I'd imagined. In fact, I was fascinated by the beautiful geishas and the cherry trees filled with pink blossoms; fascinated by the modern looking cities, cars, and trains; and most of all, fascinated by Mount Fujiyama. When I read that Mount Fujiyama was a volcano revered by all the Japanese people, my fears of Japan disappeared altogether. I was used to volcanoes. I liked volcanoes. Rabaul was surrounded by volcanoes, and volcanoes were familiar to me—as familiar as the ocean.

"If Japan has a volcano, and the Japanese people like their volcano," I thought to myself, "then the Japanese people must be nice and not mean. Maybe," my thoughts continued, "all of the bad Japanese had died in the war."

When Dad came home from the office that afternoon, I told him that I knew all about Japan.

"That's good, pet," he said. "I'll just get my tea, and you can tell me all you know so I can know too. Then I won't have to read anything on Japan."

"Japan has big cities that have trains like in Brisbane," I told Dad, "and all Japanese ladies paint their faces white, and they wear dresses that look like dressing gowns. And guess what, Dad," I added, "there is a big volcano in Japan—bigger than Matupit and the volcano has snow on it."

Dad was impressed with my newfound knowledge of Japan. He smiled and said, "That's very good, pet, you are a clever girl. Did you learn all that at school?"

"No, Dad," I said, "I found out about it in Mum's *National Geographic*. There are lots of photos, and the photos are very pretty."

I was very young when Dad went to Japan. To me, Japan was a very different place. I had only ever known Rabaul and to some extent Australia. When we visited Sydney on holidays, I found the whole holiday experience exciting. However, Rabaul was always home to me, and I could not imagine living in a place that did not have palm trees, native people, and coral reefs. I felt very lucky, and in my heart, I felt sorry for the Japanese people because they did not have what I had.

Dad's trip to Japan proved to be long and arduous. The trip involved days of travelling. Dad had to fly to Sydney, stay overnight in Sydney, and the next afternoon board an international flight for Tokyo. It was winter in Japan at that time of year, and the cold weather posed a problem for Dad.

We had lived in Rabaul for a number of years, and Dad didn't have any winter clothes, let alone any business-type winter clothes. Mum reminded him, however, that his Sydney business suit was somewhere in the house. His suit, I remember, was a Fletcher Jones, made to measure—a very expensive light grey suit. Fletcher Jones was a large Sydney department store that specialised in men's and women's business attire. The clothing was usually made to measure and very expensive. Anybody who was anybody in business *always* dressed in Fletcher Jones.

The next day, after Dad had left for the office, Mum located Dad's suit on the top shelf of his bedroom cupboard, and for the first time in many years, Dad's Fletcher Jones suit saw the light of day.

After many years of storage, Dad's suit was still in perfect condition. Mum told me later that she was surprised that, given the high humidity in Rabaul, the suit was mould-free. Later that evening, Dad tried on his suit and was elated that the suit still fitted him. He insisted the suit, plus a few long-sleeved shirts, were all he needed for his trip.

The morning before Dad left for Japan, Mum laid out Dad's clothes on their bed. The suit, Mum noted, smelt of mothballs, so she decided to hang the pants and coat on the back veranda to air. As Dad needed some last-minute items for his trip, Mum decided to pack Dad's suitcase after she had been shopping.

Our *haus boi* Buut had never seen a suit before, and when he saw Dad's suit, he asked Mum who owned the clothes and why the clothes were on the back veranda.

"Oh," said Mum, "those are *Masta's* clothes, and they smell. *Masta* is leaving tomorrow on the airplane, and I have to pack the clothes. They smell, so I have put on the veranda to get rid of the smell."

Buut nodded.

"Buut," Mum said, "I am going shopping. I have to get a few things for *Masta* before he leaves tomorrow. I don't need you again until four o'clock."

When Mum returned from shopping, she packed Dad's suitcase, and as it was very hot, she decided to rest. She retreated to her bedroom, switched on the fan, and picked up her book to read.

"I remember it was a Wednesday," Mum related to me later. "Your father always played golf on Wednesday, and sometimes he had lunch at the golf club instead of coming home for lunch. So, that day, I didn't have to bother about lunch for him. So I just went to my bedroom and lay down instead."

My mother's intuition was razor sharp, and as she read her book, a feeling of unease niggled within her. Unable to ignore the feeling, Mum put aside her book and swung her legs off the bed. Suddenly, Mum remembered Dad's suit. She raced to the back veranda. The pants and coat were missing.

"Oh my God," she muttered under her breath, "where the hell is Father's bloody suit?" She leant over the veranda and shouted in the direction of the *boi haus*, "Buut! Buut, come here, please."

Buut galloped up the back stairs. "Yes, *Misis*," he said breathlessly.

"Buut, where are *Masta's* clothes? The ones that were hanging up here," she pointed to the empty hangers, "the ones he is taking with him tomorrow."

Buut's face split into a wide grin. "Oh, *Misis*," he said, "*Masta's* clothes had a bad smell, so I washed them this morning."

"What?" The hairs on the back of Mum's neck bristled. "You washed them? With what did you wash them with, for goodness sake?"

Buut scratched his head and shuffled his feet. "I washed them with soap, *Misis*," Buut replied. "I put them in the washtub with plenty hot water and soap, and I scrubbed them good with the big brush."

Mum gasped, "Oh my God, Buut, you washed *Masta's* clothes? Are they still in the washtub?"

Buut shook his head. "No, *Misis*, I put them on the line and hosed them with the garden hose. Now they are clean good. They are hanging on the line now, and they dry quick time. When they are dry, I can iron them nice for *Masta*."

Mum nearly fainted. "Oh my God, Buut," she said as she rolled her eyes skyward. "Whatever possessed you wash *Masta's* suit?"

Buut stared at Mum with a blank look on his face. He thought he'd done the right thing. *Masta's* clothes were smelly, so he had washed them. It was that simple.

"Well, that's it," Mum muttered under her breath. "The thing's probably buggered now. Father will be furious." Mum paused a moment and shook her head. "Oh well," she added, shrugging her shoulders, "so be it. Father will just have to buy himself a new suit when he gets to Sydney. Buut, when *Masta's* clothes are dry, you bring them to me."

Mum dismissed Buut again, walked into kitchen, and made herself a cup of strong black coffee.

Later that afternoon, when Dad's suit was dry, Buut showed the suit to Mum. Mum eyed the suit in trepidation. To her surprise, the suit, although a little crumpled, looked much the same as it had before Buut's "treatment." The suit was clean, smelled fresh, and appeared not to have shrunk.

Mum sighed. "Buut, you iron *Masta's* clothes, and you put them on my bed when you have finished."

Buut nodded and trotted off.

After dinner that evening, the last before Dad left for Japan, Mum, Dad, and I sat together on the veranda. Mum suggested Dad try on his suit again. Dad resisted and said it was too hot. Mum then had no choice but to tell Dad the story of Buut, the suit, and the wash tub. Dad's face drained of colour and then turned purple with rage. He interrupted Mum midsentence.

"What!" Dad spluttered and jumped to his feet. "What did you say? Did you say Buut washed my suit? Did Buut *wash* my good Fletcher Jones suit?"

Mum pressed her lips together and nodded. "Father," she said, "you know what Buut is like. I hung the suit on the back veranda this morning to air, and when I returned from shopping, the suit was missing. Buut thought your suit was dirty, and you will just have to buy a new one in Sydney."

Dad was in no mood for excuses or advice, for that matter. His voice rose in anger.

"Why, for Pete's sake, *why* did Buut wash my suit? It wasn't dirty. I had the thing dry-cleaned before we left Sydney. Who told him to wash *my suit*? Damn it, for Pete's sake, who?"

Dad's voice rose higher. He jumped to his feet and stared at Mum.

"Is my suit ruined? I bet it's ruined now, after being washed … shrunk, I bet it's half the size now. I can't go to Japan if my suit doesn't fit. Without my suit, what am I supposed to wear, for Pete's sake? My shorts, damn it, my shorts? I can't wear my shorts in Japan. I have to have a suit. I'm going to Japan for *business*, for mercy sake. What will my business associates think of me? I'll tell you what they'll think: they will think I'm a hick, a bushy." Dad sat down again and buried his head in his hands.

"Oh, for goodness sake, Father," Mum said, rolling her eyes, "aren't you being a bit melodramatic? The suit is old anyway. It doesn't matter if it has shrunk. You can go straight to Fletcher Jones as soon as you land in Sydney and buy a new one. You'll have time. You don't leave for Tokyo until the next afternoon, so what is the problem?"

"Oh, for mercy sake," Dad yelled, "it's a Fletcher Jones suit, they don't get old. *Fletcher Jones*, for Pete's sake. They are expensive. You wear them for years. I can't just go and *buy* a new suit."

Dad's temper was at the boiling point. "Oh, for Pete's sake," his voice rose again, "how can I do that, I ask you? What about my short arms?" Dad thrust his arms at Mum. "They will have to alter the coat, and you know what a hoo-ha that is. I'll miss my Japan flight."

Mum glared at Dad as her temper flared. "Father. Go and try on your suit," she snapped angrily.

To Mum's way of thinking, the answer was simple: if Dad's suit had been ruined; he simply went to Fletcher Jones and purchased a new one. Dad caught Mum's look, grumbled loudly under his breath, and stomped off to put on his suit.

I must say, I agreed with Mum about Dad's suit situation. I also thought he was making a fuss about nothing. I couldn't see why he just couldn't walk into Fletcher Jones and buy a new suit just like that. It wasn't until I grew up and discovered I too had shorter than normal arms *and* had to have my business jackets altered that I understood Dad's dilemma.

Dad was taking ages and ages in the bedroom. Finally, Mum grew impatient.

"Father, what is going on?" Mum called loudly. "For goodness sake, come on out so I can have a look at the suit."

The bedroom door open slowly, and Dad poked his head out. He wore his silly grin that we knew so well. Was the grin because Dad had caught sight of his image in the mirror, pants halfway up his legs, and had seen the funny side of the whole debacle?

"Come on, Father," said Mum, "stop standing there like a shy schoolboy, let's have a look."

Dad jumped out and threw open his arms. He strode up and down the veranda, just like a model on the catwalk. Dad smiled from ear to ear and chuckled loudly. Dad had thrown the suit jacket on over his T-shirt, pulled on the pants, and—not bothering about socks—slipped on his shoes. We could see Dad's suit was a perfect fit. The sleeves were the same size as before, and the trousers were just the right length. The suit looked clean and fresh and was ironed to perfection, and Dad looked like a Hollywood star as he walked the "red carpet" of our veranda.

"My goodness," exclaimed Mum. "There's nothing wrong with the suit. How on earth? That's extraordinary! Buut scrubbed it with the brush in hot water, and there's nothing wrong with it!"

"Yes, and it didn't shrink one little bit!" Dad nodded as he stuck out his arms. "It's a damn fine suit, my Fletcher Jones suit, and Fletcher Jones is a damn fine company."

Dad trotted off to the drinks cabinet and poured himself a brandy.

Brandy in hand, Dad—still in his suit—sat down again, lit his pipe, and sucked in a few times.

"You know," he said to Mum, "this suit is as good a suit as a Saville Row suit. Fletcher Jones really knows its onions. I made a smart choice when I bought this suit from Fletcher Jones all those years ago in Sydney!"

Mum said, "Right." She knew full well it was *she* who suggested, all those years ago in Sydney, that Dad buy a Fletcher Jones suit and not a cheaper brand of suit.

Fletcher Jones held its exalted position with Dad for many years to come, and I think, from memory, Dad even wrote to the general manager of Fletcher Jones and told him the story.

In the years to come, Dad wore his Fletcher Jones suit on a few more occasions. He wore it to "give me away" when I was married. Dad's suit was washed and ironed again when he and Mum met Her Majesty Queen Elizabeth II and the Duke of Edinburgh when they visited Rabaul as part of Her Majesty's tour of the Commonwealth for her Jubilee.

On August 11, 1986, my Dad passed away. He wore his Fletcher Jones, totally indestructible, very expensive, made to measure, light grey business suit on his journey to heaven.

Dad's visit to Japan proved to be very successful. His associate, Mr. Ogawa, visited Rabaul many times in the next few years. Our family became very fond him and formed a bond of friendship that lasted many years.

When Dad returned from Japan, he told me that when he was in Japan, he visited a factory that had manufactured an oven that would change the way we cooked our food. The oven was so advanced, Dad said, that it cooked and heated food in an instant. Dad also told me that when you put your hand inside the oven, the food was hot but the plate was not. I thought Dad was kidding me. The oven, of course, was a microwave oven.

Dad came home from Japan with his suitcase laden with gifts for

Mum and me. I still many of the gifts today: a small jewellery box with a cultured pearl on the lid, a small ball woven in multicoloured silk, and a dried seahorse in a lacquered box. Dad also bought Mum a beautiful strand of cultured pearls. When my daughter Leanne became engaged, Mum gave her the pearls as gift.

"Your grandfather bought me these pearls," Mum said, "fifty years ago when he went to Japan on business. Wear them often—I did—and if you have a daughter, I hope you will pass them on to her."

CHAPTER 16

Robin and His Sticking Plaster Ear

Most businesses in Rabaul employed a native chauffeur, a *draivaboi* as they were known. The *draivaboi* generally ran errands or delivered goods around town. When Dad was the manager of the Rabaul Trading Company, Dad employed Robin, a middle-aged *Toloi* native man, as the office *draivaboi*.

Robin was rather tall for a *Toloi*, of slim build, with an easy smiling face. He wasn't a big head or cheeky, and he was very loyal to Dad and our family. Robin, you'll remember, very kindly gave me my chicken *Buai*. Robin was classed as a very good *draivaboi*. He didn't crunch gears or accelerate too fast or screech the tyres. Very importantly, Robin adhered strictly to Dad's speed limit rule: fifteen miles per hour in town and twenty on the open road.

Naturally, Dad led by example and applied this rule to his own driving. Just for the record, when I attained my driver's licence, Dads rule applied to me as well.

Robyn also took great pride in the fact "his" car was a nice car. Dad always insisted on a white Holden station wagon as an office car, which incidentally was traded in for a new car every two years. The new office car had to be ordered from Australia, and Dad changed the interior colour every time—either blue, red, or green. Much to

Dad's delight, Robin lovingly washed and polished the car, inside and out, religiously every Monday morning without being told.

As an office *draivaboi*, Robin's tasks were many and varied, but the task I remember him best for was a private chauffeur to me ... or so I liked to think! We didn't have any public transport in Rabaul, so whenever I wanted to go somewhere, I'd just ring Dad at the office and ask him to "please send Robin." Within ten minutes, the office car would pull into our driveway. I'd jump in, tell Robin where to take me, and off we'd go. When it was time to come home, I'd phone Dad again and ask him to "please send Robin" to collect me.

Most of the time, Dad was happy for Robin to drive me wherever I needed to go, and he only chastised me if I'd phoned for Robin too many times in one day. Dad often reminded me that we were lucky to have such a dedicated *draivaboi*, because *officially*, Robin was the office *draivaboi* and his duties were to run office errands, not ferry me around town.

For the six years I attended Court Street Primary "A" School, Robin picked me up every afternoon after school and drove me home. Robin always parked in the same spot and hunted anybody away who stole his spot. Every afternoon as I ran out of the school gate—rain, shine, or monsoon—Robin stood by the car with the back door open. He always sported a wide grin and waved madly at me just in case I didn't see him.

In the ten years or so I knew Robin, he always wore a piece of white sticking plaster on his right ear. The piece of plaster was always nice and clean, and the plaster fully encased the top part of his ear from front to back. The fact that Robin was never without his plaster aroused my curiosity, and as an inquisitive child, I'd often ask Robin what was actually wrong with his ear. Periodically, I would ask Robin if his ear was getting any better, even though I knew full well what his answer would be. Robin always replied that his ear was *bruk pinis*. *Bruk pinis* meant that his ear was broken for good and would never get any better.

I often urged him to attend the native medical clinic to have his ear looked at by a doctor or nurse. Robin always shook his head and said his ear was *bruk pinis*, and that was that. Robin was embarrassed about his ear and covered it whenever I drew attention to it. Even when I pressed him for an answer, he would not elaborate any further.

Robin's repeated refusal to tell me why his ear was *bruk pinis* really annoyed me. Every so often I'd try a differed tactic to coax an answer from Robin. I once told him that Dad was going to sack him because he suspected that Robin was a leper. When Robin asked why the *masta* thought he was a leper, I pointed to his ear and told him that "only lepers" wore sticking plaster all the time to hide their weeping wounds.

When Robin heard that Dad was going to sack him because he thought that he was a leper, Robin was really upset. Panic marred his face. He covered his ear with his hand and said over and over again that he was not a leper. His voice quivered with emotion as he told me that he was happy that he was a *draivaboi* for Dad and did not want the *masta* to sack him. He told me to hurry up and get in the car, because as soon as he had dropped me home, he was going straight back to the office and tell the *masta* he did not have leprosy on his ear.

The fact that Robin was going to talk to Dad frightened me. If Dad ever found I had lied to gain information about Robin's ear—or indeed, if Dad even thought I had treated Robin disrespectfully by making such a silly accusation—Dad would be very angry. Apart from that, I was genuinely sorry I had upset Robin. I hastily assured him that *I* knew he wasn't a leper and that I would talk to *Masta* that night and settle the matter once and for all.

To intimidate Robin as I did that day was silly and childish. Whenever I recall my conversation with Robin, l am truly mortified by my behaviour. To think that I upset Robin to such an extent fills me with remorse and embarrassment. Robin was a true and loyal *draivaboi* who genuinely respected Dad and cared deeply for Mum and me. I wish now I had the opportunity to apologise to Robin.

On another occasion, I tried to bribe Robin with a handful of European cigarettes that I had stolen from Mum. Robin looked longingly at the cigarettes. He scratched his head and said that even though he liked European cigarettes better than his native ones, if it meant telling me about his ear, he would rather smoke his native ones. As I was now stuck with the stolen cigarettes and scared that Mum would find out that I had pinched them, I gave the cigarettes to Robin anyway. Robin grinned and tucked the cigarettes into his *laplap* pocket. He knew he had outfoxed me.

After another *bruk pinis* answer from Robin, I him that I would never speak to him again unless he told me what had happened to his ear.

"All right, *Pikinini Misis*," he said as he shrugged his shoulders.

To amuse himself in the car on the drive home, Robin drummed his fingers on the steering wheel and hummed a mindless tune as we drove along.

When I was a child, Mum often told me that I was tenacious. The question about Robin's ear plagued me no end. My childish curiosity fired my imagination, and Robin's repeated refusal to elaborate on his *bruk pinis* ear gnawed at my insides.

Once I even tried to bride Robin with a pay raise. I told him that *Masta* had agreed to give him pay raise if he told me what had happened to his ear and why he had to cover his ear with plaster. At the suggestion of more money, Robin didn't even flinch. He just hung his head and said the *masta* paid him enough money, and he didn't need any more. It was as simple as that.

The question of Robin and his *bruk pinis* ear also aroused Dads curiosity. At dinner one evening, Dad, in conversation, raised the question of Robin's ear. My dad was a wonderful storyteller and had a few theories of his own. Jokingly, Dad said that maybe during the war, a Japanese soldier had shot the top off of Robin's ear in frustration, while trying to teach him how to drive. Mum was not amused.

"Oh, for goodness sake, Father," she said, "I refuse to discuss

Robin's ear at the dinner table. It is of no business of yours anyway. Let the poor man be and stop putting silly ideas into Suellen's head."

Dad ignored Mum and said, "Maybe one of Robin's cousins was a cannibal and chewed on Robin's ear when he was asleep, or perhaps his wife became a bit carried away and bit it off."

I didn't quite know what Dad meant by that, but Mum told Dad that the matter was closed.

Whatever the story was, the family never found out what had happened to Robin's ear, and I'm sure if I met up with Robin again today, he would still have the plaster on his right ear.

Robin was Dad's *draivaboi* for many years, and when Dad retired to Australia, Robin retired too. Robin said he did not wish to work for anybody else, as he had worked for the best *masta* there was.

Rapindik, Robin's home village, was situated at the base of Tavurvur Volcano. Rapindik, along with the whole of Rabaul, was buried under tons of volcanic ash when Tavurvur erupted in 1994. Many of the villagers lost their lives in the eruption, and those who survived were offered relocation elsewhere. However, a few of the villagers chose to return to Rapindik and remain there today.

On my last visit to Rabaul, I drove to Rapindik (it was a heartbreaking journey) and enquired about Robin's family. As I was unsure of his native name, I was unable gain any information. I sincerely hope that Robin and his family survived the eruption and are well today.

CHAPTER 17

Buut, the Knife, and the Fork

Our dear friends the Hayeses were leaving Rabaul. Uncle Max had been transferred to Lae on the New Guinea mainland. Our family was very sad they were leaving, especially Mum, as Aunty Betty was one of her dearest friends. Apart from that, the Hayeses had been part of our lives for many years, and we knew would miss their company.

One afternoon, just before the Hayeses left for Lae, Auntie Betty dropped in for coffee with Mum. She asked Mum if she knew of anybody who needed a good *haus boi*. Obviously, the Hayeses couldn't take their *haus boi* with them, and Aunty Betty was loath to leave Rabaul without finding him a job to go to. Mum wasn't particularly happy with our current *haus boi*, for some reason or other, so she gave the *haus boi* his marching orders and when the Hayeses left Rabaul, we inherited Buut.

"Buut the Cannibal King" was well known to us, especially after what Dad termed "the scotch episode," and Auntie Betty was pleased he was going to a "good home." She assured Mum that Buut was very good at keeping the house clean and tidy and was as honest as the day was long. Auntie Betty also casually mentioned to Mum that Buut kept his body odour in check by applying liberal amounts of deodorant and showering daily.

On the first day Buut was with us, he set the table for dinner, and the family sat down for the evening meal. Dad picked up his knife and fork, looked at implements in puzzlement, and frowned. He held the knife in his left hand and the fork in his right. Buut had placed the cutlery the wrong way around.

Dad sighed and drew a deep breath. He then changed the knife to the right and fork to the left, pushed his fork into the mashed potatoes, lifted the food to his mouth, and chewed quickly. Irritation marred Dad's face. He muttered under his breath to nobody in particular and finished his dinner.

Buut set the table for breakfast the next morning. As you know, Mum only came to breakfast on the weekend, so as usual, Dad cooked bacon and eggs, and Dad and I sat down to eat. Dad picked up his knife and fork and frowned. Buut had set the knife and fork on the wrong side again.

"Oh, for Pete's sake," Dad said, "Susie, can you please ask your mother to teach Buut how to set the table correctly with the knives and forks? I can't eat my food like this, can I?"

Dad picked up his knife and fork, crossed his hands over his plate, and attempted to cut his bacon.

Dad was clearly annoyed, and I did not want to inflame the situation, so I tried not to laugh. Dad looked very comical with his hand crossed over his plate.

"OK, Dad," I said, "I will."

Dad uncrossed his hands, stabbed at a piece of bacon, sliced off a bit of his egg, and put the whole lot in his mouth. In between mouthfuls, Dad muttered under his breath that he thought Auntie Betty had said that "this fellow Buut" knew how to do things around the house.

"Well," Dad snorted half to himself, "Betty was wrong. Buut is a cannibal, and everybody knows that cannibals don't use knives and forks!"

At dinner that evening Mum, Dad, and I sat down for dinner.

Buut, as usual, had set the table. As we sat down, Dad looked at his knife and fork and muttered, "Oh, for Pete's sake, not again." Buut had set the knife and folk on the wrong side again.

Dad would never ask Mum whether she had spoken to Buut about the correct way to lay a table, so he laid the blame fairly and squarely on Auntie Betty's shoulders.

"Betty was wrong about this fellow Buut," he said to Mum in annoyance. "Buut is a cannibal, and I can't eat my food like this." Again Dad held up his knife and fork, crossed his arms over his plate, and attempted to cut up his salad. "Only Betty," he added, uncrossing his hands, "would employ a cannibal and say he knew how to lay a table."

Mum glared at Dad. She was visibly annoyed at Dad's comment about Auntie Betty. Or was Mum annoyed, perhaps, because she thought Dad was having a dig at her for employing Buut?

"All right, Father," Mum replied in a clipped tone, "that's enough, thank you. I'll show Buut tomorrow how to lay the table properly. Now may we eat please? Suellen and I are hungry."

After breakfast the next morning, Mum showed Buut the correct way to lay the table: knife on the right side of the plate, fork on the left. Buut practiced again and again, and after a while, he and Mum were confident that Buut now knew what side of the plate to place the knife on and what side of the plate to place the fork.

Buut set the table for dinner that evening, and Mum, Dad, and I once again sat down to eat.

"Oh, for mercy sake," groaned Dad as he held up his knife and fork. Buut had forgotten what Mum had taught him that morning and laid the knife on the left side of the plate and the fork on the right side.

Dad decided he was going to fix the problem of the knife and fork once and for all. He held his knife and fork in the air and yelled loudly in the direction of the kitchen, "Buut, come here, will you please."

Buut ran from the kitchen and stood beside Dad's chair, "Yes, *Masta*," he said as he wiped his hands on his *laplap*.

When Dad became agitated with our native staff, he spoke to them half in English and half in pidgin. Dad's "English/pidgin" only confused our staff, and Dad very rarely managed to get his message across. As a result, Dad became increasingly frustrated with them and the language.

Dad crossed his hands over the plate and attempted to cut his fish. "Buut," he said, "I no can eat my dinner like this."

Buut looked at Dad, shuffled his feet, and scratched his head.

"You understand, don't you, Buut?" Dad tried to cut his fish again. "I no can eat my dinner like this. The knife and fork no work."

Buut nodded and said, "Yes, *Masta*," even though I'm sure Buut didn't have a clue as to what Dad was talking about.

"I can only eat like this." Dad uncrossed his hands and cut his fish. "You understand now? Like this. Put the knife and fork so I can eat my dinner like this." Dad cut a piece of fish with his knife, pushed the fish onto his fork, and put the fork in his mouth.

Buut grinned. "Yes sir, *Masta*," he said and scratched his head again. "I understand now."

"Good." Dad waved Buut away.

"Dad," I said. "I don't think Buut understands what you mean. He looked a bit confused."

"Oh, for Pete's sake," lamented Dad, "this business is becoming annoying, and I just want to eat my dinner in peace and quiet. I don't want a circus. Get him back here, will you, and explain to him so he understands."

Buut was summoned again. "Buut," I said in pidgin, "put the knife and spoon on *hansuit* and the fork on *hankais*."

The light came on in Buut's eyes. "Oh, yes," he grinned and scratched his head again. "*Misis* showed me today. Now I remember. Knife and spoon *hansuit*, fork *hankais*."

Dad dismissed Buut again with a nod and a wave, and we resumed eating our dinner.

Buut's voice floated from the kitchen: "Knife and spoon *hansuit*, fork *hankais*. Knife *hansuit*, fork *hankais*, knife *hansuit*, fork ...."

After dinner, Mum and Dad retired to the veranda. "Can't the man be quiet?" Dad said to Mum. "All I hear is *hansuit hankais hansuit hankais*. He sounds like a broken record, for Pete's sake, and I want to listen to the BBC."

Mum reached for a cigarette. "Father, for God's sake," she said, "just turn up the bloody volume."

"I will," Dad said and spun the radio dial a full turn. "For all I care, the whole damn neighbourhood can listen to the news."

Buut set the table for breakfast the next morning. As usual, Dad cooked breakfast and called me to the table.

"Oh, for Pete's sake," shouted Dad as he sat down. "Buut ... Buut ..."

Buut ran from the kitchen as if his heels were on fire and stood beside Dad's chair. Dad held up his knife and fork and sighed deeply. Buut shuffled his feet, scratched his head, and looked puzzled. Dad crossed his hands and attempted to cut his bacon. Buut's face split into a wide grin. He took the knife and fork from Dad's hands, crossed them over and handed them back. Dad shook his head and waved him away.

Buut set the table for dinner that evening, and we all sat down to eat. Dad looked at his knife and fork, and his face turned purple. Just before he exploded, Mum took the situation in hand.

"Father," she said, "just eat your dinner please and leave Buut to me."

Dad drew in a long sharp breath, changed over his cutlery, and sliced into his tomato. Dad ate his dinner in silence and, when he had finished, excused himself and retired to the veranda with his brandy, pipe, and book.

"Oh dear," said Mum to me, "your father is really cross about the knife and fork thing. I have to think of something to make Buut remember what goes where. This situation is getting out of hand. I don't know why Father gets so upset. It's such a silly thing."

Mum had dealt with household help all her life and at times had to think outside the square for a solution to a problem. In a sticky situation, Mum had a few tricks up her sleeve. That afternoon, she drove to the Rabaul news agency and bought a large piece of white cardboard and a thick black marking pen. Mum then drew a typical table setting on the cardboard: large plate in the middle of the cardboard, knife and spoon on the right of the plate, and fork on the left. She then added a smaller plate to the left of the large plate, and above the knife she drew a water glass. She then took the drawing into Buut in the kitchen and explained to him in her pidgin—perhaps that was Mum's first mistake—that this was how he was to set *Masta's* place at the table.

Buut nodded his head and grinned at Mum's picture. Mum asked him if he understood the picture. He nodded again and scratched his head. Mum celebrated the end of the knife and fork saga with a cigarette and good strong cup of coffee.

Mum had cooked chicken curry, a family favourite, for dinner that night. Mum called Buut to set the table and reminded him to set *Masta's* place just like the picture. Buut nodded and, picture in hand, disappeared into the dining room to set the table.

Promptly at six, Mum called me inside and told me to make myself presentable for dinner. That meant I had to wash my hands and face and brush my hair. Ten minutes later, Mum, Dad, and I sat down at the table. Dad looked at his place setting. He sat very still and breathed in deeply. Buut had indeed set his place according to Mum's drawing. However, instead of using a place mat, Buut had used the white drawn-on piece of cardboard instead, and had placed Dad's knife, spoon, fork, plate, and water glass over the appropriate outlines.

Dad looked around the table. As if on cue, Mum and I held up our knife and fork. At least Dad's cutlery was in the right place. Mum and I had to try to eat cross-armed.

Buut stayed with us for many years, and Mum tried over and over again to teach him how to lay a table in the correct manner. However, Buut was more than likely illiterate or semi-illiterate, or he just didn't know his left from right. There were times when Buut did set the table with the knife and spoon on the right and the fork on the left. Those times were rare. When the cutlery was placed incorrectly, Mum, Dad, and I just changed it over.

In time, Dad just accepted Buut's inability to lay the cutlery in the correct manner. However, each time the cutlery was placed the wrong way around, Dad grumbled under his breath about cannibals and their lack of ability to set a table correctly.

CHAPTER 18

Manakori, the TV, and the Tape Recorder

After we had lived in Rabaul for a number of years, Mum's mother, Mum's sister, and her family emigrated from Sri Lanka (Ceylon) to Australia. Mum's family settled in Adelaide, South Australia. Granny (Mum's mum) was at that time in her seventies, and Mum always travelled to Adelaide once a year and spent a whole month with her family.

I had finished boarding school the year before and was employed in a local bank, so it was just Dad and I at home. Dad prided himself on being a good cook, and he was, to a certain extent. He cooked breakfast to perfection and also managed to whip up a great vegetable curry. However, most of the time when Mum was away, Dad and I lived on salad, or we went to the New Guinea Club instead, for dinner.

This year, before Mum left for Adelaide, Mum decided to teach our *haus boi* Manakori some basic cooking skills so that if Dad and I decided not to eat at the club, Manakori could cook dinner for us instead. Manakori was delighted with Mum's plan and agreed to learn how to cook. To make things a little easier for Manakori to remember, Mum devised a plan. She decided to record her cooking instructions on the cassette player. Manakori could then listen to the tape and follow Mum's instructions step by step.

The cassette player was assembled on the veranda, and over a number of days Mum explained, in easy steps, the method of making a pot of tea, frying fish, making salad, and a few other simple dishes. Mum told Manakori that he was play the tape until he found the recipe for whatever *Masta* wanted for dinner and just follow her instructions. After many trial runs, Mum was satisfied with Manakori's progress. Manakori had fried fish, made a salad, and cooked macaroni and cheese. In fact, Manakori had exceeded Mum's expectations. Mum was also confident that Manakori knew how to start the tape recorder, pause the recording, and restart the tape if needed.

On the first evening Mum was away, Dad said to Manakori, "The *misis* is away. Now, the *misis* said that you know how to cook dinner, so we will have fried fish and salad for our dinner tonight, thank you. Now you understand how to do all that? The *misis* showed you on the tape recorder. Just do as the *misis* says. You understand now?"

Manakori grinned from ear to ear. "Oh yes, *Masta*," he said, "I will cook the fish and make the salad."

As Dad stepped on to the veranda, Mum's voice boomed out from the tape recorder.

"Good evening, Manakori," said the tape, "you are now going to make fish and salad for the *masta's* dinner."

Manakori stood poised and ready. "Yes sir, *Misis*," he replied.

I had the use of Mum's car while she was away, and as I pulled into the driveway, Dad leaned over the veranda.

"Hello, pet," he called to me, "how was the bank today? Your mother should be in Adelaide by now, so it's just you and me until your mother comes home. Manakori is cooking dinner. I have told him to cook the fish your mother left in the fridge and make a salad. Is that all right?"

"Hello, Dad," I called back. "I'll be up in a minute."

As I stepped onto the veranda, Mum's voice filled the house. "Open the fridge, take out the fish, and get out the big fry pan from the cupboard."

Manakori opened the fridge. The tape continued talking. "Turn on the stove, and ..."

"Wait, *Misis*." Manakori looked at the recorder and scratched his head. "I'm still looking for the fish. I'll get the fry pan in a minute."

Manakori located the fish on the second shelf of the fridge. He slammed the fridge door shut, grabbed the fry pan from the cupboard, and stood, fish and fry pan in hand, as he waited for his next instruction.

"Put the fry pan on the stove and turn the stove on. Put some oil in the pan, and when the oil is hot, put in the fish and fry the fish until it is cooked. When the fish cooked on that side ..."

"Wait, *Misis*, wait! I forgot the oil." Manakori said. He dumped the fish on the counter, threw the pan on the stove, opened the pantry door, and located the cooking oil. He poured the oil into the fry pan, threw in the fish, and spun the dial on the stove to high.

The tape carried on talking. "Get the tomatoes, lettuce, and cucumber out of the fridge and wash everything in the sink. Get the salad bowl, board, and knife. Cut everything up, put everything into the salad bowl, and put the salad on the table."

Manakori became flustered. "Wait, *Misis*, wait!" he yelled from across the kitchen. "You are talking too fast, *Misis*. You wait. I have to get the salad bowl."

"Now," Mum's voice rang clear and loud from the recorder, "if the fish is cooked on that side, turn the fish over. Get out the bread and butter and put the bread and butter on the table."

Manakori became flustered. Beads of perspiration slid down his face and dripped off his chin. Things were getting out of hand. The fish was burning, and the kitchen was fast filling with smoke. Mum was prattling on, and he still hadn't turned the fish over. Manakori reached for the salad bowl and slammed the bowl into the kitchen counter. He flung open the fridge door, found the salad vegetables, threw the vegetables into the sink, and turned on the tap full bore.

As Manakori stood at the sink, he cupped his ear and tried desperately to hear Mum's next instruction. The fish, meanwhile, hissed and sizzled in the pan and turned black. A large bubble of air, trapped under the fish, escaped sideways and sprayed the stove with hot oil. Manakori cursed loudly.

Suddenly, he remembered he had to turn the fish over. He dropped the tomato in the sink, grabbed a spatula from a nearby drawer, and flipped over the fish. As the fish landed in the pan, hot oil splashed all over Manakori's hand.

Manakori yelped in pain as his skin sizzled. He'd had enough of the *misis* and her tape recorder. He ran over to the kitchen bench, stuck his face close to the speakers, and screeched in a high-pitched voice, "You machine, you shut up. You shut up now. *Misis*, you talk too fast. You wait now. You shut up."

Dad and I, alerted by Manakori yelling at Mum to shut up, burst into the smoke-filled kitchen.

"For Pete's sake, Manakori," Dad bellowed, "what is going on? What is burning? You will have to whole damn fire department here soon."

Mum's instructions echoed amidst the chaos. "Now, Manakori, put the fish on a plate and call the *masta* and tell him his dinner is ready."

Manakori looked at Dad with wide eyes. Dad picked up the burning fish pan and flung the whole lot in the sink. He turned off the stove and hit the stop button on the tape recorder.

Manakori slumped against the fridge and rubbed his burnt hand. His face was contorted by frustration and pain.

"Manakori, what on earth happened? What happened to my dinner?"

Manakori began to yowl and point at the machine. "The *misis* talk too fast, *Masta*, she all the time talk too fast, and me no ..."

"Oh, for Pete's sake, Manakori," Dad interrupted, "why didn't you turn off the damn machine? If *Misis* is talking too fast, turn off the bloody machine. *Misis* showed you, didn't she, how to turn off the machine?"

Manakori scratched his head and shrugged his shoulders. "The *misis* didn't tell me to turn off the machine if she talk too fast," he mumbled.

Dad covered his face with his hands and sighed, "Oh, for Pete's sake, Manakori … it's going to be one hell of a month," he muttered under his breath. "Manakori, tomorrow I will show you how to turn off the machine when the *misis* talks too fast. All right?"

Manakori grinned and sucked on his hand. "Yes, *Masta*, thank you."

"Dad," I said, "I'll tell Manakori to clean up the kitchen and then he can finish up for tonight. We can make a salad together and have some cheese and crackers for dinner. We'll see how it goes tomorrow. We can always have dinner at the New Guinea Club."

When Dad returned from the office the next afternoon, Dad gave Manakori another lesson on how to use the tape recorder. After a few attempts, Manakori mastered the art of pausing Mum's recording when he became bogged down with instructions and re-starting the tape again when he had everything sorted and was ready to resume cooking.

The next evening, Dad stood in the kitchen with Manakori. Manakori practiced turning the recorder on, pausing the recording, and restarting the recording again when he was ready for the next step.

"Right," said Dad. "Manakori, do you understand everything now?"

Manakori puffed out his chest and nodded.

"Good," said Dad, "there is some more fish in the fridge. The little *misis* and I will have fish and salad for dinner, thank you. Now, you sing out when it's ready, please."

Manakori's voice filled with confidence. "Yes sir, *Masta*," he grinned. Manakori hit the start button on the tape recorder, and Mum's voice filled the kitchen. Dad disappeared through the door and made his way towards the veranda.

An hour later, Manakori called Dad and me to the table. Our fish looked fried to perfection, and the salad was cold and inviting. As Dad sat down and unrolled his serviette, Manakori hovered in the background.

"Thank you, Manakori," complimented Dad. "This looks very good."

Dad waved Manakori away and picked up his knife and fork. He sliced into his fish, lifted the laden fork to his mouth, and began to chew. At the first bite, Dad screwed up his face and gagged as a strange taste filled his mouth. Dad resisted the urge to spit out his fish and swallowed quickly. Dad he lifted the plate close to his face and sniffed at the fish. "Manakori," he bellowed, "what, for Pete's sake, have you done to my fish? The fish smells like ... like a bad *muli* or something."

Dad reached for his water glass, took a gulp of water, and wiped his mouth with his serviette. In frustration, Dad flung his serviette onto the table and buried his head in his hands.

Manakori appeared at the dining room door.

"Manakori, for Pete's sake," sighed Dad, pointing to the plate, "what ... what in heaven's name have you done to my fish? It tastes terrible. Show me what you have cooked it in."

"Yes sir, *Masta*," said Manakori. He fled to the kitchen and returned with a tall glass bottle filled with a yellowish liquid.

Dad face turned purple at the sight of the bottle. He grabbed the bottle from Manakori's hand and shook the bottle in Manakori's face.

"Oh, for Pete's sake, Manakori," he spluttered, "that is not oil, that is Rose's Lime Juice Cordial. You drink it in water. You *do not* fry my fish in it. That's it, Manakori." Dad stood up and looked Manakori square in the face. "I have had it. Tomorrow, you understand, tomorrow I cook my own dinner. Tomorrow, you stay in your *boi haus* until I call you. I just want peace and quiet, not a bloody circus. You stay in your *boi haus* until I have cooked my dinner, and then you come and clean the kitchen."

"Yes sir, *Masta*." Manakori hung his head and grinned. The next evening and every evening for a month, Manakori enjoyed a very welcome night off.

After the lime juice cordial episode, Dad decided he did not want Manakori to cook dinner anymore. So Dad devised his own version of vegetable curry. Dad and I ate vegetable curry every night for two weeks until Dad complained to our friends that he missed Mum and her cooking. Our friends took pity on us. Most nights, we were invited to join one family or another other for dinner and enjoyed a home-cooked meal almost every night until Mum returned home.

When Mum returned from Adelaide, she was furious and embarrassed that Dad and I had imposed on our friends night after night. She asked Dad what would happen if she was to die first and he was left to fend for himself?

The following year, Mum made arrangements to visit her family again in Adelaide. As Dad and I usually helped Mum with dinner every night, we were confident we could cook a reasonable meal and not have to eat vegetable curry night after night or impose on our friends. Apart from that, Mum's tape recorder, with her cooking instructions, was nearby, ready to use if Dad and I needed any help. Mum packed her bag and left for Adelaide. For the first time in nearly a year, Dad and I were home alone.

One afternoon, Dad decided Manakori had led a sheltered life and a little education was in order. He decided that he would explain to Manakori exactly what television was.

Television had not yet arrived in Rabaul, so Manakori had no idea what television was or what it was supposed to do. We did, however, have a two picture theatres in Rabaul. Both theatres were well attended by the native and European population alike.

Manakori, like most of the native population, went to the pictures every Saturday night without fail, regardless of what was showing, so Dad told Manakori that TV was just like the picture theatre, only it was much smaller and you could watch the TV at home.

At the end of Dad's television conversation with Manakori, Dad was well pleased. He was pretty sure Manakori had grasped the idea of TV and how the TV worked. Dad also told Manakori that the *misis* had a TV in her house in Adelaide. Manakori's eyes grew wide at the mention of Mum's TV. He asked if the *misis* could watch the pictures anytime she liked. Dad assured him the *misis* could indeed do just that and did so on a regular basis. Manakori wanted to know what the *misis* watched. Dad told him the *misis* only had to turn on the TV and she could see anything she liked at any time.

Manakori scratched his head and drew in a sharp breath. After a moment or two, his face lit up, he puffed out his chest, and he let out a long low whistle. A grin split his face from ear to ear. He told Dad he was very glad the *misis* had a TV in her house in Adelaide, especially now that he knew how the TV worked.

The next afternoon, when Dad arrived home from the office, Manakori was waiting for him on the veranda. A deep wide grin spread across his face as Dad strode up the stairs.

"Good afternoon, Manakori," Dad greeted him. "You're all dressed up. Going to church or something?"

Manakori shook his head and danced backwards on his toes as Dad stepped onto the veranda. Manakori did indeed look smart. He had on a newly pressed *laplap* and sported a clean brightly coloured shirt. His face shone like ebony, and his newly clipped hair was neat and tidy. A strong smell of sweet aftershave wafted around him.

"Good afternoon, *Masta*," Manakori announced with flair, "come and look inside."

Manakori swept his arms in a wide arc and pushed open the glass lounge room doors.

The lounge stood out like a showroom. The furniture had been dusted and polished, the cushions were fluffed, magazines and books had been tidied, and Manakori had even cut a few flowers from the garden and stuffed them into a vase. Dad's mouth fell open.

Manakori led Dad into the bathroom. The bath, shower, and hand basin had been scrubbed free of soap scum, and clean towels hung on the towel rail. In the bedroom, Manakori had changed the sheets, swept under the bed, and dusted Mum's dressing table.

"My my, Manakori," said Dad, "What has happened here?"

"*Masta*," replied Manakori, "the *misis* is watching me on the TV. So I clean the house and everything good today. The *misis* can show all of her friends on the TV that she has a very good *haus boi* that can clean and look after things good while she is away!"

"Manakori," Dad patted him on the back, "you are indeed right. The *misis* will be very pleased to see what a splendid job you have done with the cleaning, and I am sure all of her friends will be very impressed to see she has such a good *haus boi* to take care of things while she is away."

"Thank you, *Masta*," replied a pleased Manakori.

"Manakori the movie star" kept up his housecleaning vigil for the whole month Mum was away. Every now and again, when Dad was home, he caught Manakori as Manakori waved and said hello to Mum. After all, Mum was checking on him on her TV to make sure Manakori did a good job with his household chores.

CHAPTER 19

Shopping Rabaul Style

Even though Rabaul was a small town, we were blessed with a perfect blend of Eastern and Western shops from which to choose our goods. For our family, given our background, the mixture of Oriental and European foods and Oriental and European goods allowed us to cater for and indulge ourselves in both worlds. In fact, the shopping in Rabaul, be it food or otherwise, was so "not so ordinary" that Mum often said that Rabaul was the only place she knew of that offered Australian tinned Bully Beef and Chinese silk pyjamas in the same shop on the same shelf.

The many Chinese trade stores in town that I frequented as a child stocked all sorts of weird and wonderful things to eat, fiddle with, and look at. Chinese food items crammed the wide painted shelves, including packaged dried big-eyed fish and tinned fruits and vegetables I had never heard of, nor was I game to try, as well as big drums of brine-soaked goodness-knows-what, packets of noodles, and cloth bags of rice. The trade stores also stocked a wide variety of the snacks I enjoyed: red hot chili-soaked ginger pieces (yum), dried salted mango, and pawpaw strips. And of course, the trade stores always sold the one thing all New Guinea kids bought with their pocket money: Chinese dried salted plums.

Apart from the assortment of Chinese food items, some of the trade stores also stocked brightly coloured bolts of material, sewing cotton, elastic, pins, needles, buttons, and zips at very reasonable prices. Mum was talented seamstress and sewed most of her dresses, as she did mine. Some of the more upmarket Chinese stores also stocked bolts of beautiful silk material. Mum frequented these trade stores whenever she and Dad had to attend a do, to buy the silk material to make a new dress. In fact, when Her Majesty Queen Elizabeth II and the royal family visited Rabaul in 1974, Mum purchased the cream and gold silk material for her dress from a well-known Chinese trade store.

I still have the dress, shoes, and hand bag Mum wore for Her Majesty's visit. I also have the very simple fine gold chain and small gold pineapple Mum wore around her neck. In later conversation, Mum said to me, "I dressed very simply for her Majesty's visit. How could one compete with the Queen anyway? Her dress was beautiful, and her jewels alone outshone everything else, so I just made my dress myself and wore my gold chain and my little gold pineapple."

The trade stores also did a roaring trade with the native population. The stores offered native tobacco, tinned fish, tinned Bully Beef, and bags of rice as well as tin plates, cups, and cooking utensils. All in all, be you native, Chinese or European, the Chinese trade stores formed an integral part of everyday shopping.

Of all the trade stores in Rabaul, T. C. Wee and Sons, owned and operated by the Chan family, was a Holland family favourite. The store was situated on Malaguna Road, about five minutes' drive from home, and was open from the crack of dawn till well after dark every single day of the year—a convenience store in the true sense of the word.

As you stepped through the open door of T. C. Wee's, a feast of wares lay before you. The wide glass counters were crammed with little jade ornaments, delicately carved wooden Chinese figurines, penknives, boxed coloured pencils, and silk pyjamas. Behind the glass counters, sturdy wooden shelves lined the walls. The shelves, which seemed to disappear into the ceiling, were stocked with tins of fish, tinned Bully Beef, rice, tinned butter, bolts of cloth, and native *laplaps*, as well as kerosene lanterns, light globes, and Chinese paper umbrellas. Apart from all that, T. C. Wees also sold fresh bread (baked on the premises) and freshly boiled peanuts. Suffice to say, T. C. Wees had it all. Best of all, it stocked the fattest and saltiest Chinese dried salted plums. The salted plums were considered to be the best in town.

T. C. Wee's had been in Rabaul for sixty or so years. Mr. Tee Chee Wee arrived in Rabaul from mainland China sometime in the early 1900s. He was just eighteen years old. Soon after his arrival, he met and fell madly in love with a pretty Chinese girl called Lam Wo Oi. Even though Lam Wo Oi was two years older than him, they married. Mr. and Mrs. Tee Chee Wee proved to be astute businesspeople, and over the next thirty years, they amassed a considerable fortune.

When the Japanese Imperial Forces occupied Rabaul in World War II, the land and business owned by the Wee family were confiscated, and Mr. Wee became a prisoner of war. Upon his release after the war, the Australian Government granted Tee Chee Wee enough funds to buy a portion of land on Malaguna Road. Not long after that, T. C. Wee and Sons opened for business. When Tee Chee Wee passed away, his wife and their daughter Irene (who later married Bernard Chan) maintained tradition, and over the next sixty years, T. C. Wee and Sons became one of the most successful trade stores in town.

Bernard and Irene Chan pursued a number of business interests in Rabaul, and like many of the affluent Chinese in town, relied on family and extended family to keep their interests close at hand. Even though they had five children, it was their second eldest daughter, Grace, who more often than not served us whenever we went into T. C. Wee's.

While most of the children in Rabaul enjoyed free time after school, Grace, under the watchful eye of her maternal grandmother and still in her primary school uniform, tended shop. Young Grace also sorted the tins of food, bagged sugar and rice, shelled peanuts, boxed phone orders, dusted and cleaned, and whenever there was a lull in the store, spread her schoolbooks on the counter and did her homework.

When Grace completed her primary school education, she was lucky enough to stay in Rabaul and attend Rabaul High. She was not subjected, like most of us, to boarding school in Australia. Unfortunately, Rabaul High only provided lessons to the fourth form, and so Grace was sent "south" to a school in Sydney to complete the last two years of her high school education. We still saw Grace in the shop when she came home for holidays, although we noted that Grace had changed. She had abandoned her school uniforms of yesteryear and was dressed in the very latest (Australian) fashion: a bottom-hugging mini skirt!

When Grace finished high school and returned home, she gained employment at a local bank. Only a few of us returned to Rabaul to work after we had finished school. When I joined the same bank, Grace was promoted, and I was given her position of trading bank typist. Grace was proficient typist; I, on the other hand, was not. I found the typing and retyping hard work, to say the least. Suffice to say that as I languished at home after a "hard day at work," Grace— as usual—was behind the counter at T. C. Wee's, still in her bank uniform, stacking shelves, cleaning, and dusting.

For the many years we lived in Rabaul, Dad favoured T. C. Wee's above all the other trade stores in town, and there was a very good reason for that: whenever Dad went to T. C. Wee's, Grace gave Dad preferential treatment. Dad often said Grace worked too hard and that he felt sorry for her being stuck in the shop for hours on end. Nonetheless, Dad dropped in daily for bread or cigarettes, and whenever he encountered Grace behind the counter, he afforded her the respect she deserved.

Dad always waitined patiently to be served, and asked, in his quiet cultured English voice, if he might bother her or "Please, Grace, if it's not too much trouble, may I have some …?" Dad's politeness obviously struck a chord with Grace, as she always attended to Dad first if there were other people in the trade store.

Dad also valued Graces' opinion on his health matters and presented himself at T. C. Wee's whenever a mossie or sandfly strung him. Grace always recommended *Tiger Balm*; it was the best remedy for insect bites, she maintained, and that's why the Chinese always used it. On occasion, Dad also went to Grace for something Mum wholeheartedly disapproved of: to buy a tin of Bully Beef to have with his lunch. As far as the tinned Bully Beef was concerned, Mum refused to even look at the tin, much less open it. She declared that Bully Beef was disgusting and full of animal fat. Dad, however, loved the stuff and said that "Australian soldiers lived on tinned Bully Beef during World War II, and if it was good enough to win a war on, it was good enough to have for lunch!"

Grace Chan was in Darwin when Cyclone Tracey swept through the town on Christmas day 1974. Grace lost everything. However, when she returned to Darwin to rebuild her life, she met Harry Smith. Grace and Harry married in 1982 and soon after moved to Hervey Bay in Queensland. Harry built a house, ironically quite close to my mother's. I often visited Grace and Harry whenever I visited Mum, and when I did, Grace and I spoke about the good old days, sipped Chinese tea, and sucked Chinese salty plums.

When I was a young child, the Chinese trade store known as Lam and Sons, situated at the very end of Mango Avenue, held great delight for me. The shelves positively bulged with the best selection of children's toys in town. Not the toys that I saw in the department shops in Sydney, but *Chinese* children's toys.

Mr. Lam beckoned to me each time I entered his shop and steered me towards his new "just arrived today, made in China" novelty-shaped transistor radios, music boxes, or windup toys. Mr. Lam had been blessed with many sons, who in turn produced a number of grandchildren, so Mr. Lam knew exactly what plaything appealed to which child. He opened the boxes and wound up the toys and said, "I get this for my grandson, he like, if you like, you tell your father to come soon before they all sell and buy for you. I take cheque from Mr. Holland anytime!"

I often left Mr. Lam as he sat at his counter, chuckling to himself, surrounded by crumpled paper and open boxes, while I raced off to Dad's office to beg Dad to come quick with the chequebook because Mr. Lam said he would "take a cheque anytime!"

One Christmas when I was about seven years old, Santa shopped at Lam's for my new red bike (red, of course, is a lucky colour for the Chinese people, and I've often wondered if Mr. Lam was the one who chose that colour. He kept my bike hidden for weeks in his back room and never said a word as I looked longingly at the other bikes in the shop window.

As I grew older, my interest in the toys at Lam's waned, and I began to seek and explore the more sophisticated shops in town. Increasingly, I felt drawn, more often than not, to one shop in particular: Uncle Jock Ping's.

Uncle Jock's was an emporium in the true sense of the word. It was filled with wonders from afar: an Eastern Aladdin's cave that bulged with jade, ivory, and silk.

As you entered through the wide doorway, the sweet, pungent, never-to-be-forgotten smell of camphor wood swirled around you. The heady aroma settled like a cloud and chased away the odours of musky human sweat and street dust. Once inside, the treasures of the Orient surrounded you. The walls were lined with silk paintings of long-legged water birds, Chinese boats, and old men in long flowing robes, the brushstrokes soft and delicate against glossy black lacquered frames. The glass-topped counters were crammed with exotic wonders: silk pyjamas, robes, jackets, slippers, purses, and hankies, as well as glass ornaments, red-and-black lacquered jewellery boxes, and camphor-wood jewellery boxes.

Lion dogs stood in neat rows, and imperial dragons guarded jade necklaces and rose-quartz earrings with matching bracelets. Wooden sampans and houses with upturned roofs nestled among mother of pearl butterflies and ivory letter openers. Towards the back of the emporium, a bed of silk carpets lay in quite slumber. The carpets, stacked a metre high, were arranged from largest on the bottom to the smallest on top. Their delicate threads, soft and sleek, beckoned a touch, a stroke, as the light danced over hues of jade, cerise, and Ming blue.

However, the central focus of Uncle Jock's emporium was a neat square of open glass shelves that dominated the middle floor space. The shelves were filled with rosewood carvings of Chinese fishermen burdened with baskets of fish, ceramic figurines of tigers and black panthers, and landscapes fashioned from cork housed in glass boxes. On the very top of the shelves, statues of Lord Buddha took pride of place: Buddha sitting cross-legged with folded hands; Buddha with eyes closed, sleeping in peaceful repose; and Buddha, ever happy, with a laughing face, outstretched arms, and fat belly.

Of all the treasures in Uncle Jock's emporium, I loved the carved camphor-wood chests and boxes most of all. I loved the satiny feel of the wood and the stories carved into each panel. I loved the big brass hinges and the elongated skinny locks, their keys trussed in long red tassels. Most of all, I loved to lift the lid of biggest chest of all and bury my head deep inside. The wonderful aroma of *Cinnamomum camphora*, the most fragrant wood of all, filled my nostrils.

When my Mum passed away I inherited her large beautifully carved camphor-wood box that sat in our lounge room at home. Mums box now sits in my lounge room, under a large window that overlooks my veranda and front garden. Inside the box are some of

Mums treasures...the memories I hold so dear. Every Christmas I top the box with a hessian sack, just like we used to do at home and as am unable to find a wooden nativity scene, place my Christmas tree on top instead...

I am, in my heart, more Eastern than Western. A psychic once told me I was a Chinese sage and or herbalist (she couldn't tell which) in a past life. Could this be true? Quite possibly; I am not comfortable in the popular supermarkets, with their wide sterile aisles and electronic scanners that buzz and ping, nor do I like the furniture warehouses that are stacked with melamine and plastic. I prefer a Chinese trade store any day, or an emporium filled with exotic treasures where I can lose myself in camphor and rub my face on silk carpets. where I can suck madly on a Chinese salted plum and fill my trolley with noodles and rice and dim sim wrappers, sweet thick soy sauce and pungent salty fish sauce, dried mushrooms, water chestnuts, and bamboo shoots, Peking duck and red BBQ pork, packets of dried shrimp and salted mango strips, coriander, and watercress; and where I can fiddle with transistor radios and marvel at array of Chinese children's toys.

I still hunger to sit with Mr. Lam in his trade store and visit Uncle Jock's emporium again. However, in 1994, Mother Nature robbed me of that privilege. Those wonderful childhood times, along with many other treasured memories, now exist only in my mind.

There is a large Chinese trade store not far from where I now live. When I last visited, I noticed a pile of large woven plastic mats stacked against the back wall. The plastic mats filled me with nostalgia as I remembered that every trade store in Rabaul had offered plastic woven mats for sale. The mats came in every size and colour imaginable. Before I left the trade store that day, I purchased a large yellow and green plastic mat. When I arrived home, I placed the mat under the glass table on my back veranda.

When we first arrived in Rabaul in the early 1960s, there were two department stores we shopped at. Burns Philp (BP's, as everybody called it) and Steamships (Steamies, as the shop was known). After a few years, a new department store, the New Guinea Company, opened for business.

BP's was situated in the main part of town, halfway down Mango Avenue. The building was a large cream-painted double-story building of wooden construction with the shop part on the ground floor and offices on the top. Oddly enough, BP's was the only shop in town fitted with large canvas punkers. The punkers hung from the ceiling like stiff horizontal banners and swept back and forth, back and forth, fanning you each time you walked under them. I can still hear their slow rhythmical wooshhh … wooshhh … woosh.

BP's offered a limited supply of European-style clothing for men, women, girls, and boys, as well as school and office stationary, expensive make-up and perfume from the very best of the French and European cosmetic houses, and household electrical goods like electric fans and eggbeaters.

At the back of the store, almost forgotten, stood a few shelves haphazardly stocked with grocery items imported from Australia: potatoes (which were dirty and sprouted eyes), onions (the size of softballs), pumpkins (which I loathed as a child), apples and oranges (who would buy apples and oranges when you had a wealth of tropical fruit on offer at the local *bung*?), tinned goods (such as spaghetti, baked beans, and sardines), and assorted boxed breakfast cereals. Sometimes, however, on a rare occasion, we'd find a few tins of yummy Dutch biscuits or boxed Scottish shortbread—and, if we were lucky, an assortment of mustards or pickles.

Once, to Mum's delight, a whole case of black Russian caviar came to light. The caviar, obviously forgotten, was offered at a reduced price and housed next to some boxes of soap powder. Mum purchased the whole case, all forty-eight bottles of the sturgeon's black roe, for the princely sum of one pound! For weeks, Mum, Dad, and I enjoyed Russian caviar for lunch.

A few years ago, Mum reminded me of this tale. One day, my

best friend Ruth had joined us for lunch. Mum placed a few bottles of caviar on the table, and as I heaped the caviar on my plate, Ruth asked what it was.

"Try some," Mum said.

Ruth took a teaspoon of caviar and popped the teaspoon into her mouth.

"It's yummy," she said. "It tastes like sea water. What is it?"

"It's caviar—fish eggs," Mum said. "Have some more."

Later that afternoon, a very concerned Father Haley phoned Mum and asked her why Ruth had eaten fish eggs for lunch. Mum chuckled and informed Father Haley that the fish eggs were indeed Russian caviar. Mum said Father Haley was somewhat relieved. However, he stated that he and his family lived very simply, and as such, Russian caviar was *not* in Mrs. Haley's housekeeping budget.

BP's also had a small cold room that housed a delicatessen selling plastic wrapped cured meats and assorted small goods, as well a butcher counter offering a section of frozen meat. Given our background, Mum and Dad and I very rarely ate red meat. However, one day Mum purchased a beef roast. That evening, after Mum had cooked the roast, she cut away the string that bound the meat; the roast sprung apart and revealed a gristly strip of fat.

Mum was revolted at the sight of the gristle and showed the roast to Dad. Dad commented that the meat resembled something only a hyena would eat. Mum cut the roast into chunks and called our dogs. They wolfed down the roasted beef, licked their plates clean, and wagged their tails with enjoyment.

Steamies stood at the other end of Mango Avenue. The shop was in a cream-painted wooden double-story building like BP's and carried similar goods at similar prices, although Steamies did not stock grocery items. However, in order to be different, Steamies had a high-topped glass fronted freezer cabinet that stood just inside the front door. The cabinet was filled with stainless steel trays that advertised different flavours of ice cream. Most of the time, however, much to everybody disappointment, the only flavours readily available were vanilla and chocolate. The other flavours always seemed to be "out of stock". I never had the pleasure of tasting one of Steamies ice creams, as Mum said the ice cream was never frozen properly, and if I ate the ice cream I would get sick.

Our dogs came with us everywhere, even shopping. Whenever Mum shopped at Steamies, she bought each dog an ice cream. I looked on longingly as the dogs lapped the melting ice cream from the pavement, and I grumbled loudly at the injustice of not being allowed to have an ice cream as well. My grumbles, as usual, fell on deaf ears.

Between BP's and Steamies, most of our needs and those of the townsfolk were catered to. Nevertheless, one day when Mum and I were out shopping we noticed that the New Guinea Company store had closed down. The New Guinea Company was once a ramshackle tin and wood building that sold commercial refrigerators, electrical generators, and spare parts for all types of motors. The building was to be demolished and rebuilt as a variety department store.

The townsfolk were very excited at the prospect of a new store. It had been a long time since we'd had anything new in town, and as the weeks went by, everybody waited in anticipation as the new store took shape.

The New Guinea Company opened for business about six weeks or so before Christmas. Our new department store celebrated the opening by offering specials on all grocery items, electrical items, clothing, and (much to Mum's delight) a huge array of books. The new store was also air-conditioned, large, and open-plan.

As an added attraction, it boasted the availability of ultra-modern shopping trolleys. Compared to the trolleys offered by either BP's or Steamies, the New Guinea Company trolleys were large, had deep wire basket, and were fitted with a child's seat at the front. The store manager told Mum that "his" trolleys were fitted with castors and not wheels, and therefore the trolleys were guaranteed to roll with ease.

I remember that Mum appeared very interested as the store manager pointed to the castors. However, as we walked away, Mum muttered under her breath, "Bloody idiot. What would he know? I bet he's never pushed a shopping trolley in his life!"

The grocery section of the New Guinea Company was comprised of a number of wide linoleum-covered aisles, free of the usual boxes and cartons and housing long deep shelves filled with all sorts of yummy eats we hadn't seen for a while: boxes of imported biscuits, packets of German black bread, tins of New Zealand strawberries, as well as sweet-smelling English soaps, toilet water, and fancy shampoos that promised shine and bounce. Behind the groceries stood a row of large stainless steel glass-topped freezers that positively bulged with frozen foods, including ice cream in all flavours; imported fish, such as haddock, Dover sole, and trout; and packets of "snap frozen" Geisha brand oysters.

Dad said the oysters were rejects from the Japanese pearl farms. Rejects or not, Mum and I loved the oysters and devoured them with glee each time Mum purchased a packet. The well-stocked freezers also boasted plastic-wrapped parcels of Australian and continental meats, whole chickens, plump turkeys, and the odd goose or two.

After we had finished our grocery shopping that day, Mum paid for the goods and asked for them to be delivered to the house after four o'clock.

"That will give Suellen and me time," she said to lady on the checkout, "for us to have a look around."

For the next two hours, Mum and I ambled around the shop. Our mouths gaped at the goods on offer. The walls were lined with brand new stoves—no need to wait now for six weeks for a stove to be shipped from Australia; electric cookware, such a deep fryers and pressure cookers; pedestal fans; and portable air conditioners on wheels. Our new department store also had something I had never seen before.

"Mum," I asked as I pointed to a round object on wheels, "What is that used for?"

"Oh," replied Mum, "they are hair dryers. The hair salon has one. You sit under it to dry you hair. The thing is bloody awful: it burns your scalp. I hate it and refuse to go anywhere near it in the salon. I just walk out with wet hair and let my hair dry by itself."

The hair dryers were bonnet-shaped, sat atop a pedestal, and were lowered over your head and switched on. A blast of hot air circulated inside the bonnet and dried your hair. The enamel painted hair dryers came in pale pink, baby blue, or sea green. Mum looked at the hair dryers with disdain and muttered, "Who in their right mind would buy a hair dryer in the tropics?"

My mum had beautiful thick dark wavy hair, and after Mum had washed her hair, she just combed her waves into place and left her hair to dry naturally. Unfortunately, I did not inherit Mums waves. My hair was dead straight, with not a wave to be seen.

We soon moved on from the pedestal hair dryers, and for the first time in many years, feasted our eyes on goods we had only seen in catalogues or "down south" in Australian department stores: smart-looking fashions for the whole family; fashion accessories, such as belts, scarves, woman's hats, and shoes; crisp-looking Irish linen tablecloths; and place mats and serviettes in every colour of the rainbow. Fluffy towels, for bath or beach, sheets, pillow cases, and satin-trimmed cotton blankets. Stainless steel pots and pans, trays and cake racks, and French kitchen implements that Mum greatly admired.

There was also a large area dedicated exclusively to children's toys. The toys were not the made-in-China brands like Mr. Lam sold, but the rather more upmarket brands from England or America. There were model trucks, cars, and airplanes; tricycles, bikes and pull-along go-carts; dolls and dollhouses, and—set up in the corner—something else I had never seen before: a children's swing set. The swing set was painted green and yellow, and it was enormous. It held two separate swings, a long horizontal swing with seats attached at each end, a seesaw, and a long metal slippery dip. Wow!

As a child, we did not have television in Rabaul and reading was an integral part of my life. Mum and Dad encouraged my love of the written word, and all though my childhood always included a book or two as gifts for my birthday or Christmas.

Mum was very pleased to discover that our new shop had tables and tables of beautiful books to choose from. There were reference books on stamps of the world, seashells of the Pacific, and animals of the Artic; history books filled with pictures of faraway little-known places and peoples; mystery novels of murder and mayhem; and children's adventure stories of piracy on the high seas. There were cooking books and books featuring "three easy step" a la carte menus and a wealth of "how to make" volumes on model ships and airplanes.

The tables were stacked high with atlases—pocket-size to blackboard-size—and books on astronomy and strange alien space beings. It was indeed a book lover's feast. In fact, Mum said there were enough books at New Guinea Company to keep us occupied for many birthdays and Christmases to come.

When Dad came home from the office that afternoon, I swooped in on him and told him of my big day shopping with Mum. Dad was very interested as I prattled on, and he expressed surprise when I told him that if Mum needed a new stove, he could simply go to the New Guinea Company and buy one, because there were lots of stoves there to choose from.

At dinner that evening, Mum told me that she and Dad had decided that I was old enough to choose my own books for Christmas that year. A few days later, Mum and I visited the New Guinea Company again. I chose two new books, and Mum ordered our Christmas turkey, cheeses, crackers, nuts, and glacé fruit. Mum left instructions that she would pick up our Christmas food and my books a few days before Christmas.

In the early hours of the morning, three days before Christmas, Dad—a light sleeper—awoke to a loud explosion. As he walked onto our veranda, an enormous ball of fire lit the night sky. A few seconds later, our *haus boi* Joseph ran up to Dad and said, "*Masta*, has the volcano erupted?"

"No, Joseph," Dad said, "I don't think so. It's in the wrong direction. Go and get Wadiya and wait here. I will go and wake up *Misis* and *Pikinini* and go in the car to see what it is."

Joseph nodded and ran to wake his wife.

Dad ran into Mum's bedroom and shook her awake.

"Darling," he said, "there is a big fire somewhere in town. I'm going to see what it is."

The sound of the explosion had also jolted me awake. I jumped out of bed and called out to Mum.

"I'm on the veranda, Suellen," Mum said. "There is a big fire somewhere, and Father has gone in the car to find out where it is."

There had never been a big fire in Rabaul before, and we weren't the only ones awake. The whole neighbourhood was ablaze with lights. People spilled out into the street, shouted to each other or stood in huddles, and pointed to the distant fire.

The night air was electric with chaos and noise. A steady stream of natives ran past our front hedge screaming, "*Paia, paia, bikpela paia*" as they raced by. Cars blasted their horns, and dogs yelped in terror.

The dark sky was aglow with flames. The fire had really taken hold. The ground rocked as explosion after explosion echoed in the distance, and the air turned pungent as black smoke billowed like a mushroom and settled over the town.

Suddenly, a loud bang echoed in the distance. A ball of flame shot sky high followed by a shower of sparks. The sparks lit the night sky and plunged the town into darkness.

"There goes the electricity," said Mum. "I bet the poles are on fire. It's a bad one. I wonder where it is."

A short while later, we heard our car horn blast at the front gate. Mum and I rushed out to meet Dad.

"What the bloody hell has happened?" said Mum. "What's on fire? The whole town is running down our street."

"Well," Dad said, "you'll never guess what's on fire. It looks like it's that New Guinea Company shop in Mango Avenue. The fire truck is there at the scene doing a splendid job, but I doubt the shop can be saved now. It's well and truly alight. In fact, the "fire brigade" [which comprised of one very old water tanker, a European fire chief, and four native fire *bois*] will have a devil of a job. I think the adjoining shops will go too. Jock Ping's water trucks are there are well. Jump in, and we'll go and have a look."

Mum was aghast. "The New Guinea Company? Is the New Guinea Company on fire?"

"Yes, I'm afraid so," replied Dad. "It certainly looks that way, I'm afraid."

Joseph and Widaya hovered nearby, and Mum told them to get into the car. Their eyes were wide with fright. "*Masta*," said Joseph, "*bikpela paia.*"

The roads to town were filled with cars and people, all yelling and honking their car horns at the same time. Dad made his towards Mango Avenue and parked the car in a side street.

"Stick together," said Dad. "We'll see if we can get closer. Go back to the car if we get separated, and stay out of the way of the fire trucks."

Mango Avenue was awash in people and water. Our one fire truck and Uncle Jock's tankers sprayed a steady stream of water onto the burning building. The air was thick with smoke, ashes, and sparks. However, the situation was hopeless. The New Guinea Company was a funeral pyre of epic proportions.

Our brand spanking new department store burnt to the ground that night. The fire consumed all the books, bikes, dolls, and dollhouses. It sizzled the Christmas hams and turkeys and the odd goose or two. It melted the hair dryers and the fancy French pots and pans, and it reduced the shiny new supersonic-castor-driven shopping trolleys to globs of blackened metal.

The New Guinea Company fire had far-reaching consequences. Almost everybody in town had lost something, including Christmas food and Christmas gifts. Most importantly, quite a few people were now unemployed.

The family still had a cracking Christmas that year. We gathered what little resources we had and joined our friends for a "league of nations" type of feast: Indian, German, a bit of Dutch, a touch of Chinese, and some Aussie stuff thrown in as well. And even though, much to Rudolph's relief, Santa's sleigh was somewhat lighter than normal, Santa was more than generous with gifts for my family. Only my poor old Dad missed out. He had to settle for everyday food instead of his favourite much anticipated eat-only-at-Christmastime cheeses, rainbow trout, and whatnot.

Work to rebuild a new New Guinea Company store began in the New Year. And just like last time, our third variety-type department store opened for business six weeks or so before Christmas.

Suffice to say, I had lost interest in the New Guinea Company and its European wares and declined Mum's invitation to accompany her shopping. Instead, I found myself back at Lam's Trade Store and Uncle Jock's Emporium again. When Mr. Lam saw me, his face split into a wide grin. He clapped his hands with glee and welcomed me like a long-lost daughter.

CHAPTER 20

Pidgin English and Mum and Dad: a Never-Ending Saga

Neo-Melanesian or Pidgin English, as the language is known, is an internationally recognized native language. Melanesian in idiom and grammar, the language evolved, over many years, through a natural integration of white man and native. Recognized as the lingua franca of Papua New Guinea and its many surrounding islands, Pidgin is spoken along with English in the House of Assembly in Port Moresby, studied at Port Moresby University, and offered as a foreign language at the Queensland University.

Although classed as a native language, "Pidgin English"—everybody just referred to it as Pidgin—is comprised of English words with a smattering of German words thrown in and place talk, the local dialect pertaining to that particular location.

The mixture of the three languages makes Pidgin an interesting tongue. When spoken in its pure form, Pidgin is difficult to grasp, as the English words used have, over the years, been changed, limited, and/or extended in their meaning. For example, *kilim*, from the English word *kill*, means "to put out," as in douse a fire or strike a heavy blow. *Blankit*, from the English word *blanket*, means "floor rug or table placemat," and *kisim,* from the English word *kiss,* means "bring to me" or "fetch."

Pidgin also contains a some English swear words that are used in everyday conversation, as well as other English words that have a different meaning altogether. My parents found the English swear words disdainful and refused to use them. Mum and Dad often substituted an English word for a Pidgin word, and that sometimes changed the context of the conversation. As a result, whenever Mum or Dad spoke to any of our native staff, their requests were often lost in translation: for example, *As,* pronounced *arse,* means "at the back of or behind something." To urinate is *pispis,* a fish is a *pis,* and *dai* refers to the past. *Tok i dai nau* means "the matter is settled."

The German words used in Pidgin are a legacy of the German occupation (1884–1914), and over the years, many of those words have been changed to a Pidgin word. At times, however, both the old German word and a new Pidgin word are used: for example, *kaput* is a German word that means something is broken or not working and is often used when conversing with an older native. On the other hand, the new Pidgin word *bruk* is used if conversing with a younger native.

To add to the confusion, the use of "place talk" words often comes into play. So at the end of it all, if one really wanted to *tok pisin* correctly, you either had to study the language at length (which few people bothered to do); be born in Papua New Guinea *and* converse in Pidgin; or have lived in PNG from a very young age. Quite frankly, if one failed to fit any of the above categories, Pidgin proved to be a difficult language to master. Therefore, unfortunately, the language often suffered the injustice of bastardization.

As child, I don't remember ever actually *learning* to speak Pidgin. However, within a relatively short period of time after arriving in Rabaul, I became fluent in Pidgin and often switched from English to Pidgin in my everyday conversation. I still do.

My parents, however, found Pidgin difficult to grasp, and they often struggled to make themselves understood. As one would imagine, though, through necessity, Mum and Dad found themselves in situations where they had to speak with the local natives, and on those occasions, they often failed to get the message across. As a result, instructions and messages conveyed by Mum and Dad to our native staff and vice versa were often misinterpreted or misunderstood altogether. The lack of understanding placed Mum and Dad at a disadvantage. Sometimes, much to my amusement, this led to acute embarrassment for both my parents.

Our very first *haus boi* in Rabaul was a *Toli* named Johanus. Johanus was in his early thirties. He was not married and, as I recall, had a passion for all things American cowboy or Wild West. He also enjoyed listening to and singing along with (in heavily accented American/Pidgin English) American country and western music.

Mum said Johanus was none too pleased when he learnt that the new *masta* came with a *misis* and girl *pikinini* and that none of us enjoyed American country and western music. The previous manager of Rabaul Trading Co. was a single middle-aged gentleman who only messed one room, never used the kitchen, and played Johnny Cash records all the time. Needless to say Mum and Johanus never really hit it off.

One morning, not long after we had arrived in Rabaul, Mum noticed that the lounge room floor was dusty. She also noticed that a thick layer of pumice dust had settled behind the sofa. Mum was going shopping and asked Johanus to, while she was out, dust everything, mop the floor, and mop behind the sofa. When Mum returned from shopping, she noticed that Johanus had dusted the furniture and mopped the lounge room floor. However, he had neglected to mop behind the sofa.

Mum pulled the sofa away from the wall, called Johanus, pointed to the dust on the floor, and asked him, in her Pidgin, to get the mop and bucket and clean "behind" the sofa. Johanus nodded his head and trotted off. Some hours later, Mum noticed the sofa was still askew and the floor behind the sofa was still dusty. Again she called Johanus and again asked him, in her Pidgin, to clean behind the sofa. Johanus looked at Mum in puzzlement, scratched his ear, said, "Yes, *Misis*, you have already told me," and trotted off. Mum waited for Johanus to return with the mop and bucket. When, after some minutes, Johanus had not returned. Mum sought him out and found him at the back of the house pumping water from the water tank.

"Johanus," she said quite crossly, "you did not mop the dust from behind the sofa. I asked you to mop it, and it's still dusty."

Johanus stopped pumping, looked at Mum, and frowned. "Yes, *Misis*," he replied, "I will. You told me already."

Mum sighed. She sensed something was not quite right. She turned away and left Johanus to finish his pumping.

As the days rolled by, the pumice dust behind the sofa thickened. Mum became more and more annoyed as she made her repeated requests for Johanus to mop.

One morning, Mum's friend Phyllis Skinner dropped in for morning tea. Mum pointed to the dust behind the sofa and complained to Mrs. Skinner that, even after repeated requests, her lazy and inefficient *haus boi* had not mopped behind the sofa. Mrs. Skinner had lived in Rabaul for a number of years, and she roared with laughter when Mum used the word *behind*.

"Poppy," Mrs. Skinner said, "no wonder your *haus boi* hasn't mopped behind the sofa. You are confusing the poor fellow. You are telling him to do it *later*, and so he is. *Bihain* or *behind* is the Pidgin word for "later." If you want Johanus to clean behind the sofa, you have to tell him to clean its' *as*."

Mum sat bolt upright in her chair. She reached for another cigarette, flicked her lighter, and held the lighter to her cigarette.

"What do you mean, clean its *arse*, Phyllis? That's a disgusting word. What sort of language would use a word like that, I ask you? *Arse*. What sort of person would teach a native to use a word like that? My Indian servants would never use that word. How can I tell my *haus boi* to clean the sofa's *arse*? I simply refuse. That's preposterous. What will Cyril think if he hears me telling Johanus to clean the sofa's *arse*? He'll think I've gone mad and commit me to an asylum."

Mrs. Skinner chuckled again. "Poppy," she said, "*arse* is not a swear word in Pidgin. The word simply means "behind" something. If you want Johanus to clean behind something, you have to tell him to clean its *arse*. It's as simple as that."

A disgusted look crossed Mum's face. She stubbed her cigarette in the ashtray and reached for her coffee.

"Well, that may be, Phyllis," Mum said as she cupped both hands round her cup, "but I simply refuse to ask anybody to clean any thing's *arse*. How disgusting. I have never used that word before, and I won't use that word just because I *now* live in New Guinea! I will think of some other word to use instead."

Thus was Mum initiated into Pidgin. Little did she know, however, that her refusal to accept Pidgin for what it was—a recognized native language that just happened to use English swear words—placed her at a disadvantage. In the years to come, Mum was true to her word and refused to use any English swear words whenever she spoke in Pidgin. As a result, time and time again, Mum experienced the utter frustration of misunderstood instructions or misinterpreted messages.

When we lived in Rabaul, commercially prepared pet food was not available. Our animals therefore enjoyed a diet of brown rice and tinned fish. The tinned fish was either mackerel or pilchards, or brown rice and meat offcuts; the meat offcuts were a rarity and were only offered at BP's every so often.

Mum always insisted our dogs and cats be fed well before the family sat down for our evening meal. More often than not, our *haus boi* cooked the rice in the afternoon, assembled the dog and cat plates on the back veranda, and doled the rice and fish or rice and meat onto each plate.

However, whenever we changed our house staff and Mum had

to train our new *haus boi* to do things the Holland way, trouble prevailed.

The only English swear word I ever heard Mum use was "bloody." Mum said "bloody this" or "bloody that" whenever she was angry. Apart from that, I never heard her swear.

The Pidgin word used to describe any type of fish, be the fish tinned or fresh, is *pis*. Mum just substituted the Pidgin word *pis* with the English word *fish* whenever the need arose, or she just told our *haus boi*, "Put fish with the animals' rice."

This evasive reference to the tinned fish would usually suffice. However, one afternoon, our new *haus boi* Joseph forgot to add the tinned fish to the animals' rice. The dogs just sniffed at the rice and walked away. Later, I overheard Mum trying to explain to Joseph (in her half Pidgin/half English) that the dogs didn't like just plain rice, and he was, in the future, to add some fish.

"Mum," I said as I walked into the kitchen, "you have to speak to Joseph in Pidgin about the animals' food. He doesn't understand English. You have to tell him *pis*, not *fish*. *Fish* is English, Mum. *Pis* is Pidgin. Otherwise, he won't understand, and the animals will just get rice again. OK?"

At the mention of the word *pis*, Mum threw up her hands in horror. "No, Suellen, it's not OK!" she exclaimed. "How I hate this infernal language. It's disgusting. I will not say that word. I will not," Mum stamped her foot, "and I don't like *you* using that word either. That word belongs in the gutter … and," Mum added as she reached for a cigarette, "thank you very much, I simply refuse, under any circumstance, to refer to my animals' food as urine. Tinned or not!"

For the next few days, Mum policed Joseph whenever he prepared the animals' dinner, just to make sure he added some *pis* to their rice.

Poor Mum. She never accepted Pidgin, and situation after situation arose.

One afternoon, after we had been living in Rabaul for a while,

Mum settled herself on the veranda to read her book. Our *haus boi* Joseph stepped on the veranda and approached Mum.

"*Misis*," he said in Pidgin, "*i nogat susu.*"

Mum stiffened and put her book aside. She reached for a cigarette and stood up. "I beg your pardon, Joseph," she said rather stiffly in English. "What did you say to me?"

"*Misis, i nogat susu*," Joseph repeated.

Mum fell into silence. She looked Joseph square in the face and, after some thought, called out loudly, "Suellen. Quickly! Suellen, come here now please."

I must admit that the instant I heard Mum's tone of voice, I knew something was amiss, but I was in my bedroom reading, and I didn't really feel like getting up.

"Mum," I yelled back, "I'm in my bedroom. What's up?"

"Suellen!" Mum shouted. "Come here quickly! Now, thank you."

Never one to ignore my mother's commands, I pulled a face and yelled all too loudly, "I'm coming."

Annoyed, I threw my book on my bed and thought to myself, "Mum always calls me when she thinks I am doing nothing."

"What, Mum?" I said rudely as I looked from her to Joseph. "You always call me when I'm doing something."

Mum waved her hand towards Joseph and said, "I think that man is being rude … and if he is, I am going to sack him here and now." Mum sat down, crossed her legs, and glared at Joseph.

"What did he do, Mum?" I asked.

I knew Joseph to be a quiet and respectful *haus boi*, and I couldn't imagine him being rude to Mum, or anybody else for that matter.

"He …" Mum paused and lit another cigarette, "he … ask him. Ask him what he just said to me."

I turned to Joseph and asked him in Pidgin what he had said to Mum. Joseph scratched his head and looked at me in puzzlement.

"I told the *misis* that we don't have any milk left," he replied, "and *Masta* will be home soon. I have to make some milk for his tea, but there is no milk in the tin." We did not have fresh milk in Rabaul, and as such, used tinned powered milk instead.

"Joseph wants some *susu* powder, Mum. Milk powder. That's all," I said. "He wasn't being rude. He just said that there's no milk powder left in the tin, and he needs some to make milk for Dad's afternoon tea."

Mum shook her head and sighed deeply. She raised her eyes skyward and muttered between clenched teeth, "Oh, this confounded language. How I hate it. I thought ... tell him there is a new tin in the pantry. He can open that."

I nodded and relayed the message to Joseph.

As I turned to walk away, Mum said, almost to herself. "I hate this Pidgin language. It's disgusting. I thought Joseph was telling me that I didn't have any bosoms. I ..."

All of a sudden, I understood why Mum was so upset. She had misunderstood Joseph completely. *Susu* is the pidgin word for powdered cow's milk or coconut milk. In pidgin, *susu* also means a woman's breast or an animal's teat, depending on the context of the sentence. Mum, in ignorance, had completely misunderstood what Joseph had referred to. Mum thought Joseph was telling her that she didn't have any breasts!

Apart from context and English swear words, Mum also had trouble with some Pidgin pronunciations as well.

Mum often cooked with fresh coconut milk. Coconut milk is made by shredding the white flesh inside a mature coconut and adding water. The waterlogged flesh is then wrung out through an open-weave piece of cloth. The white liquid is coconut milk.

Mum always ran into difficulty whenever she asked our *haus boi* to prepare the coconut milk. The pidgin word for *shred* is *skrapim*, pronounced "cig-are-up-im." *Skrapim* also means to scratch (as in scratch an itch); however, in a "scratch" scenario, the word *skrapim* is pronounced phonetically: "scrap-im." For some reason, Mum just couldn't pronounce "cig-are-up-im" but had no trouble in pronouncing "scrap-im." So her request to *scratch* the coconut instead of *scrape* the coconut was always met with a lot of head-scratching by both parties.

Pulpul was another Pidgin word Mum had trouble understanding. *Pulpul* means *flower* or *flowers*. When we first arrived in Rabaul, Mum pointed to a bed of orchids and asked our *gaten boi* to *pull* the weeds. Mum always had a vase full of flowers in the house, and our gardener did as he was asked. Later that afternoon, he presented Mum with a big bunch of freshly cut weeds. He told Mum that in his opinion the weeds were ugly, and why hadn't she chosen some nicer *pulpuls*.

My poor mum never really grasped pidgin, but she did try (I'll give her that), and over the years, more often than not, she managed to make herself understood.

Not so my Dad. From the very first day my dear old Dad arrived in Rabaul, he struggled to speak Pidgin. As a result, he was often misunderstood. That, at times, led to a whole lot of trouble.

As mentioned before, my Dad spoke the languages of North and South India and many of their dialects fluently. However, Dad, for some reason or other, just couldn't master Pidgin.

Sometimes Dad would try, really try, to speak Pidgin. As a child, I found the process painful to watch. Dad often used words he thought were correct or changed words to other (usually English) words he thought might suit the conversation better. Alas, my dad's Pidgin rarely worked, and more often than not, his explanations or questions or instructions or intentions were (like Mum's) misunderstood and misinterpreted altogether.

When Dad first managed Rabaul Trading Co., he employed a *draivaboi* called Petrus. Petrus was a happy-go-lucky individual, eager to please and to do a good job. Petrus deserved a medal for his patience in trying to understand Dad whenever Dad spoke Pidgin, and an "A" for effort when he tried to carry out instructions that (often) just didn't make sense.

It was Saturday afternoon well after the close of business, and

Dad was especially busy. Rabaul Trading Co. had received a large order of cocoa from Cadbury. Cadbury was located in the United Kingdom, and the cocoa was due to be shipped that day. Mr. Weis, Dad's assistant manager, was in Australia on annual leave, and Dad was in the cocoa shed counting the bags of cocoa as they were loaded onto Uncle Jock's trucks.

Time was ticking by, and Dad was in a bad mood. He had a deadline to meet. All of the cocoa bags had to be stacked on the wharf by four in the afternoon, and it was now two o'clock. Dad had just received word that one of Uncle Jock's trucks, fully laden with cocoa bags, had broken down halfway to the wharf.

I was home on holidays from boarding school, and I was with Dad that afternoon in the cocoa shed. The broken-down truck posed a problem; it put Dad well behind schedule. Dad told me he had to make sure all the cocoa bags were unloaded from the broken-down truck and loaded onto another truck as quickly as possible. Dad told me to stay in the cocoa shed until he returned. As he walked away, he called loudly to Petrus in Pidgin "to catch em keys to Ute quick time."

Petrus ran into the cocoa shed, empty-handed. "Yes, *Masta*," he said as he fell in step with Dad.

"Petrus," Dad said without breaking stride, "catch em me quicktime Ute keys. You understand Ute keys?"

"Yes, *Masta*," answered Petrus.

However, Petrus didn't understand. Petrus only spoke Pidgin, and Dad was taking to him half in Pidgin and half in English. To add to the confusion, Dad used the English words for "bring me" and "Ute" and not the Pidgin words.

Petrus looked perplexed, and in Pidgin told Dad he didn't know what Dad wanted. Dad was cranky—cranky at the broken truck, cranky that he was behind schedule, and cranky because Petrus didn't know what he wanted. Dad blew his top.

"For Pete's sake," he shouted at Petrus, "bring me the Ute keys.

The keys to the Ute—you know the ones. Have you lost them? Is that what you're telling me? You've lost them. Well, where the hell did you last put them, Petrus, for Pete's sake? They must be somewhere, damn it. If you've lost them, we're in a real pickle. Jock Ping's truck has broken down, and I have to get there to see what's cooking. For Pete's sake, if I can't get the cocoa reloaded onto another truck, it's going to miss the ship."

A pained looked crossed Petrus's face. He hung his head and scratched behind his ear. He had no idea what Dad was talking about or why Dad was angry.

The fact that Dad was yelling at Petrus unnerved me. Dad never yelled at anybody, let alone his native staff.

I ran over to Dad and said, "Dad, stop yelling at Petrus. Stop. It's rude. Why are you yelling at him like that? Stop yelling. Petrus doesn't know what you want, he's confused. What do you want Petrus for? Tell me what you want and *I'll* tell him in Pidgin. Just stop yelling."

"I want the Ute keys, for Pete's sake," Dad half shouted at me, "and Petrus, the silly fool, has lost them. I have to get to Jock Ping's truck, and your mother has the office car. I have to ring her and tell her to come and get me. She'll have a fit. She's at some party or something. Ask him, will you, where he's thinks he's left the keys!"

I said to Petrus in Pidgin that Dad wanted the keys to the Ute. Petrus's face split into a wide grin. He ran off to get the Ute keys.

"Dad," I said, "you have to tell Petrus to *kisim* car keys, not *catchim* car keys, and the word for *Ute* is *hap-ka* ...half-car, see? Petrus doesn't understand *catchim* or *Ute*.

Dad almost choked. "*Kisim*," he spluttered, "*kisim*! I'm not going to ask any man to 'kiss me'! Damn it, *kisim* indeed. I've got news for Petrus. If he thinks I'm going to ask him to *kiss me*, he's got another thing coming. He can damn well learn the Queen's English if he wants to work for me, and if he doesn't like it, he can jolly well bugger off back to his village, and I'll find myself another *draivaboi*!"

Petrus returned with the Ute keys and handed them to Dad. Dad told him to get in the back of the Ute, and with a screech of tyres, they zoomed off.

For the many years that Dad lived and worked in Rabaul, he adhered to his form of Pidgin and struggled to make himself understood. However, as I stated in an earlier chapter, my dad was an enigma. On one occasion, late at night, Dad disturbed a native intruder in our home. As Dad chased the native down the street, he shouted out in the best Pidgin I have ever heard that if he ever caught the intruder, he would render not only the intruder but all of his male relatives eunuchs in five seconds flat!

After that, I knew Dad, for many years, had successfully pulled the wool over everybody's eyes. He spoke Pidgin almost as well as I did.

Mum later told me that when Dad chased the intruder down the road, he had also used *the* most disgusting Tamil words she had ever heard.

I am most fortunate to have a Papua New Guinea work colleague called Jenny. Jenny grew up in Port Moresby and now lives in Australia with her husband and daughter. I love Jenny with all my heart. She is funny and gracious and so reminds me of home. I often speak to Jenny in Pidgin, and when I do, she giggles and tells me I speak Pidgin better than she does. What a compliment!

CHAPTER 21

The Kerevat River and My Broken Elbow

The monsoon season had rolled around again, and as usual, every afternoon the heavens opened and brought a deluge of welcome rain. Mum and I still swam every day, but at this particular time of year, the sea was grubby with seaweed and debris, and the turbulent water made it nearly impossible for us to snorkel. On Sundays, rather than stay in town, we sometimes headed for the Warangoi River or Kerevat River for the day.

The Warangoi was a wide-sweeping river that was shallow in parts and rumoured to be full of alluvial gold. In fact, the local natives said that German prospectors had successfully panned the river for a number of years. My family, usually in the company of the Dixon family, often visited the river to swim and pan for gold. Of course, the only pans we had were our crockery lunch plates, and the only gold we ever encountered was the golden rays of sunlight that bounced off the shallows.

One day however, Mum found a golf ball size "pretty stone" in the shallows. The stone, Mum thought, would make an ideal paperweight, and she threw it into her beach bag. The pretty stone, much to Mum's delight, was later identified as an agate. Mum had the agate cut and polished, and our local jeweller fitted a bell cap on top of the agate to loop a gold chain through. Mum wore the agate for many years and never failed to remind everybody that she was the only person who ever found anything of value in the Warangoi River.

Whereas the Warangoi River produced gold and agate, the Kerevat produced wealth of another kind—a wealth of fun and frivolity. Of the two rivers, the Kerevat was very definitely my favourite.

The Kerevat in part, bordered the site of the old German agricultural and research Station. The station had been established during the German occupation (1884–1914). For research purposes, the German agriculturalists had established a botanical garden filled with exotic trees and plants. After the Germans were ousted in 1914, the site was abandoned, and the once lovingly tended gardens were left to the mercy of the rampant jungle. After World War II, however, a small part of the site was cleared, and a government-assisted program to aid the local native land owners was established.

It was common knowledge that some of the trees the German agriculturalists had planted still existed, although none had been found as yet, and that aroused Mums interest.

Like the ocean, the Kerevat River and its surrounding location held a fascination in one way or other for Mum, Dad, and me. My dad liked going to the rivers because he said the air was cool and refreshing and the tumbling rivers with their stony banks reminded him of the rivers of South India. The only thing missing, Dad added wistfully, was the wildlife that came down to drink.

Whenever we went to the Kerevat River, Dad parked the car high on an escarpment—just in case, he told us, the river broke its banks, The escarpment overlooked a small waterfall, making it a high vantage point, Dad also deduced, for crocodile spotting. I think the last time a crocodile was seen at this particular location was about fifty years previously.

Crocs, Dad warned me, were sneaky fellows who lurked in

the shallows waiting to grab, death roll, and gobble anything that drifted past. Dad drilled me each time we went to Kerevat that if he shouted "Croc!" I was to get out of the water immediately, run hell for leather up the bank, and jump in the car. My dad was very protective of me and quite often yelled "Croc! when the croc was in fact a half-submerged log.

Mum lectured Dad many times about crying wolf and told him that if he didn't stop, she would blindfold him and tie him to a tree. Dad, of cause, ignored Mum's threats and continued to shout "Croc, croc!" whenever he saw a suspicious-looking half-submerged floating object. Much to Dad's annoyance, his warnings fell on deaf ears.

At the height of the monsoon, the river swelled to double its size. The raging water created mini waterfalls, whirlpools, and rapids, and I loved it. I belly-scooted over fast tumbling waterfalls and screamed with delight as the wild water dumped me into spinning whirlpools. I hung on to one of Dads sneaky croc logs and rode the rapids like a white water rafter, and shrieked with victory if I stayed afloat. I waded in the shallows and collected pretty rocks and hoped like anything that one would be a rare diamond—or better still, a big fat nugget of gold.

Our old friends Mr. and Mrs. Curtis were in town for a few days, and Mum had invited them for lunch. In conversation, Mum mentioned that, at some stage, she would like to visit the old German agricultural station. The Curtis's also expressed an interest in the old German site, and it was decided that we would all visit Kerevat on Sunday.

"We can explore the old German agricultural station in the morning," Mum said, "and have a picnic lunch by the river."

Mr. and Mrs. Curtis pulled in to our driveway early Sunday morning. We loaded the picnic baskets into our car, called our dogs, and set off.

The drive to Kerevat was mostly on unsealed road, and we were thankful the overnight rain had settled the dust. An hour later, we arrived at the agricultural station.

As it was Sunday, the site was deserted. Dad parked the car under an old fig tree and said, "Righto, we are here. I wonder if we will find anything left over from the Germans."

I had never been to the agricultural station before, and I found the site quite interesting. Although there was precious little left of the German era, their influence had left a legacy that had stood the test of time. Large slabs of concrete dotted the area; the buildings had long gone, as well as concrete paths and cemented storm water drains. Thick jungle fringed the cleared area, and as we explored, Mum and Mr. Curtis identified a nutmeg tree and a cinnamon tree. The trees, although unattended for many years, still thrived. Dad found an old tractor that had almost rusted away and expressed regret that the site had been left to rack and ruin.

It was almost midday, and everybody was hungry. We decided to leave the agricultural station and head to the river for our picnic lunch.

I was twelve years old (it was the Christmas before I left for boarding school), and that day I was forced by circumstance to sit on the riverbank with Dad. Some days earlier I'd had a "slight altercation" with Mum, and in a fit of temper accidently slammed the car door against my arm. The impact from the door cracked my elbow, and as a result, my whole arm was encased in plaster from shoulder to fingertip. For a child such as me, the days of inactivity—including no swimming—were like being imprisoned in Alcatraz.

I had taken a book with me to Kerevat, and for most of the afternoon I sat above the waterfall reading. From time to time, I wandered down to the river and asked Mum repeatedly if I was "careful not to wet my plaster," could I swim? Mum's answer of course was a flat "no".

By mid-afternoon I was bored and in a rebellious mood. I was hot and wanted a swim, and I decided to sit in the water at the top of the waterfall to cool off. As I waded across the waterfall, I slipped and fell on my bottom. The force of the water spun me around, carried me over the top, and dumped me into the pool below. As I struggled to stand, the fast-flowing river swept me off my feet and carried me over the rapids and around the bend.

My plastered arm was a waterlogged mess, and by early evening the plaster had started to fall apart. Our local doctor was none too pleased when Mum phoned him at home and told him of my river swim. He ordered Mum to meet him at his surgery to have my arm replastered. When the job was done, he wrote on my plaster in thick black pen, "No swimming until further notice!"

I endured four long weeks of no swimming. Mum had little sympathy for my plight and said I was belligerent the whole time and drove her mad. My dad, however, was full of empathy.

"Pet," he said, "I know exactly how you feel. I broke my elbow when I was a boy fighting with a tiger, and Granny kept me locked up inside for a whole month until my elbow got better."

I remember that when my plaster was finally removed, my whole arm was skinny and pale, and that horrified me. I vowed never to be cheeky to Mum again.

CHAPTER 22

Christmas: a Day of Gifts and Gurias

The township of Rabaul is built within an active volcanic caldera and is, even today, vulnerable to eruptions from the five historically active volcanoes that surround the town. Seismic activity is a normal occurrence. As a child, the earth tremors or *gurias* we experienced were just part of everyday life; nothing to worry about, just something that happened, something we lived with. Most of the time, the *gurias* lasted only a minute or two and barely draw comment.

However, on the odd occasion, *a bicpela tru*—a *guria* of unnerving intensity—materialized and heralded a spate of questions throughout town. Those big *gurias* ruffled our nonchalant attitudes and often made us question our safety.

One Christmas week when I was about fifteen years old, Rabaul experienced a series of seemingly insignificant *gurias*. Day after day, night after night, we rocked and rolled, shook and rattled. Thankfully, however, the *gurias* were fairly small—just a few shakes every couple of hours or so—and as such were discussed only in passing. As nature would have it, when the big one hit, it served to remind us just how vulnerable Rabaul really was.

Christmas time was always a busy social time for my family. In the weeks that led up to Christmas, Mum and Dad attended a

Christmas party almost every night. The constant late nights taxed Mum's resolve and she often commented that she would be glad when Boxing Day rolled around. Apart from that, we always held a big social gathering at home on Christmas Day. So there was much to be done, and Mum was run off her feet.

Mum always started the preparation for Christmas in early December. She stocked the pantry with bottles of nuts, imported biscuits, and glacé fruit. She filled the fridge with cheeses and olives, slaved over the hot stove and cooked curries, made pilau, roasted the turkey, made the stuffing, and boiled the ham. Uncle Jock Ping always gave us a large ham for Christmas, which Mum boiled for hours in the old copper. Mum also organized fresh New Island lobster and mud crab to be flown in on Christmas Eve.

In hindsight, the amount of food we consumed over the festive season in those days was nothing short of sheer gluttony. But as Dad said, "If you can't be a glutton over Christmas, well, what's the use of having Christmas anyway?"

When we first arrived in Rabaul, our department stores did not stock Christmas decorations, so we made do with whatever was available. Mum always insisted we erect a Christmas tree, but all we could manage most of the time was a dead branch or a palm frond. We were very resourceful and decorated our "tree" with whatever we could find, including red crêpe paper we bought from Chinese trade stores, shells from the beach, and small pieces of driftwood. Sometimes if Mum had time, she visited the Catholic Church, made a donation, and returned home with a few white church candles. We cut the candles in half and placed them in a pot of sand at the base of our tree.

There was, however one decoration' that really symbolised Christmas for my family. Some years earlier, a local native woodcarver came to our front door. The woodcarver showed Mum a few carvings and asked if she would like to buy one. Mum liked his carvings so much she commissioned him to carve a large pig, a large frog, and a large crab. A few weeks later, the woodcarver returned with the items, all beautifully carved in New Guinea rosewood. Mum asked him if he would like to carve a few more items.

The woodcarver nodded and asked Mum if she would like a crocodile this time. Mum shook her head, opened a children's Bible, and showed him a picture of a nativity scene with Mary, Joseph, baby Jesus, a donkey, and some sheep. Mum then asked the wood carver if he could carve the same figures using the picture as a guide.

The woodcarver scratched his head and said he could try. Mum said she would pay him well—half now and half on completion. Mum also suggested that, to get a better idea of what the figures looked like, the wood carver could visit the Catholic church and look at nativity scene displayed near the alter.

Rabaul had very strict quarantine laws, and apart from a few horses on Ralabang Plantation, there were no farm animals to speak of. Mum doubted our woodcarver knew what a donkey looked like, and she said that she would provide him some money to catch a truck ride to Ralabang Plantation to see what a *liklik hos* looked like. As for the sheep, Mum added, the woodcarver would just have to rely on the picture in the Bible to carve from. The woodcarver scratched his head again, but after Mum pressed twenty dollars into his hand, he grinned widely and nodded.

As the woodcarver bade Mum goodbye, he asked if Mum wanted a pig carved as well. "No thank you," Mum replied. "To my knowledge, there were no pigs in Jesus's manger the night he was born." The woodcarver scratched his head again and told Mum he would be back before Christmas with the carvings.

To Mum's delight, the woodcarver kept his word and arrived on our doorstop a few days before Christmas. He opened his bag and presented Mum with the figures of Mary, Joseph, baby Jesus in his crib, a donkey, and some sheep (which, incidentally, looked a lot like little pigs) meticulously carved out of New Guinea rosewood.

Now that we had our nativity figures, Mum asked Barbara, our *haus boi's* wife, if she would fashion a little hut out of sticks and thatch for a manger. Barbara happily obliged, and a few days later presented Mum with a small replica of a native hut.

A large camphor wood chest stood along the back wall in our lounge room, and for a few weeks over Christmas, the chest served as a table for our nativity scene.

We laid a new hessian sack over the chest and topped the sack with clean black sand. Mum and I then arranged the figures of Mary, Joseph, baby Jesus, the donkey, and the "sheep" in the sand. As I was tropical child, I adorned our nativity scene with pieces of coral, seashells, and driftwood. Just in case Santa was hungry when he dropped in, I placed bananas and mangoes in a nearby fruit bowl.

For me, our hand-carved nativity scene symbolized the true meaning of Christmas.

The family always had a steady stream of visitors on Christmas Day. Mum graciously extended an invitation to many of the plantation assistants (most of whom were alone, as their families lived in Australia) to join us, as well as an open invitation to all our friends to drop in if they wished. All in all, it was a fun but busy day.

The family, eager to begin our day, arose bright and early that Christmas morning. We had experienced a spate of earth tremors during the week, and the tremors had persisted throughout the night. We'd been rocked, rolled, and shaken in our beds and had little sleep. However, it was Christmas Day, and we were all far too excited to be tired.

Dad and I, as usual, attended the Christmas service at our Anglican church. Mum, who held her own beliefs about Christmas, stayed at home to finalise everything before our Christmas guests arrived.

At the church service, our minister gave thanks for the birth of Christ, and during his sermon, made mention of the tremors we'd experienced this past week. At the end of the sermon, the minister knelt in prayer and asked for a safe and tremor-free Christmas day.

Our minister was new to Rabaul and, as Dad mentioned later, was perhaps, a bit unnerved by the *gurias*. When the service finished, we wished everybody a Merry Christmas and headed home to begin the day's festivities.

It was mid-morning by the time we arrived home, and Mum had all but finished the final food preparations. She had outdone herself; the dining table positively groaned under the weight of nuts, cheeses, and Christmas cake. Some of our friends had already arrived, and Dad said it was about time we started celebrating. He opened the drinks cabinet, put together his special planter's punch, and popped the corks of the champagne. Every now and again, the *gurias* made their presence known—slightly out of tune with Bing Crosby, I might add, as Bing belted out his Christmas hits on our record player. Dad made light of the tremors, saying Tavurvur Volcano must be celebrating Christmas as well, with a good belching.

As expected, our house was full of people—far too many to sit at our large dining table—and Mum had decided a buffet was more suitable. After the table had been cleared of the nuts and cake, Mum laid on a feast for a king. We helped ourselves to turkey, ham, and homemade stuffing. We scoffed curry and pilau and sucked on lobster tails washed down with Dad's punch, ice-cold champagne, and freshly made lime cordial. Even when our tummies were full, we made room for Mum's mango mousse and homemade ice cream. By early afternoon, even the greediest of us had had their fill, and one by one, we drifted out onto the veranda to sit in the cool and recover from our overindulgence.

As it was the wet season, the weather was sultry, hot, and humid. We had long since retired Bing. Everybody was sick of Jingle Bells and White Christmas anyway, and those of us who were able settled into quiet conversation.

Mum always insisted we go for a swim after Christmas lunch, and this year was no exception. However, whenever Mum mentioned the word "swim," we all just groaned.

"I'm too full to swim, Mum," I said. "I'd sink anyway. Let's go later."

A *guria* swept under us with a small shudder, soft and gentle, just enough to rattle the glasses on the drinks trolley. The tremor, momentarily, drew a pause in the conversation, but the shakes faded again quietly, as they had done many times in the past few days. A few seconds later, the second tremor hit. The house rose without warning and danced on its stilts, settled, and rose again. The timbers twisted and jived as an invisible hand jiggled our home like a child's puppet.

The fishpond on our veranda vibrated like a washing machine. Water poured over the sides and onto the floor as the house listed first one way then the other. Doors slammed shut and vibrated against their hinges. Our wall carvings swung from side to side, and Mum's hand-painted Japanese china plate, a treasured gift from Mr. Ogawa, broke free and smashed into a million pieces. The dining table tapped on its legs, the leftover turkey and ham slid off the end and rolled against the wall, the salad bowl flew across the room, our nativity figures toppled into the black sand, and our Christmas tree crashed to the floor. All around us, the house echoed with the sound of smashing crockery, breaking glass, and falling books.

As the seconds dragged by, the *guria* intensified in strength.

"Get out," Dad shouted, "everybody get out. The house is going to fall down."

The veranda was alive with dancing furniture. Nobody moved. It was impossible to stand, impossible to run.

The *bicpela tru guria* shook Rabaul like a manic cocktail shaker for four whole minutes. On and on we rattled, rolled, and shook until finally the *guria* subsided and the land around us settled once again into an uneasy calm. The air became deathly still and quiet. As the minutes dragged on, we waited silently, like an audience anticipating an encore, waiting and waiting.

Dad was the first to recover. "For Pete's sake," he whispered half to himself, "that was a beauty. Is everybody all right? Is anybody hurt?"

Thankfully, nobody was.

Mum walked into the kitchen. The mess resembled the aftermath of a food fight. Our Christmas leftovers now shared the floor with broken glass and shattered crockery. The pantry was the same—the floor was awash with liquid, broken bottles, dented tins, and brown rice.

"I don't think I can salvage much of the food," Mum said to Dad. "It will all have to be thrown out. Look at it all over the floor. Bugger. So much for leftovers, I'm afraid."

"Never mind," Dad sighed and shook his head. "Just be thankful it's only food. There is always next year, I suppose, for leftovers."

Dad asked me to check the rest of the house for damage. "I'm going to check on the water tanks outside," he added. "I hope the tanks didn't crack or split during the *guria*."

I walked into our bathroom. The scene was the same as the kitchen. The glass bottles of shampoo and conditioner had tumbled and smashed in the shower recess. I noticed that the hand basin was askew and the mirror sported a large crack. I wondered if the cracked mirror meant seven years of bad luck …or seven years of bad *gurias*.

Our beds and side tables had slid across the floor. Books and magazines lay scattered everywhere, and pictures hung like drunkards from their hooks. Thankfully, however, the damage inside the house on the whole was minimal. We were lucky.

I guess what affected us the most about the big *guria* was the fact that we had to throw out most of our leftover food. We had waited all year for the Christmas goodies, and now most of them lay on the kitchen floor.

Dad, however, refused to surrender his leg of ham. He strode into the dining room, seized the ham with both hands, and declared that he would wash it thoroughly and put it safely in the fridge.

"For the life of me," Dad declared, "I will *not* allow a silly little earth tremor to diddle me out of Jock's ham, for Pete's sake. All year," he added defiantly, "I look forward to having a few weeks of ham and not bacon for my breakfast!"

Our friends stayed well into the night and helped us clean up the mess. After we had finished, Mum said, "Is anybody hungry? I'm not. Father, can you please pour me a scotch ... and make it a double."

In the scheme of *gurias*, our Christmas Day *guria* did little damage. Rabaul stood strong that day. However, I did notice the next day as we drove to Tovarua for our Boxing Day picnic that the roads were littered with fallen coconuts.

As we left church the next Sunday, Dad joked to our minister, "I don't think the Lord was listening on Christmas Day when we had that big *guria*. I guess if we want a peaceful Christmas Day next year, we'll just have to pray a bit harder, won't we?"

The new minister puffed his chest and replied with dignity, "The Lord is not obliged to do as we ask. Perhaps He was just celebrating the birth of His only Son. After all, didn't *you* have a few drinks and fall over when Suellen were born?"

"I did," smiled Dad. "Indeed I did."

"Well," our minister replied, "what do you expect?"

At 6:15 a.m. on September 19, 1994, Matupit (or Tavurvur, as the local natives called her), a small volcano on the rim of Simpson Harbour, erupted. An hour later, Mount Vulcan, a larger volcano on the other side of the harbour, violently awoke from decades of slumber and unleashed her awesome force. Both volcanoes blasted lava hundreds of meters in the air and rained hot ash and volcanic debris over the township of Rabaul.

Vulcan grew furiously during her eruption, almost doubling in size, and shortly after her unstable sidewall gave way. Tons of mud and lava slid into the sea and covered the seabed. The mud and lava killed most of the fish life and smothered the coral reef. A river of saltwater rushed into the main crater and forced the water into a waterspout. The water spout shot sea life, pumice, and debris high in the sky.

In the aftermath, lava, pumice, and salt caked the land for kilometres around. The papers of the world would call Rabaul the "Pompei of the Pacific." My home, once described as the most gracious town in Papua New Guineas, now lay dying—suffocating and buried under tons of volcanic ash.

I had lived in Australia for a number of years when Tavurvur and Vulcan erupted. Mum phoned me at home and told me to turn on my television. For most of the day, I huddled in front of my TV. I hungered for news and was heartsick. For the second time in my life—the first time was when my Dad passed away—I experienced an overwhelming loss. I truly understood how others felt when their homelands were annihilated.

I knew my hometown was gone forever. That night, with tears in my eyes, I penned the first lines of my story.

The 1994 eruptions in Rabaul killed the Gazelle Peninsula stone dead. The aftermath displaced eighty thousand people and ruined homes, businesses, sea life, and the coral reefs. Rabaul was now a ghost town.

Tavurvur Volcano continued to spew volcanic ash for twenty years. In August 2014, she slipped into quite slumber again and fell dormant. The Gazelle Peninsula is green again. The harbour waters are clean, the sky is clear, and the land is washed by monsoonal rains. But the question is …for how long?

THE END

Printed in the United States
By Bookmasters

Printed in the United States
By Bookmasters